STREET FURNITURE DESIGN

To Linda C. R. Martin, with all my love.

STREET FURNITURE DESIGN

Contesting Modernism in Post-War Britain

Eleanor Herring

Bloomsbury Academic
An imprint of Bloomsbury Publishing Plc

BLOOMSBURY
LONDON • OXFORD • NEW YORK • NEW DELHI • SYDNEY

Bloomsbury Academic
An imprint of Bloomsbury Publishing Plc

50 Bedford Square　　　1385 Broadway
London　　　　　　　　New York
WC1B 3DP　　　　　　　NY 10018
UK　　　　　　　　　　USA

www.bloomsbury.com

BLOOMSBURY and the Diana logo are trademarks of Bloomsbury Publishing Plc

First published 2016, this paperback edition published 2018

© Eleanor Herring, 2016

Eleanor Herring has asserted her right under the Copyright, Designs and Patents Act, 1988, to be identified as Author of this work.

All rights reserved. No part of this publication may be reproduced or transmitted in any form or by any means, electronic or mechanical, including photocopying, recording, or any information storage or retrieval system, without prior permission in writing from the publishers.

No responsibility for loss caused to any individual or organization acting on or refraining from action as a result of the material in this publication can be accepted by Bloomsbury or the author.

British Library Cataloguing-in-Publication Data
A catalogue record for this book is available from the British Library.

ISBNs: HB: 978-1-4742-4561-6
PB: 978-1-3500-4481-4
ePDF: 978-1-4742-4554-8
epub: 978-1-4742-4555-5

Library of Congress Cataloging-in-Publication Data
A catalogue for this book is available from the Library of Congress

Cover design by Daniel Benneworth-Gray
Cover image © Kenneth Grange

Typeset by Integra Software Services Pvt. Ltd.

CONTENTS

List of Illustrations	vi
Acknowledgements	ix
List of Abbreviations	x
INTRODUCTION	1
1 PRECEDENTS AND BEGINNINGS: 1841–1944	7
2 THE COUNCIL OF INDUSTRIAL DESIGN: OFFICIAL ARTICULATIONS OF STREET FURNITURE DESIGN	29
3 THE GREAT AND THE GOOD: POWER AND INFLUENCE	75
4 MUNICIPAL VANDALISM: TYRANNY, CONFRONTATION AND RESISTANCE	115
5 BEYOND GOOD DESIGN: A PERIOD OF TRANSFORMATION, 1960–1974	161
EPILOGUE	197
Select Bibliography	202
Index	211

LIST OF ILLUSTRATIONS

1.1	Bandstand, *MacFarlane's Architectural Ironwork*.	8
1.2	Fountains, *Illustrated Catalogue of Macfarlane's Castings*, Vol. II (sixth edition).	11
1.3	Decorative cast iron bench on the Victoria Embankment.	12
1.4	Design by Giles Gilbert Scott for GPO telephone kiosk number 2: plan, elevations and section.	19
1.5	A view of a steel and glass bus shelter in Sutton E9, August 1937.	20
2.1	Cartoon in *Punch* magazine satirizing the Council of Industrial Design's role as an interface between designers and industry.	30
2.2	Salvage work in progress in Spencer Parade, Northampton, with iron railings being removed, the scrap metal being used for munitions, 1940.	32
2.3	'A pleasing design exhibiting all the attributes of a good concrete column'.	33
2.4	25′0″ Spun Concrete lighting column 1955 for AEI Lamp and Lighting Co Ltd.	35
2.5	Civic slovenliness: boundaries between Green Park and Piccadilly, London.	41
2.6	A wainey-edged bus shelter, in *Design*, No. 69, September 1954, 30.	42
2.7	Cover featuring Stewarts and Lloyds lamp, the *Municipal Journal*, 25 January 1952, Vol. 60, No. 3075.	44
2.8	Formalist photography: Design asked, 'should British parking meters be based on these designs?'	46
2.9	This bin was described by Design as 'typical of the neat use of steel throughout the exhibition'.	47
2.10	London Transport bus shelter designed by Arcon.	48
2.11	Pre- and post-war lamp standards at Tooting Bec, 1954.	50
2.12	Concrete bus shelter for London Transport Executive.	52
2.13	'Invariably uniform' modern railings celebrated in the Council of Industrial Design's Design Folio.	55
2.14	Two bus stops: 'one good and the other better'. Left is good, right is better.	56
2.15	Display of seating at the Council of Industrial Design and the Corporation of Birmingham Manufacturers' Competition for the Design of Outdoor Seats, 1953.	57

2.16	Members of the public visiting an exhibition of litter bins, London, 1960.	58
2.17	The Duke of Edinburgh visiting an open-air street furniture exhibition on London's South Bank, 6 July 1961.	59
2.18	Litter bins, 'Street furniture: List of Approved Designs 1963', CoID, and the Scottish Committee of the CoID, 78–9.	60
2.19	Film still from *Motoring News – London* (1956).	62
2.20	Parking meter designed by Kenneth Grange for Venner Ltd., 1958.	64
2.21	Fashion spread with parking meters, *Country Life*, 13 October 1960, 831.	67
3.1	For the *Architectural Review* this drain concealed a 'sinister underground organization that underlies the city.'	78
3.2	Street furniture in the *Architectural Review*, 1949.	80
3.3	Concrete Utilities Ltd, 'Modern Lamp Columns', List 38, 1946, 6.	81
3.4	Illustration by Gordon Cullen (cropped version), in 'Townscape: Outdoor Publicity', the *Architectural Review*, May 1949, Vol. 105, No. 629, 250.	82
3.5	'Lettering', the *Architectural Review*, January 1952, Vol. 111, No. 661, 59.	83
3.6	Illustration of an idealized piazza by Gordon Cullen, 'South Bank Translated', the *Architectural Review*, August 1951, Vol. 110, No. 656, 137.	86
3.7	Drawing of benches and litter bins by Gordon Cullen, 'Special Number on Canals', the *Architectural Review*, July 1949, Vol. 105, No. 107, 61.	87
3.8	'Townscape: Unconscious Sculpture', the *Architectural Review*, December 1952, Vol. 111, No. 672, 405.	88
3.9	Satirical poem about Royal Commissions, in Punch, 24 August 1955, 207.	95
3.10	Before and after: The Civic Trust's Magdalen Street scheme, 1959.	100
3.11	Municipal rustic: an expression of whimsy?	102
3.12	Cover, *Outrage* (London: The Architectural Press, 1955).	103
3.13	Gordon Cullen's interpretation of the 'unwitting agents treated by their authors as though they were invisible'.	104
3.14	Diverse range of concrete lamp standards, in Ian Nairn, *Outrage* (London: The Architectural Press, 1955), 373.	106
4.1	An example of inappropriate street furniture in the ordinary 'dim' places in England – in this case, Morecambe.	124
4.2	Advertisement by Concrete Utilities Ltd, 1953. CU Phosco Lighting Ltd.	126
4.3	Revo concrete lamp post, Greenwich, in 'Crooms Hill: Opposition to Design of Lamp Standards'.	129

4.4	Column designed by David Mellor – an example of the unobtrusive steel designs favoured by the Council of Industrial Design.	131
4.5	Blackheath lighting – preferred lamp post design.	134
4.6	Lamp posts in Chelsea, in 'Columns in Context', *Design*, February 1960, No. 134, 36.	136
4.7	Mr and Mrs Arnold Machin standing next to an ornamental lamp post in Stoke-on-Trent.	139
4.8	Advertisement by Concrete Utilities Ltd, 1956.	146
4.9	Ian Nairn, the shelter, 'Counter-Attack', the *Architectural Review*, December 1956, Vol. 120, No. 719, 373.	148
4.10	'Counter Outrage', *Punch*, 13 February 1957, 248.	149
4.11	The gallant fight against ugly posts and inappropriate flowerbeds.	151
5.1	'Town Number One' cylindrical litter bin: Not only a Design Centre Award winner but also attractive and 'ideal for crowded pedestrian ways'.	163
5.2	Blue road sign model made by Jock Kinneir and Margaret Calvert for a presentation to the Worboys Committee, Ministry of Transport circa 1962.	172
5.3	Green road sign model made by Jock Kinneir and Margaret Calvert for a presentation to the Worboys Committee, Ministry of Transport circa 1962.	174
5.4	Pillarbox designed by David Mellor for the Post Office, 1966.	176
5.5	Traffic light (demonstration prototype) in Cadogan Place, designed by David Mellor for the Ministry of Transport, 1965–70.	178
5.6.	'Design for Coordination' sought to eliminate 'the concept of street furniture as single objects'.	181
5.7.	Nicholas Taylor and David Watkin, 'Lamp-posts: Decline and Fall in Cambridge', the *Architectural Review*, June 1961, Vol. 129, No. 772, 425.	186
5.8.	Historic lamp posts in Manchester Square, London, in 'Lowering of Standards', *Design*, No. 245, May 1969, 28.	188
5.9.	'Cheerful' street furniture, in José Manser, 'Magic Gardens Round the Bush', *Design*, No. 273, September 1971, 54–5.	190

ACKNOWLEDGEMENTS

This book draws largely from my PhD research, a body of work that would not have been possible without the generous support of the Arts and Humanities Research Council. While researching and writing my doctoral thesis, I was hugely fortunate in the help that several people gave me. Foremost were Richard J. Williams, Miles Glendinning, Iain Boyd Whyte and Jeremy Aynsley. I benefitted in multiple ways from their advice, knowledge, enthusiasm, criticism and encouragement. Glasgow School of Art's Research Fund has been equally generous towards me, and met many of the costs associated with licensing images, for which I am truly grateful. Colleagues at Glasgow School of Art have also supported and advised me, and I'd like to take this opportunity to thank them.

The help of staff at local libraries and archives was invaluable, especially those who generously searched their archives for references to street furniture on my behalf, many without success. These archives span the distance of Britain and are too numerous to name. However, I would particularly like to thank Patricia Grant at the Mitchell Library in Glasgow, the wonderful Glasgow School of Art Library whose copies of *Design* and the *Architectural Review* were sadly lost in the 2014 fire, the British Library, Lesley Whitworth and Barbara Taylor at the University of Brighton's Design Archives, RIBA, the National Art Library, the National Archives, the National Library of Scotland, London Metropolitan Archives, City of Westminster Archives, and MoDA. I would also like to thank the staff at *Country Life*, the *Municipal Journal*, *Public Lighting Engineer* and *Punch*. Thanks also go to many of those who have helped source images and advised me, including Simon Cornwell, James Lawless, William Marques, David Pearson and Robert Richardson.

Several of the figures I interviewed for this project were instrumental in helping me understand how the debate worked in practice. I would like to thank Kenneth Grange and Margaret Calvert, who kindly welcomed me into their homes to re-tell their account of this period, and continued helping long after. I would also like to thank Ian Hay Davison, Isabelle Price and Susan Wright, all of whom were very generous with their time and their collections.

At Bloomsbury I'd like to thank Rebecca Barden, Abbie Sharman and Claire Constable for their help. I am grateful to Niels Stern for his early advice. I'd also like to extend my thanks to fellow speakers and delegates at conferences I've attended, in particular Carlos Bártolo and Javier Gimeno-Martínez. Special thanks to all my wonderful friends whose patience, generosity, hospitality, support and humour remained unstinting, in particular Erin Clarke, Jessica Kelly, Sheila McCubbin, Jennifer Olley, Kerry Spring, Lynsey Wells and Kasia Zych. Lastly, I'd like to express my thanks and love to my family, especially my mum, dad, Freya and Fred. I couldn't have done it without you all.

LIST OF ABBREVIATIONS

AJ	The *Architects Journal*
AP	The Architectural Press
AR	The *Architectural Review*
BBC	The British Broadcasting Corporation
BoT	The Board of Trade
BQR	*British Quarterly Review*
CAI	The Council for Art and Industry
CoID	The Council of Industrial Design
CT	The Civic Trust
DIA	The Design and Industries Association
FT	The *Financial Times*
GG	The Georgian Group
GPO	General Post Office
LCC	London County Council
MJ	The *Municipal Journal*
MoHLG	The Ministry of Housing and Local Government
MoT	The Ministry of Transport
NBA	National Brassfoundry Association
OoW	The Office of Works
RCHM	The Royal Commission on Historical Monuments
RFAC	The Royal Fine Art Commission
RIBA	The Royal Institute of British Architects

INTRODUCTION

Real power, especially in design terms, is often invisible. Though particular designers are sometimes celebrated for their work, many of the decisions that shape the designed environment are, if not deliberately concealed, then not entirely visible. Street furniture constitutes a significant portion of this category; after all, who among us can name the designer responsible for the poles, posts, shelters and rails in the street? Few people take much interest in why these supposedly authorless objects look the way they do, yet their anonymity and ubiquity belies the fact that someone has designed each and every one of them with particular interests and objectives in mind. In truth, a wide range of forces inform the height of lamp posts, the shape of parking meters, the colour of street signs and the style of bus shelters. Such formal decisions may seem insignificant in themselves, but they are usually made on our behalf and they make an enormous visual contribution towards the design identity of a country. Far from being simply mundane, decisions about the design of street furniture are vitally important since they reflect how we understand public space: who it's for, what it means and how it's used.

Street furniture exemplifies the way that different agents have sought to shape the street and its uses according to their own social, economic and political purposes. The term's roots lie in the area of British planning, and it is generally understood as referring to free-standing urban equipment, rather than the fabric of the street, such as pavements. The scope of what street furniture encompasses has changed over time, and would once have included objects as diverse as horse troughs, milestones and stalls for livestock. Today the term is used to describe transport and traffic management objects, like bicycle racks, traffic lights and bus shelters; security and safety objects like street lamps, bollards and railings; public health and utility objects like litter bins, urinals and signal boxes; communication objects like poster display units, signage and postboxes; as well as more overtly social or decorative objects like benches and planters. Such efforts at categorization, however, are not straightforward; a huge range of objects can be classed as street furniture and many combine several functions. Throughout history different communities and cultures have found ways to furnish the street, for a variety of reasons (not all of them practical). Identity is one reason, since street furniture has traditionally been used to beautify, improve or domesticate the street in ways that are culturally significant, both nationally and locally. Such objects also act as a cipher for the narrative of regeneration, in which – as a means of altering the identity of a space – street furniture can project a different face upon the street, renew its identity or reinstate the past. Street furniture's regenerative value can equally be understood as an expression of economic capital, or as a means of extracting value from the city. It can also function as a means of determining the social forms taking place within the street: to control public space and the behaviour of those who use it. For all of these reasons analysis of street furniture design provides a useful means through which to measure variations of patronage, influence and the balance of power in public space, from the past as well as the present.

In post-war Britain social, cultural, economic and political perspectives directly influenced decisions about street furniture design. During this time the process by which the street was shaped, and who had the power to shape it, was closely linked to the state. As part of the British government's attempts to rebuild the social order and improve standards after the Second World War, considerable attempts were made to modernize the country. New Town developments and expanding road infrastructure, as well as deliberate attempts to educate the public on matters of design, meant that street furniture emerged as a key element of post-war reconstruction. Ensuring that objects as ubiquitous as litter bins, benches and bollards adopted the visual language and materials of modernism was perceived as being vitally important by the authorities concerned, because it was through such objects that Britain's new social and cultural agenda was given physical expression, and good design was deliberately introduced into people's everyday lives.

However, while some people perceived modern street furniture as able to reduce clutter, manage traffic, raise standards of public taste and even civilize the country, for others the new designs were grotesque and represented a defacement of Britain's individual character. Nationwide campaigns were mounted against the new designs, angry letters were published in national newspapers, members of the public padlocked themselves to gas lamps, and even Cabinet meetings attended by Winston Churchill were held to discuss the issue. And yet, much to the frustration of government ministers and design professionals, many of the decisions that affected the post-war street were made away from the public gaze in local government committee meetings, at which few of those responsible had any design training. As a consequence, street furniture emerged as a particularly divisive subject in post-war Britain, drawing strong feelings across the country's social, political and cultural spectrum. The design profession argued with manufacturers; Cabinet and government ministries clashed with civic pressure groups; and the public quarrelled with local authorities. These different groups fought against and alongside one another about what constituted 'good' street furniture design, and the debate quickly developed a polycentric quality, reflecting the burgeoning multiplicity, complexity and contradictions of this unique period in British history.

This book aims to show, for the first time, that the intensity of the post-war street furniture debate reveals a great deal about the broader anxieties of the period. For while the debate was outwardly concerned with the style of modern bus stops and benches and their relationship to the British landscape, in fact, street furniture emerged as a forum through which anxieties around taste, class, influence and authority could be discussed. Such objects reflect the broad range of tensions and conflicts that characterize the uses and appropriation of public space by different agents, and equally our anxieties about the factors that shape public life. Anxieties about power were particularly relevant in Britain after the Second World War, a period in which design was brought under government control to a far greater degree than ever before, but which simultaneously witnessed an increase in voices participating in discussions about design. In such a context, the question of who has the authority to make design decisions on behalf of others, and the manner in which those decisions are made, becomes critical.

Illustrating how the debate on street furniture reflected these broader social, cultural and political themes provides a number of useful insights into the power balance between different groups in post-war Britain. This book will illustrate how the struggles between the avant-garde, progressive modernizers, conservative establishment forces, design philistines and the increasingly vocal 'untrained masses' came into conflict over how street furniture was designed and who was responsible. At the same time, however, it will show that boundaries between these different groups were more nuanced than conventional understandings of the period might otherwise suggest. Identities were slippery, and some groups were forced to battle on several fronts simultaneously. The debate on street furniture, therefore, reflects the complex ways in which power was expressed in post-war Britain – beyond just legislative power – and how groups drawn from out-with the elite that had determined British culture up until that point were increasingly able to make themselves heard.

The book does not seek to present a chronicle or inventory of street furniture – as much of the existing literature on this topic has done – and nor does it prioritize the designed objects themselves or the intentions of those responsible for producing them. Rather the chief concern of this book is with the multiple interests, agendas and alliances that shape the designed environment. Alongside designer's testimonies, the book expands the debate to include the wide variety of contemporary viewpoints that were expressed, both in public and in private, in response to the promotion, dissemination and design of modern street furniture. Extending the discussion beyond the official design narrative to other, equally important voices reflects a more accurate picture of the process through which street furniture was discussed, understood and even determined during this period. I propose that it is only by assessing how contemporary organizations and individuals responded to the design of objects like lamp posts, benches and parking meters that we can draw the fullest sense of their social and cultural significance. After all, how society thinks, talks and writes about design informs part of design's social construction and gives it a sense of meaning beyond its existence as physical matter.

A few words are needed to explain this approach. It is an understatement to say that records for the design of street furniture in post-war Britain are sparse. The companies that produced such objects have mostly ceased trading, and many of the designers involved have long since died. Furthermore, as a result of successive years of reorganization and departmental restructuring, official record-keeping on street furniture during the 1950s and 1960s tends to be arbitrary and fragmented at best, or entirely absent at worst. Some central government records remain, as does a scattering of material held by council archives in London. But of the twenty-three local authority archives I contacted for this study not one had kept detailed records on the way that their predecessors had discussed, designed, commissioned or selected street furniture. In the majority of cases only official minutes survived, in which decisions were merely formally recorded. They rarely explain why particular design decisions were taken, or who made them. The absence of these details may be attributed to the long-standing perception of street furniture as trivial, but it may also be linked to traditional (albeit frustrating) ideas of good record-keeping in which archival records were routinely destroyed. Alternatively, in the case of local councils, this absence may reflect the sheer scale of municipal operations during the post-war period, where the reach of each authority prevented detailed records from being kept on the minutiae of every decision for which it was accountable. Visual records proved just as elusive since historic photographs of the street tended to omit street furniture on the basis that its presence would have 'spoiled the picture'.

These factors have contributed to one of the book's more obvious limitations, namely that it focuses on London and national street furniture projects at the expense of what was happening at a regional or local level. It is a limitation imposed by largely practical constraints, however. For although the polemical material produced by privileged groups in London may have generated considerable noise, the actual enactment of their ideas about street furniture took place at a much quieter municipal level, the recovery of which proved exceptionally difficult. To circumvent the problems posed by the evidence available – and unavailable – I have tried to represent the design of post-war British street furniture obliquely: by surveying the debate around street furniture design rather than through the physical objects themselves. Using contemporary periodicals and newspapers, private letters and government memorandums, photographs, models, early sketches and design plans, interviews with designers and members of the public, as well as ephemera such as popular songs about parking meters, poems about lamp posts, satirical cartoons, advertisements and film, this book will show the extent to which external forces affect street furniture design, and underline design as a conceiving, planning, organizing and making activity.

The book is comprised of five chapters. Together they follow a loosely chronological structure; individually, each chapter presents the debate from a different perspective, drawing upon different conversations between and among different groups. Chapter 1 focuses on the historical framework to the post-war street furniture debate, and sets the scene for the chapters to follow. It introduces the reader to a set of arguments and ideas about design – from the late nineteenth to the early twentieth century – that shaped the critical debate on street furniture. It also provides the reader with a sense of how street furniture was designed before the Second World War.

Chapter 2 looks at the role of the Council of Industrial Design (the precursor to today's Design Council) in promoting modern design after the war, and its effect on street furniture. As the government's voice on matters of design, the CoID represents the most significant official body within the post-war street furniture debate. Though it had no direct powers and operated mainly through persuasion, its focus upon issues like good taste and the social and cultural responsibilities of design had a considerable effect upon how modern street furniture was understood and discussed. This chapter examines the way that the CoID's mechanisms and powers were harnessed to promote a particular interpretation of modern street furniture design, and how this interpretation was actually applied in practice, through industrial designers like Kenneth Grange.

Chapter 3 covers the other influential voices that were present in the debate, outside the official boundaries of the CoID but still situated within elite culture. It shows that the debate on street furniture design included a number of design magazines, individuals and organizations – including John Betjeman, Gordon Cullen, the *Architectural Review*, the Royal Fine Art Commission and the Civic Trust – who participated in the debate, sometimes in a semi-official capacity, and thus often had the ear of government. The lines of division between these groups – both between themselves, and in relation to central government – were ambiguous. However, they made a significant intellectual impact upon the debate, and demonstrate the multiple interests that affected it as well as the way that power during the 1950s was dispersed.

Chapter 4 takes the debate beyond the enlightened voices of the design world and the intelligentsia, to include municipal planners and borough engineers, MPs, civil servants and members of the public. Rather than merely focus on the comparatively noisy voices represented in Chapter 3, this chapter will examine the way in which these quieter voices contributed to the debate, and intersected through complex negotiations that tended to occur in private. It includes a number of high-profile controversies concerning street furniture during the 1950s and early 1960s, and the depth of hostility towards local government that surfaced as a result. As a whole, Chapter 4 illustrates the level of resistance to modern street furniture that emerged not just from the public, but also between the authorities jointly responsible for its improvement, including government. Identifying these internal divisions provides a more nuanced picture of how the debate on street furniture design was actually enacted, and the extent to which the debate was characterized by one confrontation after another, and between almost every party involved.

Chapter 5 assesses how the debate moved from questions about what constituted good street furniture design, to a critique of the design establishment itself. By the early 1960s, the links between street furniture design, taste and the establishment began to be scrutinized much more closely and on a much wider scale. Formerly accepted ideas about why street furniture was important, what it should look like, and who should be responsible, were seen as increasingly restrictive. As a result, the debate shifted to accommodate a greater emphasis on issues like standardization and aesthetic monotony, but also on questions about institutional accountability and the rights of the untrained. This chapter will address the challenge to 'Good Design' posed by writers like Reyner Banham, designers like Jock Kinneir, Margaret Calvert and David Mellor, and members of the public.

Taken together, the chapters of this book provide another perspective on post-war modernism in Britain, as well as the development of a more plural design culture. They paint a picture of the way that, at a time of immense change, street furniture design provided an opportunity to rigorously debate the political landscape of Britain, its cultural expectations and class hierarchies. Post-war discussions about the design of lamp posts, for instance, were not only concerned with what they looked like, but by questions about the taste of those responsible, their social position within society and ultimately their authority to make design decisions on behalf of a nation. What follows here then is a book about seemingly banal urban objects and their potential to reflect the systems and structures underpinning design culture, and expand our knowledge of how political power works.

Chapter 1

PRECEDENTS AND BEGINNINGS: 1841–1944

The anxiety people expressed about street furniture design in Britain after the Second World War was not unusual; indeed it had considerable precedent. Arguments about design in the late nineteenth and early twentieth centuries reflected many of the same anxieties about taste, style, nationalism, class and snobbery. As this chapter will show, many of the ideas articulated in post-war Britain about street furniture design can be traced to the nineteenth century. Located within the fastest developing industrial economy in the world at that time, Britain experienced many of the problems associated with such rapid change before her continental or US counterparts. Accordingly, design emerged as a forum to express anxieties about these social, cultural and environmental changes.

One of the key voices within nineteenth-century design debates was the architect and writer, Augustus Welby Pugin, whose polemic emphasized the importance of design's social, moral and national responsibilities. For Pugin, design was grounded in nationalistic fervour and religion, and according to historian Michael Collins, his crusade against neo-classicism contributed to the debate about the appropriateness of particular styles in a national context, and their moral value.[1] For Pugin, this sense of moral value also extended to objects; indeed any artefact could serve as a lesson in how to conduct our lives. Such an understanding was typical of the time, and in the context of street furniture, one only needs to consider the moral role played by Victorian Temperance fountains and bandstands (see Figure 1.1), which were intended to dissuade the public (particularly the working classes) from drinking alcohol, and encourage appropriate leisure activities.[2] And yet, although Pugin was unconcerned with street furniture design – as far as we know – his model of the 'object lesson' became a fundamental argument within design debates after the Second World War.

Style can be considered another entry-point into Pugin's interpretation of design and morality, and for him stylistic disorder was symptomatic of social disorder. In his 1841 essay 'The True Principles of Pointed or Christian Architecture' he objected to the 'meretricious ornament' and 'cheap deceptions of magnificence' that tempted the lower classes of society at that time.[3] For Pugin, popular taste was appalling, and he criticized the taste of the masses for 'fiddle-headed spoons, punchy racing cups, cumbersome tureens and wine coolers'.[4] Such objects, he said, 'corrupted design and decayed taste' and were therefore dangerous to the very fabric of society.[5] As a result of such badly designed objects, 'England is rapidly

Figure 1.1 With distinct moral overtones, Victorian bandstands encouraged appropriate leisure activities in nineteenth-century Britain. Bandstand, MacFarlane's Architectural Ironwork. © CSG CIC Glasgow Museums and Libraries Collection: The Mitchell Library, Special Collections.

losing its venerable garb; all places are becoming alike' and only the beautiful and the true could 'overthrow… modern paltry taste and paganism'.[6] The relationship Pugin draws among design, taste and monotony is an important precursor to the street furniture debate, since a wide range of organizations and individuals in post-war Britain shared Pugin's anxieties. However, these ideas extended beyond

Pugin, and as the nineteenth century progressed, the relationship among design, class and taste became increasingly important to the country as a whole.

An event like the 1851 Great Exhibition demonstrates the increasing importance of these ideas: not only within design culture but also for the state. The Great Exhibition may have been a means to showcase Britain's industrial might on an international stage, but it was also intended to improve public taste. And while in many respects the exhibition was a great success, not least financially, many in the design community roundly condemned the quality of the exhibits on display. For its critics, the exhibits displayed at the Great Exhibition were allegedly so poorly designed that they posed real harm to Britain's export trade. Yet many of those allegedly bad designs were not only produced to an exceptionally high standard using the best of materials, but were also extremely popular. For art historian Jules Lubbock, such criticism could only have been justified if 'the energies of the design pundits and the institutions associated with them, had indeed been directed towards improving the competitiveness of British manufacturers, with making their products more commercial, more popular, more fashionable. This was not the case. Instead, their efforts were *against* the prevailing fashions, the taste of the public at home and abroad: in short, against the market.'[7] That the argument of these reformers was not purely based on the competitiveness of British goods but on something else as well, leads one to speculate on what that *something else* was. For his part, Lubbock considers the moral and social influences of design as being the active factor in these historical debates. In other words, how the design of an object affects the public that buys or consumes it is more important than how it performs in the economic market. This tension is important for the street furniture debate, for it not only reflects the critical attitude of design reformers to popular taste, but also places the improvement of design out-with a financial system that recognizes value only in monetary terms.

These ideas about the social, political and economic responsibilities of design grew in importance as the century progressed, largely under the influence of art historian John Ruskin, and the architect, designer and writer, William Morris. Together they developed the theoretical underpinnings of the Arts and Crafts movement, but one of the most important ideas for which they are still known is that design can improve society.[8] The reason why a new society was necessary is familiar, however. Like Pugin, Morris and Ruskin perceived the society in which they lived to have morally failed, a state indicated by the poor-quality objects and buildings that nineteenth-century society produced. Morris regarded the latter as 'incurably vicious' and in need of significant social and political change.[9] In a lecture on 'The Lesser Arts' given in 1877, Morris attributed this viciousness to the ignorance of the public for wanting cheap, badly made and ugly things, regardless of the implications for the maker.[10] Thus Morris hoped the example set by his own design practice – with its focus on the vernacular, high-quality craftsmanship, 'honest' pattern and improved working conditions – would lead to a higher form of society.

News from Nowhere, Morris's novel written in 1890, offers us an insight into what this higher form of society would look like, in which the poverty of nineteenth-century mass manufacturing is replaced by a supportive community of craftsmen and women in a pastoral setting. While Morris's arguments about craft may have had less immediate impact, his belief that design could improve society had lasting consequences for British design culture. Another important idea that can be attributed to Morris is the belief that every member of society should benefit from design. Like several other figures associated with the Arts and Crafts movement, Morris was a socialist and his political views undoubtedly affected his belief that design 'must be made by the people and for the people'.[11] Good design for everyone, regardless of class or status, is a central theme within the debate on street furniture design, and will be returned to again later.

Yet the provision of design for everyone has a contradiction at its very heart, and in this respect, there are inconsistencies between Morris's ideals and their practical application. On the one hand, Morris has been described as a true prophet, largely because of his concern for social conditions.[12] On the other hand, however, Morris considered the public to be an unintelligent mass in need of education. This contradiction eventually saw Morris withdraw from reality, back to a 'world of poetry and beauty'.[13] While much of Morris's thinking was political by nature, there persisted an uncomfortable reality to his ideals. Noel Carrington, a Design and Industries Association member and brother of artist Dora Carrington, later recalled that 'most of Morris's disciples were drawn from the middle class, so too were his patrons. Though Morris could train working class apprentices to carry out his designs, he never produced in sufficient quantities to market goods at a price which the mass of people could afford.'[14] This uncomfortable reality between theory and practice meant that despite his best intentions, Morris's customers remained the elite within society. It is an important point, because it exemplifies the underlying presence of class in nineteenth-century debates about the benefits of high standards of design, and raises a question about who these improvements were actually for. After all, there is an obvious difficulty in outwardly trying to provide better design for everyone if you doubt the public's intellectual capacity to appreciate it.

Early street furniture debates

Many of the ideas outlined so far affected discussions about the design of consumer goods and architecture; but they also had some impact upon street furniture. It is worth noting that up until the mid-nineteenth century, much of Britain's street furniture was very simply designed, and objects like bollards were marked only with the monogram of the Crown.[15] However, by the time Victoria became Queen in 1838 innovations like gas lighting and the penny post exposed the need for a greater range of styles and designs. Seen together with the emerging technology to cast complex designs in iron quickly and cheaply, many British companies responded eagerly to this new market. A firm like Walter MacFarlane & Co. in Glasgow would eventually play a leading role in this industry, distributing catalogues of its products to subjects of the British Empire and other interested parties around the world (see Figure 1.2). Using this model, large volumes of cast iron railings, benches, bandstands, fountains, lamp posts and other urban equipment were exported around the world, signifying Britain's imperial reach.

Precedents and Beginnings: 1841–1944   11

Figure 1.2 Fountains, *Illustrated Catalogue of Macfarlane's Castings*, Vol. II (sixth edition). © CSG CIC Glasgow Museums and Libraries Collection: The Mitchell Library, Special Collections.

Though street furniture was mostly designed and produced by the iron foundries themselves, some professionals with design training also worked in the sector. Isambard Kingdom Brunel drew designs for street lamps, and the emblematic sturgeon lamps and benches framed by winged sphinxes and seated camels on London's Victorian Embankment were designed by George John Vulliamy, architect-in-chief for the Ministry of the Board of Works, between 1870 and 1874 (see Figure 1.3). Even Arts and Crafts designers engaged with street furniture, and in 1894 designer Charles Frances Voysey was commissioned by his brother Annesley, a City of London electrical inspector, to design a street lamp.[16] It was later manufactured by William Aumonier and exhibited at the 1896 Arts and Crafts Exhibition Society. While Voysey's lamp is a comparatively simpler design than Brunel's or Vulliamy's, nonetheless by post-war standards, each of these examples would have been considered unnecessarily decorative. Yet with so many firms competing for attention in a very lucrative global market, the style of nineteenth-century street furniture became increasingly elaborate, which inevitably led to criticism.

Figure 1.3 Decorative cast iron bench on the Victoria Embankment. Courtesy of London Metropolitan Archives, City of London. Bench designed by George John Vulliamy in 1877. Photograph from 1976.

The design of letterboxes was one of the first newly developed objects of street furniture to divide critical opinion. Following a successful experiment in Jersey, the first letterbox (or 'strong iron box') was developed by the author and Post Office employee, Anthony Trollope, and by Victoria's death, there were over 30,000 of them. Originally painted sage green, the letterbox went through various design changes – including one ornate example designed in collaboration with the Government's Department of Science and Arts to make it more attractive – but it was not until 1874 that they were painted red.[17] Despite their apparent success, however, essayist Ernest Raymond described the letterbox as 'one of the most supremely ugly things that civilization has produced', while G. K. Chesterton found 'surpassing beauty' in them.[18] The design of street lamps also roused debate. In 1880 John T. Emmett contributed an essay to the *British Quarterly Review* about the heavy-base lamp standards in Trafalgar Square, which he described as 'absurd contrivances'. Emmett derided the fact that 'the public see such things but cannot understand them, take them for magnificent and so pass by; and thus by constant habit of neglect, they have entirely lost the faculty of reasonable observation; sound discriminating criticism being scarcely known'.[19] That such lamps were mistakenly perceived by the public to be magnificent when in fact they merely sought to disguise a technological effect lay at the root of Emmett's complaint. Like others before him, Emmett blamed the public's lack of education and taste for poor street furniture design, and the following year he extended his criticism to the lamps on Euston Road. 'This seeming galaxy', he said, was 'all a sham, and wholly useless, save as an expensive daylight show' – remarks which once again draw on the notion that such objects were false.[20]

The arrival of electric light prompted further complaints. For some, the lamp posts themselves were eyesores, largely because of their overly technical appearance and many were later removed, or replaced with more ornamental varieties.[21] While for others it was the quality of light such lamps emitted that was most problematic. Novelist Robert Louis Stevenson argued in his *Plea for Gas Lamps* that electric light 'should only shine on murders and public crime or along the corridors of lunatic asylums, a horror to heighten horror'.[22] And for his part, William Morris argued that an illuminated society was not just undesirable but vulgar and disturbing. The reasons for such resistance are complex, however. For historian Chris Otter, 'a city from which darkness had been expunged to allow general omniscience was a city devoid of that most cherished value, personal privacy, or the ability to altogether escape from the gaze of others'.[23] Certainly the objection to street lamps has a long history, and is often linked to the uses of light as a means of controlling space and the behaviour of those who use it.[24] What all these testimonies indicate however is that, even in its earliest forms, modernization of the street was met with hostility.

Raising standards: making a case for Good Design

The nineteenth-century ideas discussed so far, about design's social, economic and cultural responsibilities, proved to be extremely influential internationally. And by the beginning of the twentieth century, designers and craftspeople across

Europe perceived British design culture, and the writings of Morris in particular, as providing an ideological model for their own efforts to raise design standards. Groups like the Deutsche Werkbund for instance, depended on many of the same arguments already discussed, particularly the idea that well-designed goods could benefit people's everyday lives. Unlike their British contemporaries, however, the Werkbund recognized that they would need to establish a practical alliance between art and industry, for it was only by working with industry and government, and influencing their decisions, that widespread design reform could become a reality.[25] The efforts of the Werkbund were so influential that by the early twentieth century, Britain's design profession was beginning to realize that the cooperation of government was essential in order to improve design standards. Borrowing the Werkbund's example, several organizations and prominent individuals emerged in Britain that were wholly committed to this task. Their efforts preceded, contributed and informed post-war debates about street furniture design, and the involvement of the state.

One group that was particularly important was the Design and Industries Association (DIA). Founded in 1915 by 'a handful of practical enthusiasts', the DIA is important because it disseminated a set of existing arguments and ideas about design, as part of its efforts to raise design standards.[26] Several of its members later became pivotal figures within the debate on street furniture design and in some cases, members of the central organizations involved, like the Council of Industrial Design and the *Architectural Review*. Like them, the DIA balanced a concern for aesthetics with an awareness of social, aesthetic and economic practicalities. Its slogan was 'Nothing Need Be Ugly', and it worked to break down the barriers that separated well-made and beautiful design from everyday people.[27] Two prominent members, the architect and historian William Richard Lethaby and head of the London Underground Frank Pick, shared the view that it was a mistake to think of art as a special matter dealt with by special people like architects, painters, collectors and connoisseurs.[28] Rather, as Pick repeated in lectures held during the First World War, art must have a relationship with 'the common things of life, the things of everyday use and enjoyment', and as 'painstaking a care for the crowd that seems to pass it by'.[29] Art, he said, was 'of the people and by the people, and for the people'.[30] The idealism underpinning Pick's position is familiar, having featured in Morris's polemic about design and it continued to be relevant in discussions about street furniture after the Second World War.

In undertaking this idealistic project, the DIA employed a language that would later come to be known as Good Design discourse.[31] Good Design is a discourse that represents a sequence of ideas, beliefs and practices that were consolidated in the early twentieth century, and which functioned in order to attribute or recognize value in design. As a qualitative judgement, it is often based upon anxiety over the social, moral and economic consequences of design, and while Good Design has never been an objective method of discerning quality, it has often been used as if it were. This was certainly the case with the DIA, which published a report in 1917 arguing that good design was 'well fitted to its purpose', and 'good design and good workmanship produce beauty in all objects of use'.[32] Good design meant plainness, unity, order, symmetry, simplicity and proportion. Bad design, by contrast, was aligned with bad workmanship, ornament, fashion and barbarism.[33]

Strong opinions about design were common among the cultural elite at the start of the twentieth century. In 1912 Roger Fry, art critic and founder of the Omega Workshop, described the decorative features of a railway station café as representative of the maker's 'horrible toil' and a culture of oppression. The excessive volume of ornament in the café reflected 'an itchy, dissatisfied culture whose decorative efforts looked like eczematous eruptions' breaking out over the skin of England.[34] Fry was not alone in seeing ornament as a cultural sickness. For Austrian architect Adolf Loos it was symptomatic of degeneracy and for Le Corbusier decoration was 'a sensorial and elementary order, as is colour, and is suited to simple races, peasants and savages'.[35] The removal of ornament signalled both inner and outer cleanliness. In stripping it back and producing cleaner, tidier objects, many early modernists believed they were simultaneously committing themselves to a more honest and democratic future.

However, the value of good design was not only measured in aesthetic terms. By the interwar period, the notion of a responsible public service grew in importance, and Good Design was perceived as able to serve such ends. The DIA promoted this understanding and applied pressure upon the British government to support Good Design in state-funded projects. The DIA can be understood as a motivating agency: including the state within design debates, and influencing nationally accepted standards of design and notions of taste. Its methods of operation were discreet, with business-like committees and benign propaganda, and one of its biggest successes lay in recognizing design's relationship to industry, and therefore to the economic health of a nation. The DIA also wanted to address the poor quality of goods produced by British industry and the lack of taste expressed by the domestic market. Both issues were related of course, for without a demand for better goods from British consumers, industry was likely to resist pressure from either government or the DIA. While its own literature reinforced the view that the DIA, 'could do much towards encouraging a more intelligent demand amongst the public for what is best and soundest in design', it acknowledged that it was probably only the professional classes who would support the production of 'attractive and carefully designed modern work'.[36] Though there was allegedly plenty of design catering to the upper echelons of society, standards were low in the field of industrial design catering for the needs of the lower/middle classes. The central question then was how best to raise design standards and improve the public's taste?

For someone like Pick who was already interested in how these questions affected civic design and even street furniture, the first obstacle to be cleared concerned the absence of visual consciousness. Like John T. Emmett's objection in 1880, Pick complained in 1923 that 'we see very little. We train our eyes to see only that which interests us. What surrounds us every day we learn to let go by unheeded.'[37] Pick suggested that travel was one solution, since only strange surroundings could wake the mind up and teach the eyes to see again.[38] Were we to adopt the quizzical air we wear abroad, he later added, we would be able to compare and contrast our cities, which would lead to a rise in standards.[39] But before design improvements could be made, Pick believed that the country needed an education in taste, and he lamented the fact that no modern standard of taste was widely recognized.[40] Good taste, affirmed Pick, might be 'personal and elusive', but it was 'confined within limits set by the understanding. Get a proper understanding and right and wrong are divided, good and evil are discerned.'[41] Yet Pick's view exposes a contradiction, for at the same time as members of the DIA encouraged the public to become 'missionaries throughout the length and breadths of the land for the conversion of things from bad to good, or from good to better, or from better to best, if that is possible', it simultaneously sought to overcome their 'atrophied taste'.[42] In this sense, the DIA's perception of the public is consistent with the examples cited earlier, in which the public were routinely castigated for having little or no taste. Seeking to improve the public's taste, while at the same time deriding it, placed members of the association in a deliberately superior position, and reflected a tension within design debates that would continue long after the war.

From the documents published by the DIA, it would appear that the organization believed in cultural hierarchy. The Englishman, the DIA observed in its 1922 report, was 'fond of saying that he knows what he likes when he sees it. But there he is usually mistaken. Men have to learn to know what they like.'[43] Educating the public on matters of taste became a cornerstone of the DIA's programme, and it encouraged them to awake their critical faculties and take nothing for granted.

Yet for the DIA, education was useless unless something was done about the quality of the products available. This was particularly pressing because the public's taste was 'subject to suggestion; and if beset with articles ill made and ill designed but following some new and violent fashion, it will come to believe that these are the articles which it wants'.[44] Thus the public's perceived vulnerability in matters of taste convinced the DIA that it could only persuade this malleable group to desire superior products, if those products were available. As such, before it could persuade the public, the DIA would first have to deal with those responsible for producing ill-made articles.

One of the key qualities to design debates is a tendency to attribute blame. For the DIA, there were many groups guilty of perpetuating bad design, including designers, manufacturers and commercial travellers.[45] The latter was widely perceived to know what the public wanted, and the DIA regretted that 'it is his taste that controls design… so design is controlled by no taste at all, by any actual likes or dislikes, but only by a general desire to follow some imaginary standard'.[46] Evidently, the DIA perceived the taste of the commercial traveller to have little substance, while its own taste was beyond reproach. Unsurprisingly, reaction to the DIA's policing of taste was hostile, and some within British industry questioned who they were, and what their objective was. Even as early as 1916 members of the organization recognized that their approach was unpopular.[47]

Addressing the poor taste of manufacturers has been a constant issue within design debates since at least the nineteenth century. In the 1930s and alongside the work of the DIA, a number of other figures also became involved, one of which was the art critic Herbert Read. In 1934 Read published an essay titled *Art and Industry*, in which he attributed the rise in poor taste to inertia between manufacturers and consumers who 'continue to pass the buck to each other – the buck in this case being the responsibility for the perpetuation in nearly every trade except engineering, of design that has neither beauty nor efficiency'.[48] Both the manufacturer and the consumer were equally to blame, according to Read, and he anticipated the standard defence of the manufacturer as representing the view that, 'from a highbrow artistic point of view… my products may be bad; but they are what the public wants, and if I were to adopt your good designs I should lose trade. If you will first educate the public then I will produce articles of good design.'[49] Likewise, Read also regarded the salesman with disdain: 'He is usually a middleman of some kind… He, Mr. Jones, the head salesman of Smiths Universal stores, is a middle-middle class man with a nice little home in the suburbs, and every suggestion that comes before him he mentally compares with the comforts of that nice little home.'[50] Once again, Read's argument can be understood through a social lens, in which the superior cultural position was occupied by a well-educated professional, and the lower position, by a member of the public concerned more with status and comfort than with ideas, however noble. Read's social snobbery is difficult to overlook, and it illustrates the continuous presence of class in debates about design, as well as the social perspective of those providing most of the commentary.

The notion of class was also present in how the DIA approached public participation. According to Raymond Plummer, a former DIA member, the association was 'all for democracy, but the thought of democracy influenced by "the pictures"… is a gruesome thought.'[51] That popular culture was so distasteful to the DIA reflects the social, cultural and even economic distance of its members from the general public. According to historian D. L. LeMahieu, 'many intellectuals held contradictory or unconsciously ambivalent views about commercial culture' during the interwar period.[52] Some of those complicated individuals believed that 'their own tastes should appeal universally', while others deliberately set their tastes at a remove from what was popular. For LeMahieu, 'aversions to cultural phenomena often became as important a barometer of cultural refinement as preferences', and he defined cultural hierarchy in Britain as having involved two specific discourses.[53] The first of which involved a reaction to commercial culture 'that permitted intellectuals to distance themselves from the crowd and what was widely perceived as its generally debased instincts'.[54] The second discourse meant establishing certain boundaries to defend what intellectuals felt was a superior culture, a difficult task when subjectivity was often at the root of those preferences. Even harder was the task of establishing when that culture proved successful, since unlike the movie box office, high culture 'possessed no such convenient, reasonably certain mechanism to determine the aesthetic merit'.[55] The most significant threat to culture, according to contemporary perceptions was the concept of egalitarianism, and LeMahieu's interpretation of the interwar period was that intellectuals believed that 'the creation and appreciation of art required talent, training, and experience none of which the general public shared in equal proportions'.[56]

This interpretation of the interwar period suggests a tendency on the part of cultivated elites to position themselves at odds with mainstream culture, so disgusted were they by the taste of their fellow men. The argument presented by these different voices – between campaigning to educate the untrained public, but simultaneously highlighting the authority of design specialists – reflects the same tensions identified by Renato Poggioli in his 1968 study of the avant-garde. For Poggioli, the avant-garde can be understood as a highly specialized, intellectual body of observers whose behavioural codes amount to a series of positions or 'poses'.[57] Such poses are predestined to be unpopular – and indeed, are often deliberately so – since the avant-garde actively opposes the culture and taste of the majority. While Poggioli calls this pose 'snobbism', he also claims that avant-garde groups tend to be formed outside of class distinctions, or at least on 'the margins of, or over, the other classes'.[58] This explains, he says, the mixed feelings towards the avant-garde from which 'radicals and conservatives look on at it from opposite sides'.[59] There are significant parallels between Poggioli's understanding of avant-garde culture and the issues that dominated the design debates discussed so far, concerning popular culture and public opinion, and high culture and the elite.

However, by the 1930s anxiety about the separation between elite and popular culture began to be expressed within the design profession. Writing in 1934, the design writer and DIA member John Gloag, attributed it to a perception that the designer 'is still outside the scheme of things, still a queer, outlandish, incalculable creature in the view of most ordinary people'.[60] While Gloag might have understood how this separation occurred historically, he condemned its perpetuation in the twentieth century. Though he acknowledged that 'the public doesn't know itself what it wants', he argued that the designer could not continue to stand at a distance from his fellow man since it was incompatible with the social, economic and political problems of the 1930s, and the ideals of democracy.[61] Aligning such an approach with the 'dictatorial highbrow', and accusing it of being no better than the commercial approach, Gloag questioned the methods harnessed by idealists.[62] While he might have respected the honesty of the intellectual critics and reformers who believed that 'people ought to like good design', nevertheless, Gloag stated that,

> to impose the taste of the few on the many is tyranny; even though it is done in the interests of improved design. In a democracy, people must be educated and persuaded, so their interests may be carried to the point of observing and comparing before they choose and buy the things they have to use and live with in their homes. This is a long job.[63]

Gloag's observation that such impositions would be seen as tyrannical was perceptive, and similar accusations would be made about local authorities in the post-war era. Equally perceptive was his point about the size of this project, for persuading the public that good design meant modern design had a number of considerable obstacles to address first.

'A special body of men trained in aesthetics'

Despite its alleged virtues, modern design was not universally popular in interwar Britain, and though the DIA had some successes, few of the most well known civic or street furniture design projects of this time show much engagement with what became known as the international style. Until Giles Gilbert Scott won a competition to design a standard telephone kiosk for the whole country in 1921 – inspired in part by the tomb designed by architect John Soane for his wife – Britain enjoyed a variety of idiosyncratic call-box designs. The Post Office took over Britain's telephone network in 1912, but before this there was no monopoly in the telephone service and rival companies competed for business by trying to make their kiosks look particularly attractive or cosy.[64] In an effort to help them blend in with their surroundings, some were even thatched. Despite the visual confusion, many people were happy with their individual designs, and a standardized call-box proved surprisingly unpopular. Gilbert Scott's 1924 K2 design for the telephone kiosk was certainly not modern, however (see Figure 1.4). While it may have rejected the previous century's interest in stylistic theatre in favour of symmetry, uniformity and restraint, it remains a monumental, classical conception. For those who supported modernism, the K2 design was merely a scarlet obstruction.[65]

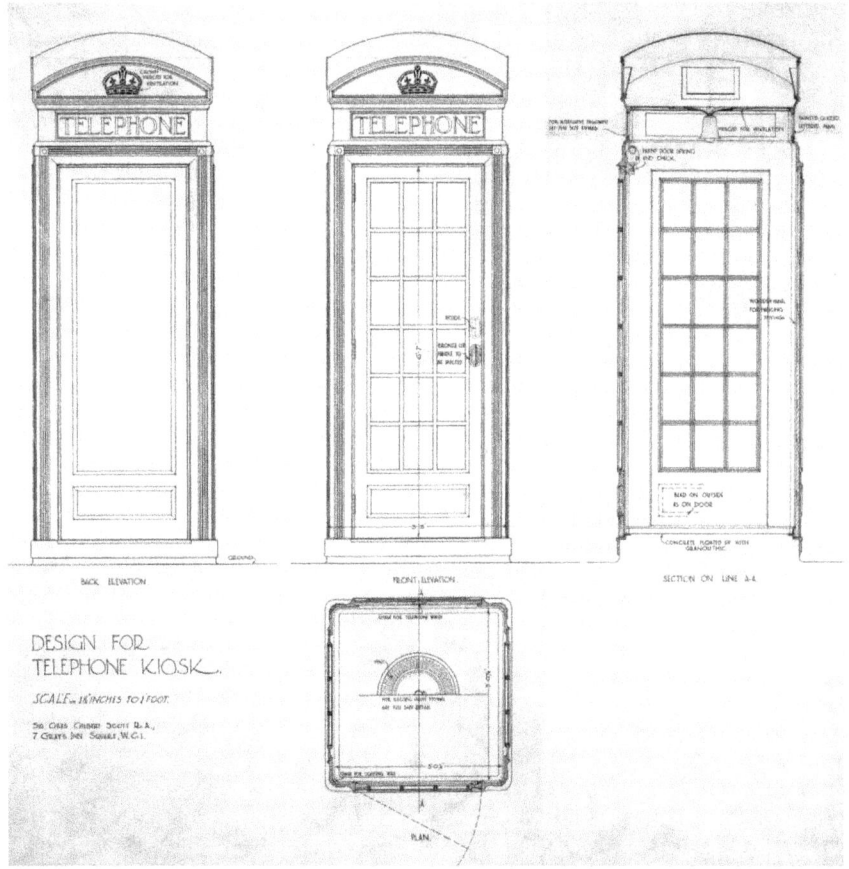

Figure 1.4 Design by Giles Gilbert Scott for GPO telephone kiosk number 2: plan, elevations and section. RIBA Library Drawings & Archives Collections.

Britain's negative reaction towards modern design was also symptomatic of a general dissatisfaction with the forms and materials with which it had gradually become aligned. Concrete for instance made a significant contribution to one of the most disliked qualities of modern design: its apparent ability to erode local differences. For the same reason the use of steel was also disliked, and in 1939 residents in the villages of Surrey and Sussex complained that their new slim tubular steel roadside bus shelters were out of harmony with their surroundings (see Figure 1.5). Following considerable local protest, the steel shelters were eventually replaced with an alternative made from oak, a design which critics said looked 'grotesquely out of place' and had arrived there through the action of 'handicapped people who had lost the power of seeing'.[66]

Figure 1.5 A view of a steel and glass bus shelter in Sutton E9, August 1937. © TfL from the London Transport Museum collection.

Throughout the 1930s many British people perceived modern design as uncompromising, continental and often ugly. Even some members of the cultural community felt constricted by Modernism's minimal language of form and fought to recognize the value of history, locality, ornament and eccentricity. As Alexandra Harris's book *Romantic Moderns* points out, cultural figures like John Betjeman, John Piper, Nicolete Gray and Paul Nash looked for ways to reconnect with the past, searching out the vernacular, the idiosyncratic and the exuberant – all qualities modern design purists rejected, and even deliberately shamed.[67] Even Herbert Read, who played a significant role in facilitating modern design's eventual acceptance in Britain, felt in 1934 that the public's reaction was justifiable given modern design's bleak, pioneering functionalism.[68] Read would later help set up Britain's first design consultancy, the Design Research Unit, which acted as an advisory body to government and industry alike, and pioneered a model for interdisciplinary design practice and corporate design.[69] For German art historian Nikolaus Pevsner, however, English modernists like Read were missing the point. Modern design might be cold, but it was ultimately pioneering. Accounting for the apparent neutrality of modern design in a typically unemotional style, Pevsner claimed that 'only ideologies differ… as for the West, a certain democratic sameness must be accepted'.[70]

Pevsner is an important figure within the design debates of the 1930s and 1940s, and his book *Pioneers of Modern Design* represents the consolidation of Good Design discourse with modern design. His impact on design debates of the twentieth century can also be measured through his 1937 report *An Enquiry into Industrial Art in England* which advanced many familiar arguments. For Pevsner, the situation in the late 1930s was at crisis point: 'when I say that 90% of British industrial art is devoid of any aesthetic merit, I am not exaggerating'.[71] But the main obstacle to Britain's adoption of modern design – an apparently simple and rational style – was the country's upper class. The English aristocracy, he said, continued to prefer period decoration to modern industrial art, owing to their conservatism, 'inborn reserve and a distrust of anything that looks strikingly new'.[72] Pevsner's biographer Susie Harries claims that he blamed the lower classes in equal measure, especially those who failed to dislike 'showy, vulgar, sentimental and meretricious objects […] as thoroughly as one would wish them to'.[73] For Pevsner, taste was 'an expression of inner harmony, dignity, cleanliness'; and Harries says that logically this meant that for Pevsner poor taste was 'a reflection of inner disharmony, indignity, grime, the indicator of a damaging and undesirable way of life and an ailing society'.[74] Pevsner attributed bad taste to social conditions and exploitation under capitalism, but he also believed that if the masses were taught to recognize better design, and it was made affordable, then they would learn to want it, leading to improvements in social conditions more generally.

During the mid-1930s this belief gained momentum and official channels like the British Broadcasting Corporation emerged as active forces in stimulating debate about the importance of design for the masses. In 1937, the BBC commissioned the arts and fiction writer Anthony Bertram to produce a series of broadcasts about design in cooperation with the DIA. According to Bertram good design could 'satisfy the needs of people; their need of practical, honest, cheap, lasting and beautiful things to use and see in their everyday lives'.[75] However, Bertram shared Pevsner's anxiety about taste. While he noted that 'very few of us agree as to what good looks are', he simultaneously doubted the suggestion that 'everyone is born with the capacity to judge design'.[76] Only education, according to Bertram, could lead to improvements in taste, and lift people out of the 'social crippledom' that such disadvantages caused. But he also proposed that specialists in design ought to be considered the experts that they were, and that 'the anger of the untrained must be braved'.[77] And, like Gloag, Bertram also called for 'a special body of men trained in aesthetics'.[78]

Bertram's BBC broadcasts also addressed an aspect of street furniture design that would cause considerable anxiety within the post-war debate, namely standardization. As noted already, during this period there was a considerable degree of local variety within street furniture design, and several different responsible agencies, both public and private. In the field of lamp posts for instance, civic authorities would often compete with each other over elaborate designs, and there was fierce rivalry between the gas and electric industries for illumination.[79] For Bertram, the design of street furniture was severely lacking, and he attributed this problem to the absence of any sense of unifying control over its design. Those who could act, he said, merely 'kick their heels just as they please' and as a result, the quality of objects as varied as lamp posts and tram standards were generally shocking – 'the bus shelters are usually the only good looking things in some industrial cities'.[80] As part of his BBC broadcasts, Bertram cited one listener who requested 'a controller of design in every city, an official responsible for lettering, lamp posts, refuges, subways, public lavatories, in fact everything in the street'.[81]

Condemnation of this kind had some precedent. In 1934, Frank Pick had railed against Britain's street lighting, signage and other 'equipment' in terms of their function, efficiency, rationality and unity.[82] Pick criticized the fact that most street equipment was clearly an after-thought and not the care of one body but of several, which had devastating effects on the architectural quality of the street. In a conversation with Gloag in 1934, Pick noted that the quality of bollards were particularly poor, and he reported that, 'their deplorable variety may be attributed to the fact that our local authorities, even when socialistic in politics, are confirmed individualists in design – and London has many local authorities'.[83] For Pick, as the head of a large organization like London Transport, modern design meant standardization, which left little room for individualism, and he called for 'a review of all the miscellaneous things, both useful and decorative, that a finished street ought to contain and for a scheme that will provide for them all harmoniously and concisely'.[84] Every street he said, 'should be deliberately planned from the start with all its equipment properly located and co-ordinated, for all these things may be wanted'.[85] For Pick, better design would not only cure the problems of the street but also transform it into a work of art.[86] A central question remained, however: how would these ideals be achieved and who would be responsible?

Aligning Good Design with government

The late 1930s represents an important shift in British design culture, because at this point, the elite voices which had positioned themselves at a discreet distance from popular taste, sought to extend their influence upon it. One of the central ways in which this was achieved was through strengthening Good Design's relationship with government and lobbying for greater powers. Many within the design profession recognized that only the state had the resources to engage in comprehensive control and raise design standards on a mass scale. And some within the DIA believed that their campaign would benefit from the appointment of an independent body endowed with 'executive powers', rather than simply 'an advisory board'.[87] In a report submitted to the government on the proposal, Roger Fry observed that 'many manufacturers are utterly at sea in the matter of design. For one thing they have lost contact with educated taste.'[88] Establishing a central council would, implied Fry, remedy this problem by advising manufacturers and acting on behalf of the public, whose taste was 'neither cultivated nor discriminating'.[89]

The appointment of a Council for Art and Industry testifies to the success of this campaign; nevertheless, it was short-lived. The start of the Second World War in 1939 put a temporary stop to these advances and the CAI fulfilled very few of its supporter's hopes. Wartime did, however, provide the unique conditions for state-supported design reform, and the comprehensive dissemination of Good Design. For instance, the style of products produced as part of the Utility Scheme reflected DIA recommendations, and the preferences of those who actively pressured for improvements informed by European modernism – a foreign association that was later parodied by *Punch*.[90] It also effectively provided an opportunity for important interwar design figures to finally apply their ideas in practice. As a result, by 1943 Cecil Weir's sub-committee report on *Industrial Design and Art in Industry* was able to announce that 'since there *is* such a thing as recognizably good design, and since there *is not* a fundamental conflict between "giving the public what it wants" and good design, then a Central Design Council, not directly responsible to a government department should start work'.[91] Yet the Weir report, as it became known, acknowledged the difficulties that might ensue as a result of the formation of such a body, particularly concerning the perception that the government was effectively censoring taste and installing an aesthetic dictatorship. In its defence, the report observed that,

> The state already acknowledges the principle of discrimination in matters of taste, which not only operates in all purchases for museums and galleries, but in selection for international exhibitions, etc. If the State is to accept its responsibility towards design as an end in itself, as an amenity for the consumer and as an essential tool in our economic life, the existence of an authoritative body is inevitable.[92]

That body would emerge as the Council of Industrial Design the following year, and would use the ideas discussed in this chapter about Good Design as the basis for its campaign to improve street furniture. However, as the next chapter will discuss, suspicions about its motivation would persist. The Council of Industrial Design would face many of the same challenges that its predecessors had – particularly concerning Good Design's relationship with the public, government and industry – and would rely on the same set of ideas about taste, style, class and expertise in order to tackle them.

Notes

1. Michael Collins, *Towards Postmodernism: Design since 1851*, 2nd edn (London: British Museum Press, 1994), 13. See also Augustus Welby Pugin, *An Apology for the Revival of Christian Architecture in England* (Edinburgh: John Grant, 1895. First published by John Weale, London 1843).
2. See Hazel Conway, *People's Parks: The Design and Development of Victorian Parks in Britain* (Cambridge: Cambridge University Press, 1991).
3. Augustus Welby Pugin, *The True Principles of Pointed or Christian Architecture* (Edinburgh: John Grant, 1895. First published by John Weale, London 1841), 27.
4. Ibid., 29.
5. Ibid., 51.
6. Ibid., 47 and 56.
7. Jules Lubbock, *The Tyranny of Taste: The Politics of Architecture and Design in Britain 1550–1960* (New Haven, CT and London: Paul Mellon Centre for British Art by Yale University Press, 1995), xii.
8. William Morris, 'The Nature of Gothic', in *The Works of John Ruskin Vol. II The Stones of Venice: The Sea Stories*, eds. E. T. Cook and Alexander Wedderburn (London: George Allen, 1903–4), 460–2.
9. Nikolaus Pevsner, *Pioneers of Modern Design: From William Morris to Walter Gropius* (Middlesex: Penguin Books, 1960 First published by Faber and Faber in 1936 as 'Pioneers of the Modern Movement'), 24.
10. William Morris, 'The Lesser Arts', in *The Industrial Design Reader*, ed. Carma Gorman (New York: Allworth Press, 2003), 35.
11. William Morris cited in Pevsner, *Pioneers of Modern Design*, 23. See also Noel Carrington, *Industrial Design in Britain* (London: George Allen & Unwin Ltd, 1976), 24.
12. Pevsner, *Pioneers of Modern Design*, 22.
13. Ibid., 24.
14. Carrington, *Industrial Design in Britain*, 22.
15. Edward Lucie-Smith, *A History of Industrial Design* (Oxford: Phaidon, 1983), 44–5.
16. Wendy Hitchmough, *C.F.A. Voysey* (London: Phaidon Press, 1997), 62. See also Chris Otter, *The Victorian Eye: A Political History of Light and Vision in Britain, 1800–1910* (Chicago and London: The University of Chicago Press, 2008), 249–50.
17. For further information on the design evolution of the letterbox, see Postal Museum and Archive. Available online: http://www.postalheritage.org.uk/collections/pillarboxes/(accessed 31 July 2015).
18. Asa Briggs, *Victorian Things* (London: Penguin, 1988), 335.
19. John T. Emmett, 'On the Profession of an Architect', *British Quarterly Review*, April 1880, 343.
20. John T. Emmett, 'The Bane of English Architecture', *British Quarterly Review*, April 1881, 403.

21 Electric Lighting in the City of London, *Engineering*, 57, 16 February 1894, 235, cited in Otter, *The Victorian Eye*, 247.
22 Robert Louis Stevenson, 'A Plea for Gas Lamps', in *The Travels and Essays of Robert Louis Stevenson*, Vol. 13 (New York: Charles Scribners Sons, 1895), 169.
23 Otter, *The Victorian Eye*, 9.
24 For further reading, see Mark Bouman, 'Luxury and Control: The Urbanity of Lighting in 19th Century Cities', *Journal of Urban History*, Vol. 14, No. 1 (1987 November): 7–37; Wolfgang Schivelbusch, *Disenchanted Night: The Industrialization of Light in the 19th Century* (Berkeley, Los Angeles, London: The University of California Press, 1988), translated from German by Angela Davies; A. Roger Ekirch, *At Days Close: Night in Times Past* (New York: W. W. Norton and Co. Inc, 2005).
25 See Frederic J. Schwartz, *The Werkbund: Design Theory and Mass Culture before the First World War* (New Haven, CT and London: Yale University Press, 1996); Joan Campbell, *The German Werkbund: The Politics of Reform in the Applied Arts* (Princeton: Princeton University Press, 1978).
26 C.H. Collins Baker, *Design in Modern Industry: The Year Book of the Design & Industries Association* (London: DIA, 1922), 9.
27 Lord Jeffrey, 'An Essay on Beauty', in *Industrial Art Explained*, ed. John Gloag (London: George Allen and Unwin Ltd, 1946. First published in 1934), 71.
28 Lethaby in Raymond Plummer, *Nothing Need Be Ugly* (London: DIA, 1985), 27.
29 Frank Pick, 'Art in Commerce and in Life', 8 March 1916 (LTM PB2a), 6.
30 Frank Pick, 'Standards of Art and Standards of Trade: The Art Teachers' Guild Record, no. 34', September 1917 (LTM PB7), 12.
31 'Good design' was an expression used by the DIA from 1917 onwards. Its application was as a value judgment rather than a representation of Good Design discourse. While the work of the DIA was instrumental in giving shape to Good Design discourse, it would be anachronistic to suggest that at this stage the expression was meant in that way. For evidence of its early application by the DIA, see Arthur Clutton Brock, *A Modern Creed of Work: The 4th Pamphlet of the Design and Industries Association* (London: The DIA, 1917).
32 Ibid., 4.
33 Ibid., 12–17; Collins Baker, *Design in Modern Industry*, 12.
34 Roger Fry in Alexandra Harris, *Romantic Moderns: English Writers, Artists and the Imagination from Virginia Woolf to John Piper* (London and New York: Thames and Hudson, 2010), 42.
35 Le Corbusier, *Towards a New Architecture* (London: Architectural Press, 1989. First published 1927), 143.
36 Collins Baker, *Design in Modern Industry*, 3–4.
37 Frank Pick, 'The Art of the Street. Mainly Illustrated from London', 9 March 1923 (LTM PB13), 1.
38 Ibid.
39 Frank Pick, 'Holiday After-thoughts', *DIA Quarterly Journal*, October 1929, New Series, No. 9 (LTM PB20), 13.
40 Frank Pick, 'To the Master and Brethren of the Art Worker's Guild', 15 February 1916 (LTM PB1), 20.
41 Frank Pick, 'Art in Household Things: A Paper for the Art Workers Guild, Ladies Evening', 23 February 1917 (LTM PB6), 12–13.
42 Frank Pick, 'The Meaning and Purpose of Design', 19 June 1933 (LTM PB49); Collins Baker, *Design in Modern Industry*, 10.

43 Ibid., 16.
44 Ibid., 6.
45 Ibid., 8.
46 Ibid., 10.
47 Frank Pick, 'An Edinburgh Address on Design and Industry', October 1916 (LTM 1998/105574 B6 BOX 4), 8.
48 Herbert Read, *Art and Industry* (London: Faber and Faber Ltd, 1952. First published 1934), 7.
49 Ibid., 188. Read's reference to 'good designs' also suggests that by 1934, it was emerging as a meaningful expression.
50 Ibid.
51 Plummer, *Nothing Need Be Ugly*, 13.
52 D. L. LeMahieu, *A Culture for Democracy: Mass Communication and the Cultivated Mind between the Wars* (Oxford: Clarendon Press, 1988), 103.
53 Ibid., 104–5.
54 Ibid., 107.
55 Ibid., 121.
56 Ibid., 120.
57 Renato Poggioli, *Theory of the Avant-Garde* (Cambridge, MA: Belknap Press, 1968), 2–4.
58 Ibid., 85 and 90.
59 Ibid.
60 Gloag, *Industrial Art Explained*, 141.
61 John Gloag, ed., *Design in Modern Life* (London: George Allen and Unwin Ltd, 1934), 17.
62 Gloag, *Industrial Art Explained*, 156.
63 Ibid.
64 See Gavin Stamp, *Telephone Boxes* (London: Chatto and Windus, 1989); John Timpson, *Requiem for a Red Box* (London: Pyramid Books, 1989).
65 Pick, 'Holiday After-thoughts'. Gilbert Scott allegedly wished the kiosks to be painted silver and greenish-blue inside. However, a decision was taken to paint the kiosks 'Post Office red' for purposes of visibility and its compatibility with dirt. For more information, see The Story of the British Telephone Box. Available online: http://www.the-telephone-box.co.uk/story/ (accessed 31 July 2015).
66 Christian Barman, *The Man Who Built London Transport: A Biography of Frank Pick* (London: David & Charles, 1979), 237–8.
67 Harris, *Romantic Moderns*.
68 Read, *Art and Industry*, 7.
69 Michelle Cotton, *Design Research Unit 1942–72* (Köln: Walther Koenig Books Ltd, 2011), 6.
70 Pevsner in Matthew Aitchison, ed., *Visual Planning and the Picturesque: Nikolaus Pevsner* (Los Angeles, CA: Getty Research Institute, 2010), 181.
71 Nikolaus Pevsner, *An Enquiry into Industrial Art in England* (Cambridge: Cambridge University Press, 1937), 12.
72 Ibid., 206.
73 Susie Harries, *Nikolaus Pevsner: The Life* (London: Chatto & Windus, 2011), 181.
74 Ibid., 184.
75 Anthony Bertram, *Design* (Harmondsworth, Middlesex: A Pelican Special, Penguin Books Ltd, 1938), 19.

76 Ibid., 13–4.
77 Ibid., 13.
78 Ibid., 18.
79 See 'The Game Continues', *Public Lighting and Public Lighting Engineer*, Vol. 1, No. 4, December 1936. Also available online: http://www.simoncornwell.com/lighting/home.htm (accessed 31 July 2015).
80 Bertram, *Design*, 27–8.
81 Correspondence in *The Listener*, 6 October 1937, 711.
82 Frank Pick, 'The Design of the Street', in Gloag, *Design in Modern Life*, 102.
83 Ibid., 103.
84 Pick, 'The Art of the Street', 17 and 23.
85 Frank Pick and John Gloag, 'Design in Modern Life. The Design of the Street', 6 June 1933 (LTM PB23), 9.
86 Ibid., 18.
87 HMSO, *Report on the Production and Exhibition of Articles of Good Design and Every-Day use* (London: HMSO, 1932).
88 Roger Fry, 'Appendix: Memorandum', in ibid., 44.
89 Ibid., 46.
90 See Utility cartoon, *Punch*, 9 October 1946, 291.
91 Cecil Weir, *Industrial Design and Art in Industry*, quoted in Fiona MacCarthy, *A History of British Design: 1830–1970* (London: George Allen and Unwin 1979. First published as *All Things Bright and Beautiful*), 73.
92 'Report of the Sub-Committee Appointed by Mr. Harcourt Johnston on Industrial Design and Art in Industry', 23 September 1943, Section 12, in Jonathan Woodham, 'Managing British Design Reform I: Fresh Perspectives on the Early Years of the Council of Industrial Design', *Journal of Design History*, Vol. 9, No. 1 (1996): 57.

Chapter 2

THE COUNCIL OF INDUSTRIAL DESIGN: OFFICIAL ARTICULATIONS OF STREET FURNITURE DESIGN

By the early 1940s, the view that an official machine was necessary to ensure better standards in design was shared by many parties, both in and outside of government. Neither the Design and Industries Association nor the Council for Art and Industry had achieved their ambitious objectives and the formation of a body more closely linked to government had several advantages. According to former DIA member, Noel Carrington, the Board of Trade (BoT) believed that establishing 'an organization under its own wing and with its own officers would be more trustworthy'.[1] In the light of this, a series of meetings were held by the Board in 1944, with a view to creating a body that could be trusted to influence and encourage higher standards in British manufacturing. The Council of Industrial Design (CoID) was the product of these meetings, and is the subject of this chapter.

The organization was founded in 1944 by Hugh Dalton, president of the BoT, on an initial government grant of £55,000. According to the CoID's first annual report, its primary task was 'to promote by all practicable means the improvement of design in the products of British industry'.[2] For Dalton, the organization's role was to

> make a sustained effort to improve design, and to bring industry to recognize the importance of this task. You have to arouse the interest of ordinary men and women ... if you succeed in your task, in a few years' time, every side of our daily life will be better for your work ... men and women in millions will be in your debt, though they may not know it ... Industry itself will have much cause to thank you.[3]

The CoID was expected to fulfil this broad remit by promoting the value of well-designed goods to both the general public and the industrial sector. Indeed, as *Punch*'s cartoon illustrates – albeit satirically – one of the services provided by the CoID involved matching designers with clients (see Figure 2.1). In doing so, the CoID was also expected to perform an important economic role for the BoT because improving the public and industry's ability to 'appreciate the need for good design' was considered to be the best way to rebuild Britain's export trade.[4] By all accounts, Britain was in a very difficult economic position after the war, and therefore any attempts to reinvigorate British industry by the BoT ought to be seen in this light.

"I'd like to contact the designer of the Adastra garden rake."

Figure 2.1 Cartoon in *Punch* magazine satirizing the Council of Industrial Design's role as an interface between designers and industry. Cartoon by J. W. Taylor, *Punch*, 27 November 1946, 474. Reproduced with permission of Punch Ltd., www.punch.co.uk.

And yet the CoID's role in the field of design went beyond economics. The organization's second director – Gordon Russell – is credited as having put in place the essential structure for the CoID that remained largely intact until the mid-1980s. The organizational model was as an educational and advisory service for the public, industry and municipal authorities. The CoID's interpretation of Good Design was thoroughly endorsed through exhibitions, symposiums and conferences, publications, the Design Centre and *Design* magazine. Russell was also noted for his interest in the reform of design education, particularly where he believed it could perform better for industry. As such, the CoID also assisted in the training of designers, and provided an interface between designers and industry.

The combination of all these different services for different audiences – including the public, retailers, industry and educators – would establish a balance that the CoID strove to maintain: both serving industry and designers, and acting in the interests of the public.

Though much of its central work focused on consumer goods, the remit of the CoID extended to a wide variety of everyday objects, and in this respect it is possible to discern a relationship between Anthony Bertram's pre-war aspirations for everyday design and the CoID's post-war aspirations for street furniture. In a letter from Russell to *The Times* in August 1950, he claimed 'either we care enough to insist on well designed and appropriate things everywhere or we do not. But can we hope to satisfy increasingly critical customers in export markets or even complacently regard ourselves as civilized people if we ignore the design of the commonplace things which all of us use everywhere everyday?'[5] Justifying the improvement of commonplace things as a way of civilizing the country reflected the agenda of the CoID as a whole, and quickly extended into the wider designed landscape, particularly street furniture. Russell's interest in street furniture had considerable precedent. Even as early as 1935 he had declared: 'is it too much to hope that in learning to design our cups and gas fires, our chairs and lampposts we may in the end learn to design our lives?'[6] With no apparent irony, Russell's comment reflected a moral judgement upon the existing state of people's lives, a position the CoID would also adopt. For the CoID, street furniture was an important example of commonplace things that required attention, since 'it is in its minor equipment and detail that an age reveals its character'.[7] And while some people were emotionally attached to pre-war street furniture, its detractors believed that such objects were not only ugly and largely responsible for the messy clutter of Britain's streets; but were also representative of a stratified social system, which was increasingly seen as incompatible with post-war social reforms. As such, improving the design of street furniture quickly became one of the CoID's aims, for which it was both nationally and internationally recognized.[8]

Besides the notion that better design could civilize the country, the CoID's interest in street furniture can be attributed to a number of other factors. For a start, bombing raids during the war had caused considerable damage to Britain's built environment, and some of the country's street furniture had been damaged as a consequence. The British war effort proved just as destructive, and following the Minister of Aircraft Production Lord Beaverbrook's call for scrap metal in 1940, miles and miles of Victorian iron railings were torn down (see Figure 2.2). While some were supportive, others complained bitterly, among them the writer Evelyn Waugh for whom ornamental cast iron work was one of Victorian England's unique achievements.[9] Waugh expressed his disappointment in a letter to *The Times* in 1942 that, 'in the high mood of sacrifice with which so much is being broken and melted, it is possible to detect an undercurrent of satisfaction that national need should give the opportunity for removing what is now thought unsightly'.[10] Though many considered them to be monstrosities or even disfigurements, he argued that the railings 'which adorned the houses of all classes were symbols of independence and privacy in an age which rated liberty above equality'.[11] Waugh's

Figure 2.2 Salvage work in progress in Spencer Parade, Northampton, with iron railings being removed, the scrap metal being used for munitions, 1940. Popperfoto and Getty Images.

argument was not just a stylistic one; he saw the removal of these old railings as indicative of a political shift, in which personal freedom – or as others might have said, a stratified social system – was being threatened by an overbearing state.

Several other factors also explain the increased interest in street furniture. Over and above deliberate wartime damage, years of civic underinvestment meant that some of Britain's street furniture did need to be replaced. Street lighting across the country was moving from gas to electricity, which required new equipment. After the war, new roads also had to be built to accommodate the anticipated increase in car ownership.[12] Combined with the pervasive sense of urgency to redevelop the country and build new housing, streets, towns and cities, these factors contributed to street furniture emerging as a particularly newsworthy topic in the immediate post-war years.

Lighting manufacturers quickly took advantage of the demand, producing street lamps in much the same way as they had done before the war, albeit for electric installations and using concrete (see Figure 2.3). But for the CoID, the immediate post-war years presented a new start for the country, not least in design terms. As an organization dedicated to modern design, the CoID shared the view of another official body concerned with street furniture design, the Royal Fine Art Commission, that the damage inflicted upon street furniture during wartime provided an unexpected opportunity whereby 'every effort should be made to use to the best advantage the exceptional opportunity of starting from scratch which is presented by

Figure 2.3 'A pleasing design exhibiting all the attributes of a good concrete column' – Concrete Utilities Ltd., 'Modern Lamp Columns', List 38, 1946, 1. CU Phosco Lighting Ltd.

the creation of new towns and the redevelopment of blitzed areas'.[13] Manufacturers, they insisted, could not simply continue producing street furniture according to pre-war standards; others knew that this was exactly what industry wanted to do. In a feature on industrial design in 1946, the *Architectural Review* claimed that the CoID was ill-equipped to sell '*design* to manufacturers who must know only too well that *output*, however shoddy, cannot possibly overtake demand for several years to come'.[14]

The problem was compounded by the fact that many manufacturers held the view that that 'British made' was a marker of excellence in itself, and that design was superfluous – being one of the 'perversities of foreigners'.[15] At the time, there were a number of large manufacturing firms producing street furniture, such as the General Electric Company, Osram, Concrete Utilities Ltd. and Thorn, which perceived street lighting in particular as a rich territory. Indeed, given the urgency with which the streets required modernization and the availability of central funds to pay for that process, it represented a considerable commercial opportunity. There was, according to the industrial designer, Kenneth Grange, 'big money' to be made in street lighting.[16] These firms had departments devoted to nothing but street lighting, and according to Grange, the standard of work they produced was 'as sophisticated as anywhere in the world'.[17] Yet the CoID's perception of standards clearly differed from Grange's, and in a lecture given some years later, one CoID officer recounted that manufacturers 'rapidly produced designs based on tired, worn clichés of the day and … found no difficulty in selling these in vast quantities as there was no longer an enlightened patron interested in good taste, as the original gas-lighting boom'.[18] Raising awareness that tired, worn clichés were no longer acceptable was one of the ways that the CoID sought to educate manufacturers and improve industrial standards.

One of the great ironies within this discussion, however, concerned the design quality and serviceability of much of the existing stock of street furniture. Ornamental lamps and railings functioned perfectly well; they just didn't look modern. As such, it's worth asking, just what part of industrial standards required improvement? As the last chapter discussed, prior to the 1950s the design of street lighting was chiefly a matter for iron foundries or engineers rather than architects or industrial designers. For engineers, the design of a street lamp was a technological and practical solution to a problem, in which appearance was less important than questions of optics, height, distance, maintenance and weather resistance. While visual style is of course an inevitable consequence in the production of any object, the appearance of street furniture was not prioritized in the way it should have been, at least according to the CoID. For the CoID, improving the standard of street lighting meant improving how it looked, as well as its effectiveness, but it understood improvement in terms of an object's modern qualities (see Figure 2.4). Modernism declared design should be transferable from one place to another, that it should jettison ornament as well as the past, and be industrially produced using modern materials.

The CoID was encouraged in its efforts to improve street furniture design by the Ministry of Transport (MoT) and the Royal Fine Art Commission (RFAC). Up until the beginning of 1952 the RFAC was responsible for maintaining visual standards in street furniture design, but some years earlier, it had begun to express concern that those standards were in fact falling. In Russell's letter to *The Times*, he referenced the comments of Lord Crawford, Chairman of the RFAC, who had made it clear that 'in "passing" designs for lamp-posts and other street furniture, the Royal Fine Art Commission is often in the unfortunate position of having

The Council of Industrial Design 35

Figure 2.4 25´0″ Spun Concrete lighting column 1955 for AEI Lamp and Lighting Co Ltd. Design Council Archive, University of Brighton Design Archives and Susan Wright. Modern lamp post designed by Jack Howe for AEI Lamp and Lighting Co Ltd. 1955.

to select the least offensive'.[19] Both the RFAC and the CoID agreed that poor standards were intolerable. As such, together with the Ministry of Transport, the RFAC recommended that the CoID be given responsibility for the approval of lighting columns and brackets for Grade A roads.[20] While there was a transitional period during the 1950s – in which designs that had been previously approved by the RFAC were considered valid even if they had not been approved by the CoID – a timescale for this process was devised. Yet once the responsibility for street lamps was awarded to the CoID, it became increasingly obvious that standards ought to equally apply to other types of street furniture as well. Thus, in 1959, the MoT issued a directive to regional engineers that all street furniture, with the exception of litter bins, should be selected from the CoID's approved list of products.[21] Though there was no compulsion for them to do so – with the exception of lighting – it nonetheless meant that, by 1960, the CoID became the British government's official authority on the design of street furniture.[22]

The Street Furniture Advisory Committee

The element of the CoID which dealt with street furniture directly was the independently appointed Street Furniture Advisory Committee. It was established in 1949 and made up of ten members, who were responsible for judging street furniture designs that had been submitted by manufacturers. Members of the committee relied upon a secretary to liaise directly with manufacturers to ensure that the products they submitted fulfilled certain criteria, and those that did not meet the committee's standards were returned with recommendations for improvement. Once identified as having met those requirements, the products were included in the Design Index, which was a photographic database of all the products selected by the CoID, accessible to the public.[23] However, for some manufacturing firms this meant their products had been approved by the committee, an interpretation which caused the CoID considerable consternation. One CoID document reflects the anxiety the term caused:

> We constantly try to persuade firms whose items are accepted for Design Index to use the word 'accepted' or 'selected' rather than 'approved', explaining that as we are not ... an official approving body, misuse of the word 'approved' may lead to misunderstandings. Unfortunately our own staff members do from time to time use the word 'approved' themselves in this connection and this weakens our case when approaching manufacturers.[24]

This discussion about nomenclature indicates the level of confusion regarding the remit of the organization, both in and outside the CoID. Yet unlike other committees, the Street Furniture Advisory Committee did actually have the power to approve street lighting for some roads.

The power to approve street furniture was bestowed upon the CoID by the MoT in a combined effort to raise general standards of design.[25] Partly because of its relationship with the MoT, the committee's main purpose at first was to improve the daytime appearance of lamp posts, and approve those that achieved this aim.[26] Once items had been approved, the committee's secretary acted by subtly pressurizing local authorities to select from these designs, which were in turn expected to purchase them from the manufacturers in question.[27] Ensuring that manufacturers produced products likely to meet the CoID's approval was essential, for if the right products were not available then any influence possessed by the CoID over local government would be wasted. The MoT enforced local government compliance through policy, but there was also a financial incentive to comply, because CoID-approved designs were partially subsidized by the MoT.[28] For design historian Nigel Whiteley, such an approach exemplified the CoID's belief in government intervention, control and planning, much like the Utility scheme.[29] For others, it amounted to a bribe for Good Design.[30]

The way in which the committee operated in the area of street furniture, and its relationship with the MoT, reflects the mechanisms of the CoID as a whole. Though it did not have enforceable powers – except in the area of lighting for Grade A roads – the CoID's influence cannot be underestimated, since it had the power of the government on its side. Rather than being seen as a department of government, the CoID must ultimately be seen as a mediator between government and industry, and a way for central government to apply arms-length pressure upon manufacturers. In this way, the CoID could be viewed as a latter-day Quango: state-funded and appointed by government, but broadly autonomous in spirit. Another way of understanding the CoID is as a consultative body, which could not engage with the design process directly, but could use its independently appointed committees to act on its behalf. As such, the CoID could distance itself from its committee's decisions, but equally benefit from their supposed impartiality. For the Street Furniture Advisory Committee at least, one member later stressed that 'we did not have, nor have we ever, sought any powers'.[31] Given this statement was made during a lecture on street furniture to planning officers in 1960, it can be seen as deliberately modest, for it is likely that the CoID was keen to underplay its hand in such an environment. Instead, as the CoID's fifth annual report claimed, the committee achieved its agenda through 'persuasion and education'.[32]

The role of the Street Furniture Advisory Committee is clearly important. Its acceptance or rejection of certain designs had enormous consequences for Britain's street furniture, particularly street lighting. Unfortunately, the minutes of committee meetings were routinely destroyed by the CoID, and therefore it is impossible to know the nature of their discussions or the reasons why particular decisions were made. Nevertheless, a number of points can be made about the committee: the way it worked, how it was appointed, and what its objectives were.

Legislation and taste

The legislative changes that occurred after the war had a significant effect upon the remit of the CoID and its Street Furniture Advisory Committee, as well as much of the debate on street furniture that later ensued. The 1947 Town and

Country Planning Act is especially significant. It was introduced by the left-leaning Labour government of the time – a party which was committed to public initiatives – and put in place a wide range of state controls affecting land use. One of the most significant – and disliked – of these controls was the introduction of planning permission, meaning that land ownership no longer conferred ultimate development rights. As Lord Kennet, Heritage Minister in the late 1960s pointed out, the Act was 'the first introduction into the law of any democratic country the principle that society might forbid a man to do what he would on his own land, without compensation'.[33] Besides stripping landowners of their traditional rights, the Act also gave locally elected leaders responsibility for the urban landscape of their surrounding district, and provided financial assistance to encourage them to do so. Thus what had once been practiced in private increasingly became a public service. This had repercussions not only for architecture, but also for street furniture, which was exempt from planning controls. In this respect the Act was extremely important in inadvertently assigning responsibility for street furniture to local authorities.

Yet the 1947 Act also had an ideological agenda. It was essentially a piece of permissive legislation, which bestowed almost unlimited powers upon local government. And according to Jules Lubbock, it 'removed all statutory obstacles in the shape of bye-laws and no imposed no new statutory regulations in their place'.[34] In fact, the Act was made deliberately vague in terms of local government consent, in part because planning was considered a continuous process, but as a result, local government became more powerful than the public. It is Lubbock's view that the Act 'effectively nationalized the land by nationalizing all its development rights; in theory at least, planning authorities were placed in the position of the aristocratic landlords of the eighteenth-century, with the same freedom to promote positive development on a large scale, instead of merely regulating the developments of other people and preventing abuses'.[35] The suggestion that the post-war Labour government gave local authorities the same powers as eighteenth-century aristocratic landlords is one that some might question. However, for many besides Lubbock, the Labour ideals of collectivism and participation were a screen for what was in effect a continuation of the same approach as there had been for centuries – where powerful groups were able to act in the way of their choosing, without any mechanisms in place which could hold their actions to account. As Chapter 4 will show, local government often behaved as if it was unanswerable to the general public, whose objections were routinely ignored. According to Lubbock, the developer could act on his right to appeal within the framework of the Act, but the public had 'a capacity, not legally defined, only to make objections. They do not even have to be heard.'[36]

The Act also affected the CoID's contribution to the street furniture debate. According to Lubbock, 'because the 1947 legislation was permissive rather than regulatory, everything depended on key institutions and public bodies being under the control of the right chaps'.[37] Lubbock's point suggests that the make-up of organizations like the CoID – and its committees – was key to using the Act effectively. They were essentially another instrument of government, in which the right appointment of members was vital to frame the important issues and use their influence to effect change. As has already been discussed, many of the original members of the CoID were drawn from various committees relating to the BoT and the wartime Utility scheme, and design historian Jonathan Woodham perceives signs of aesthetic continuity in the CoID's interpretation of Good Design, largely based on its membership.[38] In his research on the subject, Woodham draws upon a number of letters which demonstrate that taste was fundamental to CoID membership. Referring to the candidate S. C. Leslie's suitability for the position of first director of the CoID, then director of the National Gallery, Kenneth Clark spoke of his concern that, 'we do not know what Mr Leslie's taste is like. It would be disastrous if, having been given a fairly free hand, he were to turn out to have bad taste.'[39] Evidently, discussions of Good Design and taste were often linked, but to what extent did this affect the Street Furniture Advisory Committee, and did the issue of taste underpin the decisions it made on street furniture?

Without the recorded minutes it is impossible to know for certain, but it is likely that taste was a factor in many of the Street Furniture Advisory Committee's decisions. CoID officers often cited taste during municipal lectures on the subject. Indeed, in an issue of *Design* from 1950, the editorial comment clarified the CoID's position on taste by stating that, 'it is no part of our purpose to belittle commercial success ... but it is no part of our job to agree that the lowest common denominator of public taste is ipso facto good design.'[40] For many manufacturers, however, the CoID had established a dictatorship on matters of taste. Certainly, the way in which the CoID's committees made their selection was not clear, and many manufacturers held a suspicion that the CoID represented a centrally orchestrated agenda. In his 1968 autobiography, Russell disputed this accusation:

> As I have already said, I have no wish to be a design dictator and during my time at the council I always strenuously avoided being associated with any measure which might appear that we were restricting the freedom of manufacturers to sell anything they cared to produce. Our job was to persuade them that a standard existed and that it was worth their while to up-grade their production so as to attain it. It is sometimes said that there is no such thing as good or bad design, that it has no real measurable standards, that it is in fact, just a matter of personal taste. But it is readily accepted that there is a standard of, say, honesty or driving or housing, so why not one of design?[41]

Russell's view was typical during the 1950s, in which cultural authority was held by a small number of men, whose personal taste was perceived as standing in for Good Design.

The taste of the CoID has been discussed from several perspectives already, and is often linked to class. Evidently, one of the CoID's tasks was to promote design as a social and economic good, but some historians have argued that it was arranged along class lines, and promoted a narrow view of middle-class taste. For Woodham, the social formation of the CoID was such that many provincial manufactures felt suspicious about the alleged cultural elitism of a body firmly rooted in the metropolitan taste-making circles of the South-East of England.[42] And it is his view that the CoID represented the 'establishment' in its promotion of metropolitan cultural authority.[43] In her book *Did Britain Make It?* Penny Sparke draws on original testimonies from CoID members that give further credibility to Woodham's argument. According to Paul Reilly, third director of the CoID, the supposed elitism of the CoID's taste and its endorsement of particularly middle-class values can be easily defended. He recounts,

> showing Aneurin Bevan round a furnished house at the Ideal Homes exhibition. He [Bevan] said that he thought the Council was quite right in furnishing in middle class taste since the working class never seem to get it out of their heads that the middle class know better than they do how to spend money. We wanted to improve everything. Of course, today working class values rate more highly than they did in the 1950s and 1960s.[44]

While Reilly's openness about the issue of class may seem particularly candid, it is important to place his statement into a broader context. Accusations that the CoID was a uniquely class-driven body are not wholly accurate, since the society in which it existed was one in which class boundaries remained relatively distinct. Many other cultural organizations operating during the post-war period were equally affected by questions of class, not least the BBC.

Representing whose interests?

Yet acting in the public's interests was only one part of the CoID's remit, for it had a number of other loyalties too. Given that the CoID represented the official design viewpoint, it would be easy to assume that it aligned itself with other cultural organizations, sharing their views and supporting their agendas. However, at least during the 1950s, this was not the case, and loyalties were often tested. An example can be drawn from an article published in 1950 by Reilly in *Art News and Review*'s regular series The Shape of Things, 'Who Cares for Street Furniture?' Reilly suggested that in fact, very few of the CoID's allies cared about street furniture, which was a 'public disgrace'.[45] He called the standard of existing street furniture 'abysmally low', which exposed a national tolerance for 'civic slovenliness' (see Figure 2.5).[46] He also accused the Royal Institute of British Architects of being a professional body 'more concerned about the welfare of its members than with the wellbeing of public amenities' and the RFAC of being an organization which 'intervenes only when requested'.[47] However, private letters held in the National Archives show that both The Royal Institute of British Architects (RIBA) and the RFAC questioned the diplomacy of the CoID's approach.[48] And if the CoID was not prepared to temper its attitude to its fellow lobbyists, then did its loyalties lie with government?

Figure 2.5 Civic slovenliness: boundaries between Green Park and Piccadilly, London. The *Architectural Review* asked sarcastically, 'is the chicken wire there to protect the holly hedge?' 'Marginalia: Excess of hazards', the *Architectural Review*, July 1949, Vol. 105, No. 107, 66. RIBA Library Books & Periodicals Collection.

In March 1958, Russell gave a paper on 'The other duties of an engineer' to the Institute of Municipal Engineers, which focused on aspects of civic design. Excerpts from his talk were published by a number of national newspapers, including the *Times* and the *Daily Telegraph*, and periodicals like the *Municipal Journal (MJ)*.[49] During his talk, Russell made a number of pronouncements on the style of street furniture, and he declared that it needed to be given 'a real sense of style, which is not at all the same thing as being styled or streamlined'.[50] He criticized some styles from the period, claiming that 'wainey-edged elm weatherboarding does not make a bus stop look rural: it makes it look self-conscious (see Figure 2.6)'.[51] Rather Russell suggested, street furniture should be 'efficient and economical to produce but had style and fitted naturally into the street'.[52]

Yet the contentious part of Russell's talk was less on these questions of style, as much as the way that he blamed those he considered responsible for bad street furniture design, namely government. For Russell, the lack of good street furniture was principally caused by the Ministry of Transport's subsidy system, and *The Daily Telegraph* reported Russell's view that 'the main difficulty now is that the best of the designs which have been achieved with much blood and sweat may never be seen by the public because they cost a few shillings more than second-rate ones, and the Ministry of Transport grants are based on the lowest tender'.[53] Russell's allegation

Figure 2.6 A 'wainey-edged' bus shelter of the type derided by Gordon Russell. Bus shelter, in *Design*, No. 69, September 1954, 30. Design Council Archive, University of Brighton Design Archives.

focused on the point that local authorities could often only afford to purchase the cheapest street furniture available, which was not always Good Design. Good street furniture, Russell said, should 'as a rule be straightforward, simple and unobtrusive', which was not (Russell implied) what local authorities were able to purchase due to meagre Ministry of Transport grants.[54] Unsurprisingly the MoT reacted badly to Russell's comments, particularly his additional view that 'power today rests in the hands of the State, local authorities and immense corporations, who usually demonstrate it by displays of such dreariness and boredom that the citizens brain is numbed'.[55] Internal correspondence within the MoT shows that several people questioned the fairness of Russell's remarks, and eventually he was invited to 'put the matter right'.[56] Russell eventually apologized in the event that he had 'embarrassed the Ministry of Transport'.[57] Evidently, relations between the CoID and government were delicate at times, and the balance of power over street furniture was not clearly divided: even at the centre there were differences of opinion.

However, as already noted, street furniture was a category of design that involved other parties, besides central government and design organizations, and the CoID was forced to work with local authorities and manufacturers as part of its project to improve standards. Here too, there were shifting loyalties. At times the CoID defined itself as 'an ally of industry', while at other times it appeared to align itself with local authorities.[58] For instance, in a lecture to planning officers in 1960, a member of the Street Furniture Advisory Committee conceded that 'we tend to feel that our work on street furniture is very much a lone battle. To come and discuss it with our allies and supporters, if I might class you as that, is of course a very welcome change.'[59] Such an opening statement might imply strategic flattery, but it might also suggest that the CoID knew the support of local authorities was key to its agenda. After all, as the main purchaser of street furniture, local authorities were the ultimate target market in terms of influencing the design of the street, a subject in which they were already intensely interested (see Figure 2.7). For the CoID, ensuring municipal support was crucial, which meant that tact and diplomacy were key to negotiations with this group. Nevertheless, at this particular lecture, the speaker accused local councils of being so thoroughly absorbed in internal politicking that the importance of furnishing the street to the best possible standards was often forgotten.[60] This view was also articulated by Reilly in a letter to Lord Snowdon (by then, a member of the CoID) in 1962, in which he noted that 'all lighting is ... paid for from the rates, therefore not only is the industry extremely cut-throat but with few foolish exceptions the Councils are very niggardly and usually spend the minimum'.[61] It is unlikely that such a view would have been expressed to the local authorities themselves, and sadly Reilly does not specify which ones he classed as 'niggardly'. In this respect, the medium of a letter is crucial in allowing Reilly's points to be made privately. Reilly also noted that the strategy often used by the salesmen of street furniture manufacturers consisted of flattering 'the ego of some empire building engineer who will not on principle use anything acceptable to his rival engineers in nearby boroughs'.[62] Thus, competition between local authorities was also a factor to be accounted for in the CoID's negotiations on street furniture.

Manufacturers were also criticized by the CoID, particularly for failing to appreciate the value of design, or for applying it too late in the production process. In his letter to Snowdon, Reilly noted that 'until quite recently there were only three professional designers regularly engaged on the problem. There is now a slight increase of professionalism but the majority are still designed by salesmen or directors... The firms who have a design policy find that at sales level it tends to be forgotten by salesmen who must have an order.'[63] Such a statement is revealing, since it suggests that even in 1962, the CoID had not managed to persuade everyone about the value of Good Design. Few firms producing street furniture employed professional designers, preferring instead to design the products in-house. It was also often the case that when lighting schemes were put out to tender, manufacturers and not local authorities made design decisions on appropriate columns and fittings. This problem was allegedly compounded by

Figure 2.7 Cover featuring Stewarts and Lloyds lamp, the *MJ*, 25 January 1952, No. 3075, Vol. 60. Photograph courtesy of *MJ* and Tata Steel. Reproduced by permission of the National Library of Scotland.

some manufacturers who, according to the *MJ*, 'do not always offer their full range to the smaller authority in remote parts but offer only a limited choice – perhaps of lines they seek to clear'.[64] Clearly the power that manufacturers had over the design of the street was significant in some parts of the country, particularly when local authorities were financially constrained. As a result, design was often left on the margins of any financial transaction between the two.

What these examples show is that the CoID's engagement with street furniture design was not a simple one. This complexity can be attributed to the multiplicity of parties that also engaged with the issue, as well as to the approach adopted by the CoID. In assigning blame upon those it considered responsible for bad street furniture design, the CoID risked isolating itself since no one wanted to take on this responsibility. As a result, the CoID was repeatedly forced to use different arguments and different methods for different groups, shifting its loyalties according to the target audience.

Design *magazine*

Published between 1949 and 1994, *Design* magazine can be considered as the CoID's mouthpiece. While the clarity of vision – in terms of both tone and visual identity – was eventually diluted, nevertheless, *Design* remains a useful means of representing the CoID's voice in the debate on street furniture. Reflecting back upon its formation in 1970, *Design* defined its early years as a 'propaganda magazine' combining a pulpit message with a crusading determination.[65] That message concerned the value of modern design, which was 'loud, clear and endlessly repeated'.[66] *Design* promoted this message to a readership that included manufacturers and designers, through a variety of ways, not least visually. Indeed, while *Design* was able to retain some degree of autonomy by publishing articles that offered alternative interpretations to the organization's agenda, the visual style of the magazine, its photographic identity and tone was entirely consistent with the CoID. Photography was used by *Design* as a further means to promote the CoID's message of Good Design, indeed, as a 1965 issue clarified, it was only 'by getting pictures and captions of well-designed products in print' that this message could truly be promoted.[67] The specific point of view that such photographic material adopted was unambiguously formalist (see Figure 2.8), and was used by Design to educate its readers on Good Design.

Design magazine was primarily used as a means of promoting the benefits of Good Design, and the very first issue in 1949 set out what this meant. The Leader comment proposed that 'good design is not simply a question of personal taste' but a question of standards.[68] The notion of standards was repeated frequently across consecutive volumes of *Design* throughout the early post-war period, and particularly the notion that such standards could only be upheld by professional organizations like the CoID. Russell wrote *Design*'s first feature 'What Is Good Design?' in which he upheld this definition. For Russell, Good Design was '*an essential part of a standard of quality*', and conversely, bad design was a 'deterrent

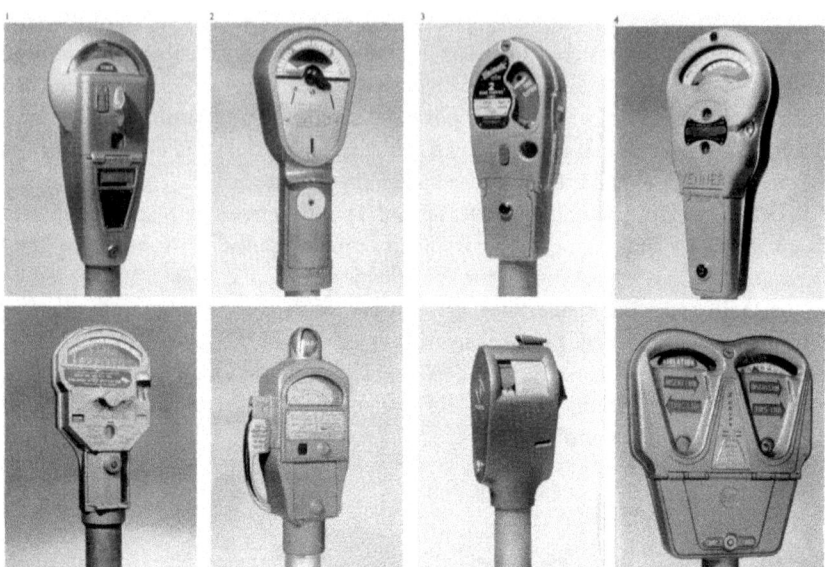

Figure 2.8 Formalist photography: *Design* asked, 'should British parking meters be based on these designs?' International parking meters, *Design*, No. 88, April 1956, 34–5. Design Council Archive, University of Brighton Design Archives.

of production and sales'.[69] A number of conclusions can be drawn from Russell's definition. In the first place, bad design was perceived as having an effect on sales. Thus in order to convince manufacturers of the value of Good Design, it was often presented as good for business, and as 'a strong selling point'.[70]

A second point that can be drawn from Russell's definition of Good Design lies in the way it was defined as much through establishing positive values as through rejecting negative ones. For Russell, Good Design was not '*precious, arty or highfalutin*', and he characterized its counterpoint as '*clichés* [which] are not the right answer to a human need'.[71] Such clichés took the form of unnecessary ornament or expressions of historic style and this approach was consistently attacked in *Design* during the 1950s, particularly in relation to street furniture.[72] Much of the language used to describe bad design can be situated in wartime propaganda of good and evil, and an editorial from 1950 claimed that 'there is still a world of difference between the *moderne* and the contemporary and there is still the old dragon of the pseudo-antique to be slain, but the day may be nearer than we think when the battle will be, not between different styles or periods, but between good and bad within the same idiom'.[73] Defining the rejection of bad design – in this case, the pseudo-antique – as a dragon to be slain, is indicative of an attitude after the war, where themes like morality, duty and patriotism were often employed by the CoID as part of its campaign to improve standards.

In 1951, the subject of street furniture first featured in *Design* as part of its coverage of the Festival of Britain, a national event supervised by Labour politician Herbert

Morrison to celebrate Britain's industrial, scientific and cultural achievements.[74] The CoID had assumed responsibility for the Festival's industrial design, and furnished the South Bank site with appropriately modern street furniture, including steel bins designed by James Cubitt and Jack Howe (see Figure 2.9), public seating by Ernest Race and Misha Black, planters by H. T. Cadbury Brown, and signage by Robin Day and Milner Gray. Writing for *Design*, the architect planner for Hatfield new town Lionel Brett, justified these modern designs to readers, reporting that 'anyone can see that if these objects are well designed you get an atmosphere of fun and gaiety instead of restriction and control. Bollards, lamp-posts, shelters, litter bins, seats, kiosks; how they can murder a scene, and how they can enliven it!'[75] Such a joyous approach to the design of street furniture is striking, and Brett even supports the use of colour in street furniture design: 'there is no need for street furniture to

Figure 2.9 This jaunty bin was described by Design as 'typical of the neat use of steel throughout the exhibition'. Outdoor litter bin designed by Jack Howe, Festival of Britain, South Bank Exhibition, 1951. Design Council Archive, University of Brighton Design Archives.

apologise for itself by camouflage colouring or tamely traditional design. If it is to be useful it must be noticeable, and England is grey enough without neglecting these opportunities for a blob of colour.'[76] Many of the examples reproduced in *Design* show the jaunty angles, freedom of line, new use of materials and whimsy that Brett and others at the CoID celebrated, but their sensitivity to particular forms and the ambiguity of their recommendations is difficult to discern from a historical remove. Identifying the differences between a good litter bin and a bad bus shelter is almost impossible, partly because the advice seems to have changed fairly regularly (see Figure 2.10). While celebrated at the time, the contemporary modern style of Festival street furniture would be thought flimsy and effeminate quite quickly, a fact that even Brett recognized in 1951.[77]

Figure 2.10 London Transport bus shelter designed by Arcon. Festival of Britain, South Bank Exhibition, 1951. Design Council Archive, University of Brighton Design Archives. The bus shelter was described by *Design* as: 'A London Transport exhibit lacking the grace of most of the incidental equipment of the exhibition'.

Much of the discourse around the Festival of Britain enforced the notion that it was intended to act as a breath of colour, pleasure and wonder in an otherwise grey war-damaged city, but there was also a subtext to the event. The whole of the South Bank exhibition site was carefully considered to allow visitors to experience modern architecture and design, in some cases for the very first time. By furnishing the site with modern street furniture, visitors could go beyond imaging the modern streetscape; they could actually sit on the benches, throw their litter in the bins and navigate using the signage. At a time when organizations like the CoID were trying to promote modernism, this was a perfect opportunity to convince the public of modern street furniture's advantages. The coverage in *Design* served a similar purpose. In 1951 international tension was escalating and Britain was re-arming for another war in Korea. Against this background the Festival also showed a distinct political awareness. In *Brief City*, a retrospective film produced about the design features of the South Bank exhibition grounds, *The Observer*'s Patrick O'Donovan, in discussion with Director of Architecture Hugh Casson, declared that that 'there were no resounding proud messages here, no one was taught to hate anything. At a time when nations were becoming more assertive and more intolerant, here was a national exhibition that avoided these emotions and tried to stay rational.'[78] *Brief City*'s efforts to present the Festival as a benign, apolitical event were somewhat unsuccessful however, and while the site would remain associated with the CoID, it was almost completely dismantled by the incoming Conservative government later that year, perhaps because it was perceived as a Labour Party project.

The political dimensions of design could be quite explicit during the 1950s. For instance, in March 1954 the aesthetic of American parking meters was criticized in *Design* for their 'thick, insensitive "jelly mould" contours and heavy handed lettering.'[79] The main argument against this particular parking meter – depicted top right in Figure 2.8 – was made on the basis of its national identity, and in *Design*'s early editions nationalism rarely seems far from the surface. This prejudice might be attributable to the propaganda issue already mentioned, but it could equally be attributed to the CoID's own emergence as a body dedicated to promoting the work of British industry at a time when the country's export market was threatened. The CoID's first annual report credits America as posing the biggest threat to Britain, since its progress 'has made many of our exports old-fashioned and less acceptable.'[80] On this basis, it seems likely that American products would have been criticized because of their negative effect on British industry; certainly the organization continued to press manufacturers to give their products a 'British look.'[81]

Design *as a forum for debate*

As a CoID channel for the promotion of Good Design, *Design*'s coverage of street furniture clearly reflected the wider concerns of the organization. Yet *Design* is also a useful marker of the public's response to modern street furniture. *Design* published letters in almost every issue, many of which concerned street furniture. And as early as 1950 there were complaints about the way street furniture looked.

Many of these complaints were initially made in the pages of national newspapers and focused on lamp posts. A particularly vocal critic was the writer and poet John Betjeman who, despite having worked for the *AR*, was seen by some as a traitor to the modern movement due to his ongoing defence of Britain's architectural heritage. Alexandra Harris argues that in Betjeman's case, it is not always clear whether 'conservatism of this kind was a retreat from contemporary affairs or a particular kind of locally oriented engagement'.[82] What is clear is that he passionately objected to modern street lighting. In 'Ugly Lamp Posts', Betjeman's letter to the editor of *The Times* in August 1950, he criticized the craze for functionalist modern lamp posts, and described them as 'gibbets', 'frightful' and 'clumsy'.[83] The columns, he said, were too thick, the colour and texture too drab, and they were painfully out of place and usually out of scale with their surroundings. By contrast, the iron lamp standard was graceful, easily accepted and harmonious feature of the street (see Figure 2.11).

Figure 2.11 Pre- and post-war lamp standards at Tooting Bec, 1954. Design Council Archive, University of Brighton Design Archives.

The response to Betjeman's criticism was immediate. While the chairman of the RFAC concurred, writing that 'the standards now being erected throughout the country have caused the Commission much concern', a member of the public from Nottingham attacked Betjeman's attempts to create prejudice: 'Such intemperate language does not assist in reaching the right solutions in matters of taste.'[84] Due to the level of interest, *The Times* responded a few days later by observing that 'lamp posts have possibly affected the life of ordinary people much more than they commonly realize... The chief need is for better educated taste among matters of lamp posts as well as in local authorities who have the choosing of them.'[85] The CoID agreed, and sought to use *Design* as a means of spreading this message.

In 'New Lamp Posts in the New Towns' published by *Design* in June 1952, the CoID tackled Betjeman's interpretation of modern lamp posts head on. While Betjeman perceived concrete lamp posts as 'sick serpents', the CoID praised their 'smooth unbroken lines'.[86] Yet Betjeman's criticism continued, and in a letter to *Design* the following year, he claimed that because of the high-mast lamp posts approved by the CoID, 'towns like Chippenham, Devizes, Wantage, Abbingdon and Wokingham, and cities like Lincoln and Exeter have been ruined by tall poles with hideous bases with jazz modern decoration on the bottom and giants' match strikes on the sides'.[87] Betjeman also disputed the aesthetic judgement of the Street Furniture Advisory Committee, writing that: 'It is not safe to say that what a committee has chosen as a decent design for one place will look well anywhere. Certainly nothing could look worse than the lamp-standards in Salisbury... and I do not like the idea of standardized designs for the whole country where anything more obtrusive than public seats is concerned.'[88] Betjeman's point about standardization is important, and will be addressed again in Chapter 5, but his central point here concerns context. While he cared little for the design of the lamp posts themselves, the bigger problem concerned their relationship to the locations in which they were situated.

For the Street Furniture Advisory Committee, however, the relationship between street furniture and its immediate surroundings was beyond the committee's remit, and it refused to accept liability for badly sited street furniture. Its job was to 'make sure that only good designs are available for local authorities to choose from', rather than approve specific objects for specific sites.[89] Such were the number of these complaints that the CoID was forced to remind readers that criticism of CoID-approved street furniture was often misdirected, and responsibility rested with the local authority concerned.[90] Complaints like these gave rise to a perception that CoID approval was based on appearance rather than function. This view was expressed by the Secretary of the National Brassfoundry Association, who wrote to *Design* in 1954 about a bus shelter designed by the architect and industrial designer Jack Howe (see Figure 2.12).[91] According to this reader, 'in that the primary function of a bus shelter is to afford protection from the elements and particularly from rain, I would describe the shelter that you illustrate as being a dismal functional failure, as evidenced by the fact that the pavement below it in the illustration is wet all over.'[92] Such an oversight was evidence enough for some that the CoID's central priority was based upon aesthetics. So did Good Design just mean good-looking design?

Figure 2.12 Concrete bus shelter for London Transport Executive. Designed for and manufactured by Spun Concrete Ltd. 1954, Photo: D. N. Zinram. Courtesy of Susan Howe. Shelter designed by Jack Howe.

For the design and architecture critic Reyner Banham, who often contributed to *Design* during the 1950s, the magazine's narrow understanding of modern design meant that it increasingly did focus on the appearance of objects. Writing in 1955, Banham claimed that *Design*'s rejection of ornament 'seems to lie in a misplaced desire for unity at a time when diversity and differentiation of product-aesthetics seem to offer the most exciting rewards in the field of design since the Bauhaus'.[93] Banham justified his point further by writing of the Swiss architect Le Corbusier, who 'saw, as Adolf Loos seems to have seen and as Ruskin and Morris failed to see, that to stretch a single aesthetic standard over expendable and perennial products indifferently was a short cut to the neurotics' ward'.[94] While Banham's point was made in reference to the automobile industry, his general argument can be extended into the context of street furniture, where a single aesthetic standard was emerging by 1955. This approach, warned Banham, was likely to end in disaster, and he encouraged *Design*'s readership 'to accept, exploit and enjoy the fact that we no longer have to trim ourselves to fit into a single procrustean aesthetic'.[95]

Banham's warning proved prophetic, and by 1956 the CoID was compelled to defend its approach to aesthetics through *Design*, which clarified that, 'from a commercial point of view pleasing looks cannot be relegated to the last place on the list of priorities and the Council's insistence on treating them as an essential aspect of good design does not run counter to a commercial bias'.[96] Placing this justification in the context of commerce was a deliberate attempt to appeal to these complaints, but it failed to succeed. In the same issue, the matter of appearance and styling was raised by another reader:

> Much as I admire the lampposts approved by Mr. George Williams and the CoID... I must remind you that the primary purpose of any lamp standard is to give light. The design of the posts, although important, is only a secondary problem... while Holborn and Westminster have well-designed lights with bad styling, Paddington and some other boroughs have badly designed lights, with good styling laid on top, I believe that the CoID has always decried 'styling'. Why does it not do so now?[97]

This reader's point about styling must have engaged *Design* sufficiently, since it also published a response by the president of the Association of Public Lighting Engineers, who said: 'Engineers are always having to make compromises; but aesthetics are outside their ken, and it is a relief to have the *imprimatur* of the CoID on certain designs. This does not stop the argument, but it keeps us out of it.'[98] The president's diplomatic response demonstrates his reluctance to criticize a body whose '*imprimatur*' was legally required for the Association's designs to be passed. Tact as well as tactics are in evidence, since publishing a comment by the Association of Public Lighting Engineers meant that *Design* could deflect the heat of the debate away from the CoID.

Sometimes the CoID used *Design* to defend its approach to street furniture. In 1956 *Design* reported that, according to some manufacturers, the level of criticism their street furniture designs received was due to the CoID's 'central interference'.[99] Such an accusation went against the grain of persuasion and education, and as a result *Design* claimed that manufacturers of street furniture

> must take a good deal of the blame for the muddle of our streets since he has largely been responsible for the 'fashionable' element in their furnishings. He has in the past, largely without professional advice, often forced upon the public through the engineer or surveyor a set of ugly styles which represent his private interpretation of modern trends. This sort of thing is evil enough in the consumer goods we buy over the retail counter... but at least we can please ourselves whether or not we buy.[100]

In this example, it is possible to argue that the CoID also used *Design* to attack those who undermined it. Other groups who failed to seek professional advice – i.e. the advice of the CoID – also came under pressure in *Design*, which was routinely used as a means of shaming local authorities for street furniture schemes which did not comply with CoID advice.

Design folio

Other channels through which the CoID sought to disseminate the values of Good Design included its design folios. Described as a 'monthly series of pictorial essays on design appreciation', such folios were produced by the CoID from 1948 onwards, and covered a broad range of topics.[101] According to design historian Penny Sparke, the object of the folios was to educate readers – particularly those considered design literate – on modern design, and encourage them to consider ways that the design of the objects in question might improve.[102] The education of the public was considered a vital means of promoting the CoID's agenda and Russell himself believed that 'to get good designs at all one must have good designers at the beginning rather than at the end'.[103] To that end, the design folios were distributed widely among educational associations and other bodies across Britain, so that by 1949 over 1,400 schools subscribed.[104] A further aspiration of the scheme was that schools would eventually compile their own library of images, like the ones included in the design folios to 'illustrate everyday objects of good design'.[105] This, it was hoped, would eventually influence the designers of the future.

As part of its interest in commonplace things, the CoID published a design folio on street furniture in 1951. It is an impressive large-scale document, complete with an introductory essay, twelve lithographs and shorter essays accompanying each plate. The folio defines street furniture as 'art made compulsory', a definition it borrowed from *The Observer*.[106] The importance of street furniture was attributed to its compulsory nature, in which, 'given ones inability to avoid street furniture, much therefore hangs on the choice of this furniture and its siting, for individually pleasant pieces can be rendered *guache* and ill-fitting if they be jumbled together without thought to scale or composition'.[107] With a view to addressing these problems, the folio encouraged its readers to engage in activities which would improve their understanding of street furniture design, including environmental analysis, sketching, collecting illustrations of different street furniture designs, and reading texts on urban design. Furthermore, through the lithographs the folio presents the reader with several examples of street furniture 'past and present, at home and abroad, from which we can draw our comparisons and on which we can start basing our judgement'.[108] Modern street furniture was presented as a means to solving the problems posed by the period examples.

The folio presents a further way to represent the CoID's position in the debate on street furniture. For instance, one of the plates depicts modern railings from a municipal housing estate built in 1949, and the folio celebrates their 'invariably uniform' characteristics, particularly because 'individualism … is avoided' (see Figure 2.13).[109] Another plate depicts a steel and concrete street lamp, and the folio explains that the materials used to fabricate the lamp rendered it unfit to accommodate ornament. 'The finished effect', the folio claims, 'is of grace and dignity, and their simplicity is such that either would look well in any setting. They are content, quietly and unostentatiously, to serve their purpose.'[110] Other examples included in the folio were considered less enlightened, and it is through such examples that the value system of the CoID is reflected. Plate nine depicts two bus stops – 'one good and the other better' – and the corresponding text is accompanied by an additional line drawing of a bad bus stop (see Figure 2.14). The folio reports that this bad example 'looks as though it reached its shape by accident', and its lettering 'can only be called vile. No component has been considered in relation to another and the complete article is singularly ugly.'[111] By contrast, the better of the two modern bus stops has been assigned this role because its superior

Figure 2.13 'Invariably uniform' modern railings celebrated in the Council of Industrial Design's Design Folio. Railings, in 'Street Furniture: A design folio prepared by the CoID. Book I', no date, Plate 6. Design Council Archive, University of Brighton Design Archives.

and simpler design makes the manufacturing process easier and far cheaper; and, as a result of fewer corners and crevices, is simultaneously easier to maintain.[112] Besides providing visual examples of good street furniture design, the folio also reflects the difficulties the CoID experienced when preparing the folio. There are a number of continental examples but London Transport is the only British firm represented.[113] The folio was clearly intended to encourage an increased respect for modern street furniture design at a time when significant stylistic changes were taking place across the country.

Figure 2.14 Two bus stops: 'one good and the other better'. Left is good, right is better. 'Street Furniture: A design folio prepared by the CoID. Book I', no date, Plate 9. Design Council Archive, University of Brighton Design Archives.

Exhibitions

While the 1951 design folio on street furniture was directed at people who were design literate or who were being trained in this capacity, the exhibitions staged by the CoID were directed at everyone. Exhibitions were an important means through which the CoID tried to promote Good Design, and the 'Britain Can Make It' exhibition held in 1946 and the Festival of Britain in 1951 were both early examples of this approach.[114] As already noted, the Festival of Britain was one of the first instances where the British public could actually experience modern street furniture design for themselves.

Figure 2.15 Display of seating at the Council of Industrial Design and the Corporation of Birmingham Manufacturers' Competition for the Design of Outdoor Seats, 1953. Design Council Archive, University of Brighton Design Archives.

One of the first exhibitions specifically centred on street furniture design was held in May 1953 in London's Victoria Embankment Gardens.[115] The exhibition was organized jointly by the CoID and the Corporation of Birmingham, and presented seventy designs of outdoor seating from forty-one manufacturers (see Figure 2.15).[116] A further exhibition on seating was held later that year as part of the Royal Horticultural Display at the Chelsea Flower Show.[117] *Design* magazine had earlier launched a competition for manufacturers to design outdoor seats for the exhibition, in which the brief clearly stated that 'reproductions of historic styles were not likely to win places'.[118] The competition was orchestrated to stimulate interest in the design of street furniture, and promote modern design. Indeed, according to internal CoID correspondence, the exhibits that were permitted to take part were 'lightweight contemporary'.[119] Despite this particular focus on modern design over other styles, there does not appear to have been much debate about street furniture design as a result of these exhibitions. Even Betjeman considered the aesthetic qualities of modern seating to be comparatively unobtrusive.[120]

Figure 2.16 Members of the public visiting an exhibition of litter bins, London, 1960. In CoID, *16th Annual Report*, 1960–1961, p. 37. Design Council Archive, University of Brighton Design Archives.

Legislation also provided the catalyst for exhibitions. Following from the 1958 Litter Act, which emphasized the shortage of well-designed litter bins, the CoID organized a competition and exhibition of new litter-bin designs at the Victoria Embankment in 1960 (see Figure 2.16). That same year another significant, and this time permanent, exhibition on street furniture was opened on London's South Bank.[121] On open-air display were lamp posts, bus shelters, seats and litter bins, and the exhibition was an opportunity for members of the public and even His Royal Highness the Duke of Edinburgh to see the best examples of modern street furniture design that manufacturers could supply in an area already associated with the CoID (see Figure 2.17).[122] The fact that exhibitions of street furniture were displayed in such central locations, and were able to draw such an exalted audience, testifies to the important role these objects played at the time.

Exhibitions like these, however, were intended as more than just publicity for the CoID; they also acted as shop windows for the manufacturers. The value of using venues like the South Bank and the Victoria Embankment – near to Westminster and County Hall – was that local authority planners and engineers could see street furniture products in a central urban setting, and later place their orders with the

Figure 2.17 The Duke of Edinburgh visiting an open-air street furniture exhibition on London's South Bank, 6 July 1961. Design Council Archive, University of Brighton Design Archives.

companies concerned. However, in order to stage these exhibitions, the CoID required the support of manufacturers, which supplied the products on display. In this respect, their relationship was crucial and often delicate, and the CoID frequently expressed concern that manufacturers could decide within their trade associations to 'gang up on us' and 'back out en masse'.[123] The threat, real or perceived, that industrial sponsors could effectively withdraw their exhibits demonstrates the power balance between the two groups. Also, there were frequent spells of anxiety, both by the manufacturers and by the CoID, that unless they had been specifically invited, local authority engineers and architects did not visit the exhibitions in great numbers.[124] But the records also show a feeling of loyalty between the CoID and manufacturers, which suggests a more nuanced relationship than might otherwise be assumed. Clearly, this relationship was not always characterized by hostility and at times the two groups might even have seen themselves as allies.

Street furniture catalogues

Besides exhibitions, the CoID also sought to influence the design of street furniture by publishing catalogues (see Figure 2.18). This method of engagement was first discussed by *Design* in 1950, which stated that 'a good catalogue, it must be remembered, has to perform two main functions: (a) to present information,

(b) to create a desire for the goods'.¹²⁵ It also added that, 'however technical the subject, an attractive and contemporary appearance is invaluable'.¹²⁶ On this basis, the CoID published an illustrated catalogue of the best British street furniture in current production every two years from 1963 onwards. The designs were selected from the Design Index, which in turn had been approved by the Street Furniture Advisory Committee. Manufacturers did not pay to be included in the catalogue, but they did contribute to the publication costs.¹²⁷

Essentially, the catalogues functioned much like working manuals on good street furniture design, since they were distributed to every local authority and civic society in Britain.¹²⁸ Many of the early catalogues contain greyscale images of approved street furniture designs arranged into categories.¹²⁹ The information given for each product is largely technical and manufacturer's contact details are provided at the back. The photography is formalistic, and most of the products are photographed against a neutral studio-like background, free from contact with real life. However, the banality of these catalogues should not be underestimated: they represent another way in which official channels like the CoID sought to influence the way that street furniture was designed and understood, without being open or transparent about how they were assembled or funded.

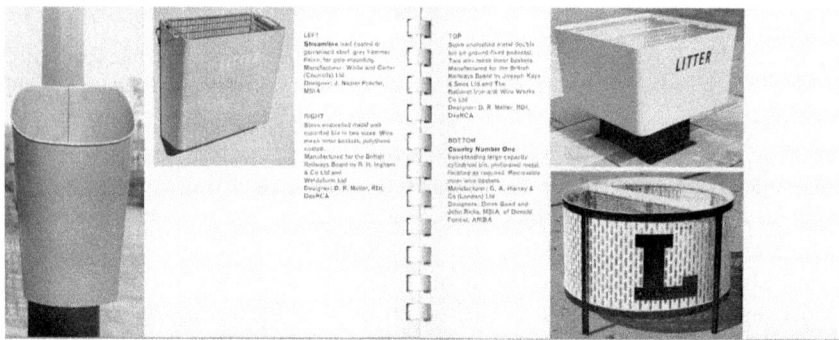

Figure 2.18 Litter bins, 'Street furniture: List of Approved Designs 1963', CoID, and the Scottish Committee of the CoID, 78–9. Design Council Archive, University of Brighton Design Archives.

The practice of Good Design

Design magazine, exhibitions, folios and catalogues illustrate how the CoID promoted good street furniture design to different audiences using different methods, but how was it actually practiced? As one of the few remaining street furniture designers who practiced during this early post-war period, Kenneth Grange provides an original account of how designers engaged with Good Design. Grange was responsible for designing Britain's first coin-operated parking meter in 1958, and his work embodied the modern aesthetic promoted by the CoID. He was also one of the CoID's recommended industrial designers, one of its judges and a serving committee member. Having designed street furniture for some years previously alongside Jack Howe – who had in turn, worked briefly as an assistant for former Bauhaus director Walter Gropius – Grange was an ideal choice to redesign the parking meter. Yet the parking meter was a particularly contentious object of street furniture. While some regard it in a public-spirited light, even as 'a life improving innovation', it was not a view shared by everyone.[130] In 1967, it was described as a 'monster', and in 2008, as 'one of the most reviled symbols of modern life'.[131] At its early development, it was perceived by some within the design elite as an American intrusion, but was welcomed by local authorities as a commercial endeavour. For the public, it was little more than a further disciplinary measure that would curtail its liberty to freely park where it liked.

The parking meter was an American invention, designed to alleviate traffic problems in the inner parts of Oklahoma City. First referred to in Britain in 1953 as a 'metering instrument', and dismissed by the Automobile Association on financial grounds two years later, the parking meter aroused considerable public interest in the early post-war period.[132] From 1954, parking meters were even regularly discussed at a senior level of government. For instance, according to a memo prepared by the Ministry of Transport on the 26th of November 1954, 'the experimental use of parking meters to ease traffic congestion was recommended in the Report of the Working Party in the Inner Area of London', but that 'legislation is required if parking meters are to be used, on however small a scale, in this country'.[133] Their value lay in inducing 'motorists to garage their cars, while keeping the streets suitable for parking available for the short term parker'.[134] A more obvious value, though one not directly articulated at this stage, was the parking meter's ability to generate revenue for the local authorities concerned.

The following month the MoT presented another memo to a Cabinet meeting in 10 Downing Street – a meeting which included the serving prime minister Winston Churchill, Anthony Eden and Harold MacMillan. The memo concerned the Road Traffic Bill and the possible inclusion of a provision 'authorizing the introduction of parking meters' in the inner area of London.[135] Those present expressed some concern that the proposals 'might well prove unpopular'.[136] Nevertheless, ministers decided that an experiment with parking meters ought to be carried out, but insisted that they were in no way 'committed to the permanent adoption of this device'.[137] That parking meters would in fact come to be a common feature of the urban landscape testifies to the success of this initial experiment.

The route of the parking meter into British consciousness began with one London borough. After Cabinet's decision to approve a pilot scheme, Westminster Council elected to run it in 1956 and approached the firm Venner for help. Venner was a British manufacturer that, according to Kenneth Grange 'owned a high proportion of the business on our streets, in terms of the clockwork mechanisms... that switched the lights on and off, and these mechanisms were stored in the posts. And if you counted the number of posts in the country, that was a big business.'[138] Venner then, was a large and well-regarded firm whose clockwork mechanisms were considered to be 'extremely reliable... expensively made and well constructed'.[139]

Grange understood that Venner was the firm Westminster decided to use in its parking meter project. According to Grange, representatives from Westminster Council and Venner travelled to America and selected an existing meter called the 'Park-O-Meter'. Other accounts suggest that Venner had in fact anticipated the demand for meters in advance of the pilot project, and had already obtained a license to produce the meter in question.[140] Certainly, Venner had begun to advertise in the *MJ* in 1956 with the claim that 'the British-made Venner Park-O-Meter is in full production' and that some municipalities were already planning their installations. Indeed, later that year the *MJ* reported that interest in the parking meter had drawn large crowds at the Public Works and Congress exhibition due to the perception that it was soon to become an important local authority purchase.[141] The invention even made the news, and short films were produced to educate the public on how the meter worked (see Figure 2.19). Nevertheless, irrespective of when and how Venner selected the 'Park-O-Meter', it was the meter to be used in the Westminster pilot project, and was described by Grange as 'a mechanically sound, banjo-shaped meter'.[142] This meter was 'the one that had been ordered and contracts had been signed and Westminster were promised a delivery of these things installed in particular parts of Westminster'.[143] They were, according to Grange, 'all set to go. They were going to import these things, doctor them slightly to suit our coinage, and off they go. Nice job.'[144]

Figure 2.19 Film still from *Motoring News – London* (1956). Footage supplied by British Pathé Ltd.

Despite preparations for the pilot scheme nearing completion the project was temporarily suspended between 1956 and 1957. As noted already, the CoID had been asked by the MoT to advise manufacturers on objects of street furniture, among them parking meters. George Williams, the CoID officer responsible for street furniture, wrote in *Design* in 1956 that the problem with parking meters concerned their 'individual *design*'.[145] Seemingly, the MoT had already permitted a number of manufacturers to develop designs for future parking meters, giving them a 'free hand' according to Williams. He added that, 'the Ministry will expect a "pleasing outward appearance" and has invited manufacturers to consult the CoID on this aspect. Those already submitted to the CoID show that much more attention to form, proportion and detail is necessary before they should be allowed to take their place in the street.'[146] The meters noted by Williams can be seen in Fig. 2.8, alongside the Venner meter soon to be installed on the streets of Westminster.

Having discussed the matter with the Royal Fine Art Commission, the CoID deemed the Venner meter unacceptable for the British streetscape.[147] Its position had barely changed since 1954 when *Design* had declared, 'alone it will not look pleasant, but seen in a row along a pavement or spaced at intervals around a London square its contribution to street furniture can only be deplored'.[148] Despite having no enforceable powers in respect to the official approval of parking meters, both Westminster Council and Venner deferred to the CoID's position. The reason why is not clear, though Grange attributes this to the respect each organization had for the CoID, which was 'the only governmentally backed institution that anybody trusted and looked to'.[149] Unfortunately, records for the CoID's decision no longer exist, but it is possible to piece together a sense of its reasoning from Williams's remarks in *Design* in 1956. Of the Venner design in question, Williams notes that, while showing 'at least some regard for appearance...the finished results are far from good and their repetition at 7-ft intervals along the pavement would, to say the least, become irksome'.[150] Terms like 'irksome' were, according to Grange, 'easily and agreeably used in those years', but it was language like this that contributed towards the suspension of the local authority pilot scheme, despite the alleged respect that Westminster Council and Venner maintained towards the CoID.

According to Grange, the result of the CoID's rejection was that Venner 'were over a barrel because they had a delivery to meet'.[151] However, because one of the services provided by the CoID involved matching designers with clients, Venner requested its help to correct the rejected design. In turn, the CoID forwarded names of approved designers to Venner, which is how Grange was awarded the commission to redesign the meter. Having been awarded the commission, Grange was provided with little more than a Park-o-Meter. His design is an inverted tear-shaped form in line with the modern style of the period (see Figure 2.20). Contrary to the view of some critics, Grange says his changes were intended to make the existing banjo-shaped design simpler, rather than more British.[152]

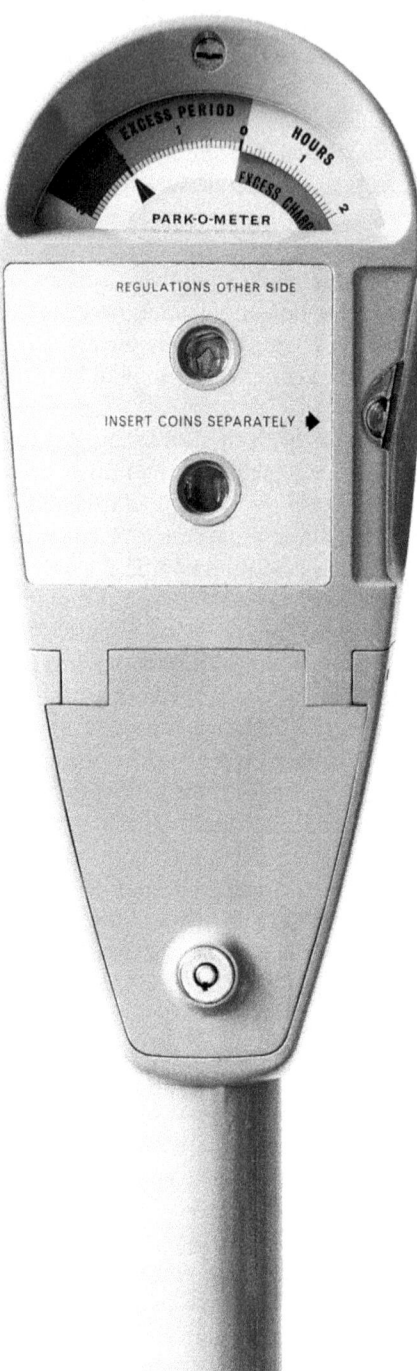

Figure 2.20 Parking meter designed by Kenneth Grange for Venner Ltd., 1958. Courtesy of Kenneth Grange.

Consensus and like-minds

During the course of redesigning the parking meter, Grange had very little contact with other organizations, apart from the CoID. Yet the extent to which the organization's ideals about Good Design came to be reflected in the parking meter is nuanced. According to Grange, the CoID did not present him with a brief, and nor did it have 'a tick-list of things to achieve at all, but somehow there was enough consensus among those of us who were either beneficiaries of the Council or came to be used by the council... I mean, we were all of like minds, there's no question about it'.[153] Grange's experience was that 'the relationship between quite a lot of big players in our industries and the Council was very good, so the actual Council of people sitting around a table always represented modernist thinking and usually a lot of good business brains from a lot of big firms'.[154] In this way, Grange clearly did not see the CoID as sitting outside industry; but rather, that the two made decisions together. Nevertheless, he does concede that individual members often behaved differently depending upon the circumstances. For instance, while CoID members were committed to modern design on a professional level, their personal taste often differed quite considerably. Their homes, according to Grange, represented an 'inherited taste' largely because antiques had 'a higher, more reliable monetary value'.[155] Furthermore, after two decades of shortages, many homes in those years were, says Grange, 'unaffected by the taste and style judgments [of today]. That we had a home at all was a reward. One value in this environment was that taste didn't much cloud judgments about what was appropriate.' Grange defines this attitude as a form of 'clear good-hearted conservatism', in which a respect for older things was a type of non-taste, in which lies 'a certain honesty'.[156]

That those who worked with the CoID were of 'like minds' is a theme that recurs throughout Grange's account of his experience in redesigning the British parking meter. He describes it as a collective 'aesthetic view' that those who worked with the CoID shared, and which even developed among the designers themselves. Despite some people's personal preference towards Georgian, everyone, according to Grange 'wanted to show themselves to be modern' and in this respect, domestic arrangements seem symbolic for the contradictions that characterize the age.[157] For Grange, those people 'understood the difference between modern American styling and modern Scandinavian design [which] represented the poles of taste'.[158] The reason why American design was caustically dismissed in Britain was due to a difference in form, a perception which was common at the time.[159] Even the *Architectural Review* doubted whether streamlining could satisfy serious designers in England.[160] For Grange, while the American streamlined designs in chrome were often 'functionally excellent', their styling was considered to be very heavy-handed, and 'more overtly theatrical than it was here'.[161] By contrast, Grange shared the CoID's position that 'what we were aspiring towards... represented European and not American' [design].[162] Indeed, the taste underpinning much modern design from the period was, according to Grange, essentially 'upper-class European'.[163] While the Scandinavians always used natural starting points, 'whether that was stones, or wood, or mountains or flowers... the American interpretation of that was just more Broadway, more theatrical'.[164] Britain, by contrast – and Grange's work in particular – has been described as reflecting 'an aesthetic sensibility that is rooted in European Modernism but enthused with a warm approachability'.[165] According to Grange, the reason for such an approach to modernity was that in Britain 'there were enough designers and enough liberation allowed by the marketplace that we could develop a wider range of detail ... I hope we've been more lenient in a lot of stuff in terms of what our modern design is. We're not so ruthlessly simplistic'.[166] The simplistic designers were 'a few stalwarts who persisted in the Germanic Bauhausian movements', represented by figures like the German designer Dieter Rams who was 'absolutely unremitting in terms of what he allowed'.[167] In contrast to Rams, Grange insists the British modern style emerged through consensus.

Grange's point about consensus is not altogether convincing however; indeed, there is plenty of evidence to suggest the opposite was true. But to understand it, one needs to contextualize the role of a designer in post-war Britain. Grange's unwillingness to speak negatively about any of the parties involved reflects the discretion of a professional, but his attitude is also typical of many designers who express themselves through their work. As a result it is unlikely that the social or political context in which Grange worked would have had much impact upon his practice. Ultimately there was a client relationship that had to be served, and the practical constraints imposed by the client – such as cost, availability of materials and so on – would have been much more influential. To some extent Grange's success can be explained because of his proximity to industry, and his ability to prioritise that relationship over others.[168] In the parking meter project, however, Grange contends that he felt a greater responsibility towards the public.[169] While it is conceivable that Grange's work on the parking meter was an act of government-sponsored beautification, for Grange the process was much more than merely a question of style: it was a matter of giving the public what it deserved, namely 'to join the modern world'.[170] This was a view, he believes, that everyone involved in the design profession shared. Each figure was trying to 'upgrade all sorts of things ... [and] pressing for better stuff generally across the country'.[171]

Reaction to the parking meter

For many people, parking meters soon became a cipher for the urban landscape, as this 1960 *Country Life* fashion spread suggests (see Figure 2.21).[172] The wardens enlisted to monitor the meters also became firmly rooted in popular consciousness, not always as figures of respect, as cartoons in *Punch* from the period testify.[173] Such was the presence of parking meters that they were even credited in popular music. For instance, the 1967 song 'Lovely Rita' by The Beatles concerns 'Rita' the meter maid, a contemporary term for female parking warden. Films too were made about parking meters, and those produced by British Pathé such as *Wardens Are So Courteous* would have been screened prior to films in the cinema, therefore reaching a wide-ranging audience.[174] The educational quality of such a

Figure 2.21 Fashion spread with parking meters, *Country Life*, 13 October 1960, 831. Courtesy of *Country Life*.

film is hard to miss, and similar films also sought to educate the public on the value of parking meters. For instance, the narrator of the 1965 film *Parking Meters* describes the 25,000 or so meters in Britain as 'worse than one-armed bandits and just as hungry for your cash', but emphasizes their export value.[175] More than fifty countries imported Britain's parking meters, thus providing a sizeable source of overseas revenue. And yet negative perceptions of meters simply would not disappear. Indeed, several feature films were produced during the mid-1960s, which used the parking meter as the symbol of an oppressive state. In the title sequence of *Cool Hand Luke* for instance, an intoxicated character played by Paul Newman carefully removes the 'heads' of parking meters, before being arrested and sentenced to prison for the crime.[176] In this context, the parking meter acts as a cipher of Newman's resistance to authority.

The negative perception of parking meters, as represented by *Cool Hand Luke*, was one that Grange rejects as being overblown, however. For Grange, protests against modern street furniture were limited, and 'it was the occasional sensational disaster that would have been covered and made a lot of noise but it didn't reflect the wider view'.[177] Documents from the time, however, indicate that there was a palpable sense of anger about the design of parking meters. For instance, in February 1957, the *MJ* questioned the extent to which the Mayor of Westminster had to search his conscience over the mounting protests, and emphasized the importance of the design of the new parking meters.[178] The *MJ* was also critical of government for only asking the CoID to advise on a 'pleasing outward appearance' for the meters.[179] Design, the *MJ* added, 'is not such a matter of individual taste as is so often expressed, there are rules of design as much as there are rules of any other art; and there are many educated in the art; the manufacturers could do well by consulting them'.[180] Other magazines like the *AR* also examined the subject of parking meters, and frequently criticized their design.[181]

So why did Grange not recognize the plurality of opinion concerning his work? Clearly some anger was expressed about parking meters but whether it was directed towards the role they performed, in which parking became a financial transaction, or their design is unclear. Equally, such a reaction may not have been widely known outside the local context in which it was expressed. While protests of this kind were regularly reported in national newspapers and design magazines, it is possible that a designer like Grange was not aware of such reports. Moreover, material produced by government would have remained confidential. Another explanation might be found in Grange's relationship with the CoID. The design culture of post-war Britain was a relatively closed world in which a small number of figures made decisions about design together. Since Grange was a designer with considerable public patronage, and powerful structures backing him up, it is possible that in such a closed world, important figures like Grange were not aware that their views weren't widely shared. Britain at that time was a state-dominated economy and in such a context few would have worried about feedback from the market, because it simply did not matter. Designers therefore could have operated with very little knowledge of the reception of their work. Such an attitude is difficult to understand in today's economy, which is much more dominated by private interests and competition. In balance, just as Grange could hold the view that a preference for Georgian was a form of non-taste, it is also possible that those who redesigned Britain after the war accepted modern design equally uncritically. In this way, one can assume that there was not an explicit consciousness of style. The like-minded attitude, the shared aesthetic view and the sense of consensus that characterizes Grange's account of the parking meter project, must be understood in this light.

But what about the *other* voices in the street furniture debate, the ones who made a lot of noise? Just as this chapter has drawn a picture of how the CoID affected the debate on street furniture at an official level – and how the public, manufacturers and local government reacted to its involvement – the next chapter will examine the other powerful voices in the debate, so as to reflect a more accurate picture of the interests and agendas involved as a whole.

Notes

1   Carrington, *Industrial Design in Britain*, 74.
2   The CoID, *1st Annual Report 1945–46*, 5.
3   MacCarthy, *A History of British Design*, 73–4.
4   CoID, *1st Annual Report 1945–46*, 6.
5   Gordon Russell, 'Ugly Lamp Posts', *The Times*, 24 August 1950, 5.
6   Gordon Russell, 'Hand or Machine? The Craftsman in Modern Industry', in *The Conquest of Ugliness*, ed. J. de la Valette (London: Methuen, 1935), 51; Stephen Hayward, '"Good Design Is Largely a Matter of Common Sense": Questioning the Meaning and Ownership of a Twentieth-Century Orthodoxy', *The Journal of Design History*, Vol. 11, No. 3 (1998): 223.
7   *Design*, No. 32, August 1951, 3.
8   For instance, in 1948 the CoID was consulted by the Östereichischer Werbedienst on 'the best means of combating unsightly excrescences, disfiguring perversions of proportions and tasteless exaggerations' in the city. See 'Translation of a Letter from Dr. Koch, from the Östereichischer Werbedienst, Vienna, to the CoID, 30 November 1948', in Royal Fine Art Commission, 'Street Furniture. Design: Correspondence and Minutes', BP 2/127 (London: National Archives of the United Kingdom).
9   Evelyn Waugh, 'Victorian Taste', *The Times*, 3 March 1942, 5.
10 Ibid.
11 Ibid. See also 'Taste in Transition', *The Times*, 3 March 1942, 5.
12 Jonathan Woodham, *The Industrial Designer and the Public* (London: Pembridge Press, 1983), 84.
13 'Design of Street Furniture', Point 26.8, 7 October 1949, 5, loose in Royal Fine Art Commission, 'Street Furniture. Design: Correspondence and Minutes', BP 2/127.
14 'Industrial Design', special number of the *AR*, October 1946, 92.
15 Ibid., 92. See also Utility cartoon, *Punch*, 9 October 1946, 291.
16 Interview with Kenneth Grange, 21 November 2012.
17 Ibid. For further information on the manufacturers operating during this period, see http://www.simoncornwell.com/lighting/manufact/index.htm (accessed 31 July 2015).
18 'Notes for a Lecture Given to Durham County Council Planning Officers on Wednesday the 27 January 1960', 1, in Council of Industrial Design. 'Street Furniture: Articles and Lectures'. Box 220 (1432.15 Part III). Brighton: Design Council Archive, University of Brighton Design Archives.
19 Russell, 'Ugly Lamp Posts', 5.
20 The CoID, *8th Annual Report 1952–53*, 9; Woodham *The Industrial Designer and the Public*, 84.
21 The CoID, *15th Annual Report 1959–60*, 23.

22 'Notes for a Lecture Given to Durham County Council Planning Officers on Wednesday the 27th January 1960', 2, in Council of Industrial Design. 'Street Furniture: Articles and Lectures'. Box 220 (1432.15 Part III).
23 The Design Index was first known as the Stock List. See the CoID, *4th Annual Report 1948–49*, 2; Catherine Moriarty, 'A Backroom Service? The Photographic Library of the Council of Industrial Design, 1945–1965', *Journal of Design History*, Vol. 13, No. 1.
24 'Use of the term CoID Approval', in Council of Industrial Design, 'Street Furniture Articles and Lectures' (1432.15 Pt III).
25 The RFAC, *9th Annual Report 1948–1949*, July 1950. London, 13, MoDA Ref. 720.6041.
26 The CoID, *8th Annual Report 1952–53*, 9.
27 David Davies, 'The Street Scene', *The Times* (1432.15 Pt III); and 'Notes on Pedestrianisation Symposium 17th April 1973', in Council of Industrial Design, 'Street Furniture: Articles, Lectures and Correspondence' (1432.15.1 Pt 1).
28 See Ministry of Transport, 1949–1967. 'Highways Engineering: Registered Files. Street Lighting. Design of Lamp Standards: Including Painting and Guidance by Royal Fine Art Commission' [Correspondence and Papers] MT 95/210. London: National Archives of the United Kingdom.
29 Nigel Whiteley, *Pop Design: Modernism to Mod* (London: The Design Council, 1987), 32.
30 MacCarthy, *A History of British Design*, 95.
31 'Notes for a Lecture Given to Durham County Council Planning Officers on Wednesday the 27th January 1960', 1, in Council of Industrial Design. 'Street Furniture: Articles and Lectures'. Box 220 (1432.15 Part III).
32 The CoID, *5th Annual Report 1949–50*, 2.
33 Lord Kennet cited in Miles Glendinning, *The Conservation Movement: A History of Architectural Preservation* (London: Routledge, 2013), 286.
34 Lubbock, *The Tyranny of Taste*, 345–9.
35 Ibid., 349.
36 Ibid., 348.
37 Ibid., 350.
38 See Lesley Whitworth, 'Inscribing Design on the Nation: The Creators of the British Council of Industrial Design', *Business History Conference* proceedings, 2005; Woodham, 'Managing British Design Reform I', 55.
39 Thomas Barlow, *Letter from Sir Thomas Barlow to Kenneth Clark*, 20 December 1944, BT64/3635, in Ibid., 56.
40 *Design*, No. 14, February 1950, 1.
41 Gordon Russell, *A Designer's Trade* (London: Allen and Unwin, 1968), 263.
42 Jonathan Woodham, *Twentieth Century Design* (Oxford: Oxford University Press, 1997), 19.
43 Ibid., 119.
44 Penny Sparke, ed, *Did Britain Make It? British Design in Context 1946–1986* (London: Design Council, 1986), 43.
45 Paul Reilly, 'The Shape of Things: Who Cares for Street Furniture?', *Art News and Review*, Vol. 11, No. 22 (2 December 1950), 6.
46 Ibid.
47 Ibid.
48 Letter from Bill [RIBA] to Godfrey Samuel [RFAC] 15 December 1950, loose in Royal Fine Art Commission, 'Design: Correspondence and Minutes', BP 2/127.

49 'Plea for Streets to Be Less Ugly', *The Times*, 12 March 1958, in 'CoID: Design of Street Lighting Equipment', N.A. Cat. Ref.: MT 109/132; 'Chaos in the Normal Town: Better Street Fittings Urged', the *Daily Telegraph*, 12 March 1958; 'Call to Redesign Street Furniture', the *MJ*, 21 March 1958, Vol. 66, 620.
50 'Civic Design in the Streets' – Paper for Spring School on "The Other Duties of an Engineer" of the Institution of Municipal Engineers, Metropolitan District, 11–13 March 1958, by Sir Gordon Russell, 3, loose in 'Discussions on the Design of Street Furniture', N.A. Cat. Ref.: BP 2/279.
51 Ibid., 5.
52 'Call to Redesign Street Furniture', the *MJ*, 21 March 1958, Vol. 66, 620.
53 'Chaos in the Normal Town: Better Street Fittings Urged', the *Daily Telegraph*, 12 March 1958, in 'CoID: Design of Street Lighting Equipment', N.A. Cat. Ref.: MT 109/132.
54 'Call to Redesign Street Furniture', the *MJ*, 21 March 1958, Vol. 66, 620.
55 Civic Design in the Streets – Paper for Spring School on 'the other duties of an engineer' of the Institution of Municipal Engineers, Metropolitan District, 11–13 March 1958, by Sir Gordon Russell, 2, loose in Royal Fine Art Commission, 'Discussions on Design of Street Furniture'. BP 2/279. London: National Archives of the United Kingdom.
56 Internal correspondence from J.G. Ashley, Highways Management and Services Division, 12 March 1958, to Mr. Eales and Mr. Gillender; internal correspondence from R. G. S. Hoare to Mr. Gillender, 17 March 1958; letter to Gordon Russell, from Reep Lintern, MoT, 18 March 1958, loose in Ministry of Transport, 'Ministry of Transport and Successors, Highways Management and Services Division: Registered Files. Street Lighting. Council of Industrial Design: Design of Street Lighting Equipment'. MT 109/132. London: National Archives of the United Kingdom.
57 Letter from Gordon Russell to Reep Lintern, MoT, 20 March 1958, loose in Ibid.
58 *Design*, No. 91, July 1956, 11.
59 Notes for a lecture given to Durham County Council planning officers on Wednesday the 27 January 1960, 1, in Council of Industrial Design, 'Street Furniture Articles and Lectures' (Box 220 1432.15 Pt III).
60 Ibid.
61 Paul Reilly, *Lamp Post Feature: Notes Sent to Lord Snowdon (Confidential), 19.3.62*, 4, in 'Street Furniture Articles and Lectures' (1432.15 Pt III).
62 Ibid., 3.
63 Ibid.
64 'Value of Experience in Street Light Planning', the *MJ*, 25 September 1959, Vol. 67, 2647.
65 *Design*, No. 253, February 1970, 56.
66 Ibid.
67 'Point of View', *Design*, No. 204, December 1965, 26.
68 *Design*, No. 1, January 1949, 1.
69 Gordon Russell, 'What Is Good Design?' *Design*, No. 1, January 1949, 3.
70 Ibid., 5.
71 Ibid., 3. Russell's definition has similarities with that expressed by Frank Pick, who claimed in 1916 that 'art must give up its preciousness. It can no longer be exclusive or seek the singular and the rare.' Frank Pick, 'To the Master and Brethren of the Art Worker's Guild', 15 February 1916 (LMT PB1), 7.

72 For example, in 1958 *Design* reported that 'many appreciate the fact that old lamp standards are now outdated, and that replacements should not merely consist of pathetic reproductions of Victorian designs which inevitably lack the true qualities and charm of the originals and misuse modern materials and production methods'. In *Design*, No. 114, June 1958, 45.
73 Paul Reilly, 'A Hallmark for Good Design', *Design*, No. 20, August 1950, 2.
74 See Mary Banham and Bevis Hillier, eds. *A Tonic to the Nation: The Festival of Britain 1951* (London: Thames and Hudson, 1976); Becky Conekin, *The Autobiography of a Nation: The 1951 Festival of Britain* (Manchester: Manchester University, Press 2003); Harriet Atkinson, *Imaginative Reconstruction: Designing Place at the Festival of Britain 1951* (PhD thesis, 2006).
75 Lionel Brett, 'Detail on the South Bank', *Design*, No. 32, August 1951, 3.
76 Ibid.
77 Ibid., 5.
78 *Brief City: The Story of London's Festival Building*, Dir. Maurice Harvey/Jacques Brunius. Richard Massingham Productions in association with *The Observer*, 1951.
79 *Design*, No. 63, March 1954, 6.
80 CoID, *1st Annual Report 1945–46*, 6.
81 'Design Council Wants a "British Look"', *Guardian*, 27 August 1962.
82 Harris, *Romantic Moderns*, 12 and 70.
83 John Betjeman, 'Ugly Lamp Posts', *The Times*, 16 August 1950.
84 Letters to the Editor: 'Ugly Lamp Posts', *The Times*, 19 August 1950, 5.
85 Leader comment, *The Times*, 25 August 1950, 5.
86 'New Lamp Posts in the New Towns', *Design*, No. 42, June 1952, 29.
87 John Betjeman, Letter, *Design*, No. 55, July 1953, 6.
88 Ibid.
89 'Suggestions for an Ideal Lantern', the *MJ*, 25 September 1953, Vol. 61, 2095.
90 Peter Whitworth, 'Street Lighting: New Designs Reviewed', *Design*, No. 114, June 1958, 46.
91 For more information, see *Jack Howe: A Designed Life* (2015). Produced by Susan Wright, Directed by Martin Mortimore.
92 Letters page, *Design*, No. 72, December 1954, 46.
93 Reyner Banham, 'A Space for Decoration: A Rejoinder', *Design*, No. 79, July 1955, 24.
94 Ibid.
95 Ibid.
96 *Design*, No. 91, July 1956, 11.
97 Ibid., 53.
98 Ibid.
99 *Design*, No. 88, April 1956, 27.
100 Ibid.
101 Catherine Moriarty, 'A Backroom Service?', 43.
102 Sparke, *Did Britain Make It?*, 34.
103 Russell, 'Ugly Lamp Posts', 5.
104 The CoID, *4th Annual Report 1948–49*, 5.
105 Catherine Moriarty, 'A Backroom Service?', 43.
106 *The Observer*, 23 July 1950, quoted in the Council of Industrial Design, *Book L. Street Furniture: A Design Folio*, no date (circa 1951), 1.
107 Ibid.
108 Ibid.
109 Ibid., 4.

110 Ibid.
111 Ibid., 5.
112 Ibid.
113 Ibid., 1; Letter from Gordon Russell concerning 'Ugly Lamp Posts', *The Times*, August 24 1950 5; The CoID, *Book L. Street Furniture: A Design Folio*, no date (circa 1951), 5.
114 Also known as the 'Britain Can't Have It' exhibition, the 'Britain Can Make It' exhibition was an important project for the CoID. See Sparke, *Did Britain Make It?*
115 The CoID, *9th Annual Report 1953–54*, 8.
116 Ibid., 10.
117 The CoID, *10th Annual Report 1954–55*, 10.
118 'Outdoor Seats: A Competition for Manufacturers', *Design*, No. 54, June 1953, 5.
119 'Letter from George Williams to P. Fellows 29.07.53', in Council of Industrial Design, 'Royal Chelsea Flower Show – Display of Outdoor Seats', Box 220 (1401.1).
120 John Betjeman, Letter, *Design*, No. 55, July 1953, 6.
121 CoID, *16th Annual Report 1960–61*, 23.
122 CoID, *17th Annual Report 1961–62*, 18.
123 'Memo from Mr Chapman to Mr Fellows 19th July 1966', in Council of Industrial Design. 'Street Furniture: South Bank Exhibition'. Box 220 (1432.21.1).
124 'D. Johnston and D. Davies, Report on visit to South Bank street furniture exhibition 16th May 1968', 1, Ibid.
125 'Planning the Catalogue', *Design*, No. 14, February 1950, 6.
126 Ibid.
127 See *Street Furniture from Design Index 1965–66* (London: CoID, 1965).
128 However, according to David Davies in 'Streets Ahead' the first list of approved lighting column designs was produced in 1954, the *MJ*, 8 January 1971, 47, in Council of Industrial Design. 'Street Furniture: Articles and Lectures'. Box 220 (1432.15 Part III).
129 *Street Furniture: List of Approved Designs 1963* (London: CoID, 1963).
130 Fiona McCarthy, 'Life in Design', in *Kenneth Grange: Making Britain Modern*, eds. Fiona MacCarthy, Gemma Curtin and Deyan Sudjic (London: Design Museum and Black Dog Publishing, 2011), 8.
131 *Parking Meters*, 12 August 1965, British Pathé. Available online: http://www.britishpathe.com/video/parking-meters (accessed 30 July 2015); Josie Barnard, 'Time Runs Out for the Parking Meter', *The Daily Telegraph*, 30 December 2008. Available online: http://www.telegraph.co.uk/news/features/4029123/Time-runs-out-for-the-parking-meter.html (accessed 30 July 2015).
132 The *MJ*, 23 October 1953, Vol. 61, 2300; and the *MJ*, 14 October 1955, Vol. 63, 2750.
133 'Road Traffic Bill: Parking Meters', Memo by the Minister of Transport and Civil Aviation, 26 November 1954, 1, N.A. Cat. Ref.: CAB 129/72 0011.
134 Ibid.
135 'Cabinet Conclusions of a Meeting at 10 Downing Street on the 2 December 1954', 4, CAB 128/27 0081.
136 Ibid.
137 'Draft Cabinet Statement: Parking Meters, 20th December 1954', 3, CAB 129/72 0051.
138 Interview with Kenneth Grange, 21 November 2012.
139 Ibid.
140 Gemma Curtin, '60 Years in Design' in *Kenneth Grange*, 38.
141 The *MJ*, 23 November 1956, Vol. 64, 2779.

142　Interview with Kenneth Grange, 21 November 2012.
143　Ibid.
144　Ibid.
145　George Williams, 'Street Furniture: A Review of the Use and Abuse of Lampposts and Parking Meters', *Design*, April 1956, No. 88, 28.
146　Ibid.
147　The Royal Fine Art Commission, *14th Annual Report – 1955–1956* (London: February 1957), 15, 720.6041.
148　*Design*, No. 63, March 1954, 6.
149　Interview with Kenneth Grange, 21 November 2012.
150　George Williams, 'Street Furniture: A Review of the Use and Abuse of Lampposts and Parking Meters', *Design*, April 1956, No. 88, 35.
151　Interview with Kenneth Grange, 21 November 2012.
152　Deyan Sudjic, 'A Modernist at Heart', in *Kenneth Grange*, 15.
153　Interview with Kenneth Grange, 21 November 2012.
154　Ibid.
155　Email correspondence with Kenneth Grange, 2015.
156　Ibid.
157　Interview with Kenneth Grange, 21 November 2012.
158　Ibid.
159　Ibid.
160　'CoID Progress Report', the *AR*, December 1951, Vol. 110, No. 660, 352.
161　Interview with Kenneth Grange, 21 November 2012.
162　Ibid.
163　Ibid.
164　Ibid.
165　Gemma Curtin, '60 Years in Design', in *Kenneth Grange*, 28.
166　Interview with Kenneth Grange, 21 November 2012.
167　Ibid.
168　Fiona McCarthy, 'Life in Design', in *Kenneth Grange*, 8.
169　Interview with Kenneth Grange, 21 November 2012.
170　Ibid.
171　Ibid.
172　*Country Life*, 13 October 1960, 831.
173　*Punch*, 19 October 1955, 464; *Punch*, 17 October 1956, 455; *Punch*, 2 January 1957, 68.
174　*Wardens Are So Courteous*, 19 September 1960, British Pathé. Available online: http://www.britishpathe.com/video/wardens-are-so-courteous/query/parking+meters (accessed 30 July 2015).
175　*Parking Meters*, 12 August 1965, British Pathé. Available online: http://www.britishpathe.com/video/parking-meters (accessed 30 July 2015).
176　*Cool Hand Luke*, directed by Stuart Rosenberg, Jalem Productions, 1967, USA.
177　Interview with Kenneth Grange, 21 November 2012.
178　'Design Must Not Be Forgotten in Creating Parking System', the *MJ*, 22 February 1957, Vol. 65, 391.
179　The *MJ*, 8 June 1962, Vol. 70, 1740.
180　'Design Must Not Be Forgotten in Creating Parking System', the *MJ*, 22 February 1957, Vol. 65, 391.
181　'Counter Attack', the *AR*, July 1957, Vol. 122, No. 726, 78–9; 'Parking Meters', the *AR*, September 1969, Vol. 142, No. 871, 178.

Chapter 3

THE GREAT AND THE GOOD: POWER AND INFLUENCE

Alongside the Council of Industrial Design (CoID), several other professional organizations and individuals wielded considerable power and influence within the post-war street furniture debate, some even on an official and semi-official basis. Magazines like the *Architectural Review* and organizations like the Civic Trust and the Royal Fine Art Commission had an enormous impact on street furniture design, and represent the wider intellectual context to the debate. The views expressed by these different agents sometimes overlapped and sometimes stood in opposition, both to each other and to the CoID. As a result, the street furniture debate developed a polycentric quality, in which power was fragmented among the design elite, and opinion divided. This chapter shows that in the absence of legislative power, soft power became extremely important for the post-war street furniture debate.

'Ivory Towers': *The* Architectural Review

The *Architectural Review* (*AR*) was an important voice in post-war design debates, but it was also extremely peculiar and contradictory. On the one hand, it maintained an aesthetic interpretation of design, celebrating the picturesque and providing critical commentary from the margins; but on the other, it doggedly campaigned for higher standards and held abuses of power to account. Founded in 1896, the *AR* was published by the Architectural Press (AP), which also owned the *Architects Journal*. Considered by those within the AP as 'the more dignified' of its publications, the *AR* had from the outset demonstrated its commitment to the 'artistic, as distinguished from the business side, of architecture', and in many ways its focus on the aesthetics of architecture continued.[1] While the *AR*'s attitude to modernism was sometimes elastic – and throughout the post-war period the magazine routinely presented ancient and modern together – nonetheless, from the 1920s onwards, the *AR* emerged as the magazine that published the latest in European architectural thinking, commissioning pieces by several of its leading figures, including Le Corbusier, Ernö Goldfinger and Walter Gropius.[2] Though somewhat looser in its interpretation of modernism than the CoID, the *AR*'s owner, Hubert de Cronin Hastings, employed several writers who shared his sympathies, including J. M. Richards (editor between 1937 and 1971), Pevsner and Banham, as well as those who sometimes didn't (like John Betjeman, former assistant editor).[3] Such figures worked together to promote what they considered to be good design from a highly self-conscious aesthetic position.

The *AR*'s aesthetic agenda can be traced to a special supplement published in January 1947 called 'The Second Half Century', in which the four members of the *AR*'s editorial advisory board – Richards, Pevsner, Hastings and Osbert Lancaster – outlined their editorial policies. They claimed that, despite being an architectural magazine, the *AR*'s remit went beyond architecture, particularly 'the right sort of architecture', and extended to deliberately 'flout good taste'.[4] That taste, particularly good taste, was a quality that the *AR* understood negatively can be placed in the context of a book published in 1933 by Betjeman. In *Ghastly Good Taste*, Betjeman defined good taste as synonymous with the conventional or the status quo; and in terms of style, with the historical or neo-historical. Gentleman architects, he said, with their knowledge of period obscured the good work of the all-important engineers with their self-conscious marks.[5] Consequently, modern design was understood as sitting outside of taste because of its association with enduring values like function and professional figures like engineers: an interpretation echoed by Kenneth Grange in the previous chapter.

In 'The Second Half Century', the *AR* defined one of its objectives as 'the need to demonstrate the unity, or rather the indivisibility, of the arts'; underneath which was the less tangible but no less bold objective, namely '*visual re-education*'.[6] The magazine's editors asserted that the only way to improve the taste of the public was through re-educating them on the values of modern design. Such a position bears striking resemblance to Frank Pick's interwar anxiety about British people's lack of visual awareness.[7] However, whereas Pick's solution was to recommend a trip abroad, the *AR* encouraged its readership to follow certain exercises, which included denying themselves 'the pleasures of historicism and antiquarianism'.[8] Rigorously following such exercises, the *AR* claimed, would lead to a visual rebirth and a 'new keenness of perception' to revitalize the modern movement.[9] Yet this approach primarily focused on re-educating the eye to appreciate the subtleties of the environment, and for its part, the *AR* promised to address, 'extravagant or surprising objects or scenes, such as a surrealist municipal seat on the front at Swanage or an exotically decorated butcher's shop on the Old Bath Road'.[10] Swanage was well known among the arts community for its visual idiosyncrasies. In 1870 the Dorset town had received a gift of architectural salvage by a man named George Burt, who intended to embellish it with ornate iron bollards and lamp posts. While based there in 1935, the artist Paul Nash declared Swanage to be a 'Surrealist dream', and documented the peculiar combination of bollards and bedheads strewn around the landscape for a feature in the *AR*.[11] Concentrating on such apparently random examples of street furniture, visual culture, landscape and townscape would, according to the *AR*, exercise the visual nerve of its readership and underline the 'importance of the pursuit of visual life'.[12]

For the *AR*, visual re-education was a call to arms for seeing, which – while not motivated by political or moral revolution at this stage – was no less evangelical, for it went beyond mere propaganda and communication. According to the *AR*, 'to those for whom visual relations matter, the capacity to *see* represents itself as a way of salvation'.[13] The *AR*'s use of terms like 'salvation' and its supposition that the process would 're-create a visual culture which will help to re-create civilization' echoes wartime propaganda.[14] But the campaign was presented as a battle for aesthetic rather than political values, which would be 'arduous and unpopular and extremely difficult to explain', as well as attracting little more than 'expense, criticism and ill-will'.[15] Nonetheless, this was a battle that the *AR* felt it could fight, based on the fact that it was 'unroped to any guide… hacking its own way up the ice-slopes of modern experience'.[16] The position cultivated in this supplement is not just independence, but self-enforced marginalization, a penance – it is implied – that had to be endured as a result of being enlightened. And yet lobbying for increased aesthetic sensitivity at a time when cities across Britain were faced with enormous challenges shows a peculiar sense of remoteness from the social, cultural and ultimately, practical concerns of modern design after the war. To what extent, however, did this distance inform the *AR*'s approach to street furniture?

Street furniture: The subtleties of the urban environment

Throughout the late 1940s and early 1950s, street furniture was used by the *AR* as an example of design that the public too often ignored, in a bid to alert its readers to the subtleties of the urban environment. One of the first instances when the *AR* used street furniture in this way occurred in August 1948, when it published a short feature on a manhole cover.[17] The accompanying black and white photograph depicts the manhole cover in the street, with little sense of the surrounding environment – i.e. buildings, people or traffic – in the frame. The text is poetic, and there is a pervading sense of animism; the manhole cover is described as having 'a life, personality; a patter and texture of its own'.[18] It is also described as being part of a body of objects that often slipped under the consciousness of the public, and unfortunately even the professional designer. There had been, lamented the *AR*, 'a total visual blackout, a conspiracy on the part of the eye to ignore whole slabs of the world out there, and though the streets are one of the most important visual elements in the townscape their objective existence, apart from the buildings, the street itself, curbs, lamp posts, hydrants, manhole covers, never swing into view'.[19] Drawing attention to a manhole cover in this way suggests that the *AR* shared the CoID's interest in everyday objects, but it also shows the *AR*'s ability to promote modern design both visually and textually.

In fact, much of this photographic material had been developed before the war, when Richards and the artist John Piper made a series of surveys of the built environment.[20] According to Alexandra Harris, their detailed examinations shared the ethnographic style of Mass Observation, the social project which engaged with the messy texture of everyday life as real people lived it, in which no subject was off limits.[21] However, unlike the scientific detachment customary to Mass Observation, Harris notes that Piper and Richards 'made fresh sympathetic judgments about ordinary places'.[22] Their motivation was to show that tradition and modernity could exist side by side, or to 'embrace modernism while hanging on tight to their histories'.[23] The material culture of the past was clearly important to them and they were not prepared to cast it aside in pursuit of the new, like so many others from this period.

In a similar example to the manhole cover, the *AR* again alerted its readers to the importance of the street floor the following year. Using the same animistic tone, the *AR* described the accompanying photograph in which, 'the granite sets

Figure 3.1 For the *Architectural Review* this drain concealed a 'sinister underground organization that underlies the city'. Drain, in Townscape, the *Architectural Review*, December 1949, Vol. 105, No. 636, 354. RIBA Library Books & Periodicals Collection.

break in waves against the cliff of the curb, the bicyclist throws a cloak of shadow as of a cloud upon the sea, the drain cover awaits the shower that will suck heedless match-ends through fifteen avid little mouths into the sinister underground organization that underlies the city'.[24] That an object as mundane as a drain could be described in such terms (see Figure 3.1), testifies to the value the *AR* assigned street furniture, as well as its own self-conscious aesthetic agenda. It was also a further example to which the town planner was allegedly blind. Such elements, 'the trivia of the visual scene' as the *AR* defined them, were essential determinants of the quality of the urban realm. The *AR* was interested in trivia, an indication perhaps of its refusal to accommodate conventional subjects and standards of taste. Instead its editors encouraged their readership to engage with 'the vast field of anonymous design and unacknowledged pattern which still lies entirely outside the terms of reference of official town planning routine'.[25] Encouraging the public to open their eyes and look at street furniture – unlike the town planner – was the first of many steps in the *AR*'s campaign to improve design standards in the street – one of the most important visual elements in the townscape.

Like the manhole cover and the drain, street furniture continued to be described by the *AR* in such poetic terms (see Figure 3.2). Banal objects like bollards were described as 'sunning themselves'.[26] Street furniture was even regarded as a form of urban sculpture by Andrew Hammer in 1951, for whom 'in a fully realized townscape every street is its own sculpture gallery'.[27] Others writing for the *AR* shared Hammer's interpretation, including Banham who observed that lamp posts had a certain surreal quality.[28] Even the celebrated architectural writer Ian Nairn – whose work on the Outrage campaign will be discussed later – had opinions about street furniture, and he once described an American fire hydrant as displaying 'unexpected virility'.[29] Drawing attention to the sculptural or humanistic qualities of street furniture like this owes a considerable debt to surrealism, in which the mysteriousness and irrationality of the everyday is elevated.[30] This sensibility is borrowed in part from psychoanalyst Sigmund Freud's work on the unconscious, in which the edges of consciousness are important despite their perceived marginality. The *AR*'s approach to street furniture appears to adopt this sensibility, which serves to emphasize its artistic and intellectual perspective on the debate even further.

Yet while many of these photographic investigations of everyday life sought to retain a sense of detachment, the *AR* also issued advice on best practice in contemporary urban development. In a feature on 'trim' – namely the treatment of junctions, verges and margins – the *AR* defined the best of these elements as being 'simple, functional and have a feeling of unassuming rightness; the right thing in the right place used in the right way'.[31] It also discussed how street furniture could be used in the wrong way, by highlighting poor examples. At the start of the 1950s, this tended to mean concrete lamp posts, which the *AR* characterized as 'among the worst offenders in the contemporary street scene'.[32] Several specific models were singled out by the magazine as part of a 1951 survey on street lighting. For

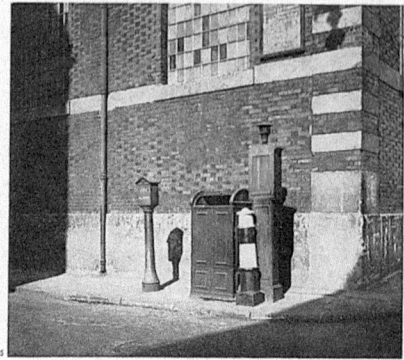

STREET FURNITURE Four objects surprised whilst sunning themselves behind St. Benets. The photograph shows the bad effect of crowding, together pieces of street furniture which in themselves are good.

GEOMETRY Sitting on a veranda at the sea, I was able to observe the curve of the horizon by sighting it along the veranda rail. I could see the rise in the centre. This simple but astonishing sight evokes the same emotion as the perception of geometry in the environment. Planes, lines and curves which have the same infallibility.

SIGNIFICANT OBJECTS The town is full of objects, trees, steeples, lamp posts, pillar boxes, pediments. On the large scale they become means of articulation, on the small scale they provide richness and possibly strangeness (as the two eyes follow you all the way down the street).

FLOORSCAPE The space between buildings is just as important in the total view as the buildings. Floors have functions to perform as well as walls, but the problem is not wholly one of convenience. If it is worth while studying the scale and texture of a wall, then it is important on floors. The type of floor can affect the scale of buildings, it can isolate a building, or make it part of a scene.

Figure 3.2 Street furniture in the *Architectural Review*, 1949. Eye as Painter, in Townscape Casebook, the *Architectural Review*, December 1949, Vol. 105, No. 636, 371. RIBA Library Books & Periodicals Collection.

instance, the Concrete Utilities Ltd. Avenue column (see Figure 3.3) was described as capable of destroying the 'character of many unassuming suburban streets'; and other columns were described as incongruous and ugly, or showing 'a coarseness of detail that is peculiar to the modern concrete lamp-standard'.[33]

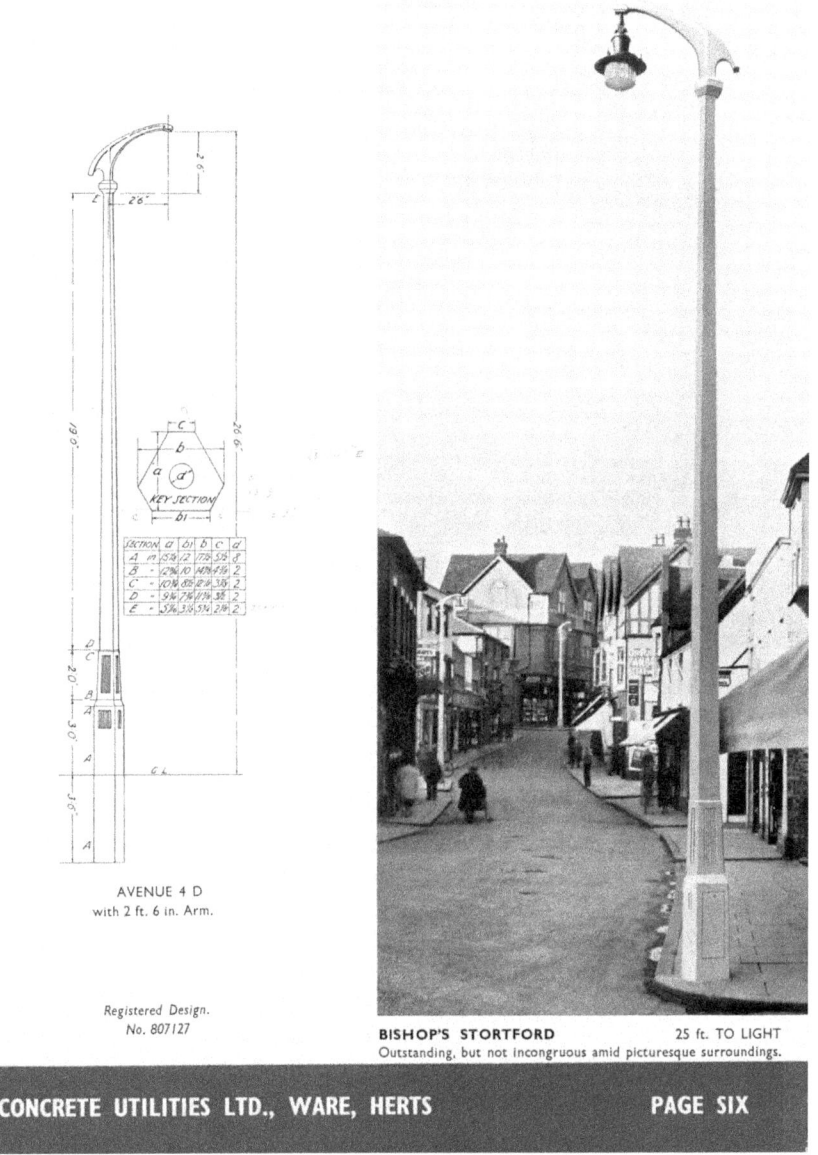

Figure 3.3 Concrete Utilities Ltd, 'Modern Lamp Columns', List 38, 1946, 6. CU Phosco Lighting Ltd.

The subtleties of the urban environment were also important to the *AR* because they reflected standards of taste and could therefore be used to improve standards. For a magazine that cultivated a position outside conventions of taste, it is interesting that the *AR* would simultaneously seek to comment on this issue. An early example can be found in a 1949 feature on the lack of advertisements

Figure 3.4 Illustration by Gordon Cullen (cropped version), in 'Townscape: Outdoor Publicity', the *Architectural Review*, May 1949, Vol. 105, No. 629, 250. Courtesy of Gordon Cullen Estate and RIBA Library Books & Periodicals Collection.

in the New Towns then under construction (see Figure 3.4). Advertisements, or outdoor publicity, according to the *AR*, represented one of the twentieth century's most valuable contributions to urban scenery. Yet to its detractors, it could only serve to 'vulgarize public environment and degrade public taste'.[34] Such views were incompatible with the *AR*, which held that to omit outdoor publicity from the New Towns 'would seem to be an act of genteelism reminiscent of the days when the designer ignored everything that didn't fall into line with his own private taste'.[35] However, despite condemning the private taste of the designer, the *AR* was willing to recognize the levels of tastes that identified different levels of society. For instance, in support of its case that publicity ought to be permitted in the New Towns, the *AR* noted that,

> Public taste is already vulgar and already has the one merit of vulgarity, i.e. vitality. To put publicity into a strait-jacket, to restrain it, will not improve public taste but simply kill off its vitality. The solution surely is to let the public express its vulgarity, for expression is itself a form of education. In this way the public and its publicity will improve together.[36]

The point made here is useful on a number of levels. Principally, it reflects the social distance of the *AR* from the public, but it also suggests that the *AR*'s visual re-education campaign was based on the premise that, despite having some positive qualities, public taste was vulgar. In other words, while the *AR* was on the one hand actively flouting good taste, it was simultaneously reinforcing the idea that the public's taste was inadequate and in need of re-education.

The *AR*'s understanding of street furniture in relation to taste can also be seen in a report it published in 1952, on the use of 'genteel' lettering in street furniture (see Figure 3.5). For the *AR*, use of the term genteel was intended to imply

Figure 3.5 'Lettering', The *Architectural Review*, January 1952, Vol. 111, No. 661, 59. RIBA Library Books & Periodicals Collection.

conventional understandings of good manners and good taste, and the negative connotations that have already been established. According to its report, 'the worst enemy of the public notice, as of the public speaker, is the soft and the sissy, and the worst kind of sissy is the genteel sissy'.[37] Helpfully, the *AR* illustrated its report with examples of genteel lettering and some lettering on a seaside warning sign, which it clearly preferred. Describing the sign, the *AR* claimed 'its stentorian voice would reach the back row and beyond in the teeth of a 60 m.p.h. gale – a splendid example of straight-from-the-shoulder visual oratory and straight-from-the-shoulder English too'.[38] Besides the nationalistic fervour with which this particular sign was celebrated, the negative references to genteel lettering serve to reinforce the *AR*'s objective to flout good taste. But the report also demonstrates a further way in which the *AR*'s coverage of street furniture can be situated in a historical context. By comparing a good example of lettering with a bad one, the *AR* was continuing a method of visual rhetoric employed by design reformers since the nineteenth century.

Such an approach was not without its critics, however. For one Liverpool-based reader in 1952, the magazine's subject matter was trivial and he asked for some proper criticism instead of just criticizing the lettering on the 'litter boxes'.[39] He added, 'we know these things are important, but surely if the REVIEW really wants to improve design it should begin not by attacking the fringes, but by striking downwards towards the very root of the problem'.[40] In response, the editors issued a denial that the magazine focused on the fringe, but nevertheless insisted that 'the treatment of the fringe is often symptomatic of what is happening at the core'.[41] Evidently, the *AR* considered street furniture as a lens through which bigger issues could be revealed – or as an 'acid test of good town design' – and later reports on bollards, lamp posts and litter bins were approached in a similar way.[42]

Townscape

One of the most important ways in which the *AR* engaged with the subject of street furniture was through the series Townscape. Developed originally in the 1940s and 1950s by Hastings and Pevsner, Townscape is more often identified with the magazine's art editor Gordon Cullen, who popularized the series and later published a book of the same name. The original idea likened the urban landscape to a painting or urban scenery, and Pevsner's research on the picturesque provided its early foundations. The principles of the picturesque – 'variety, of intricacy, of the connection of the building with nature, of advance and recess, swelling and sinking, and of contrasts in texture' – may have been formulated in the context of eighteenth-century landscape gardening, but they became embedded in the idea of Townscape as a whole.[43] While an interest in the picturesque had been steadily growing in Britain, Pevsner was instrumental in extending the concept into post-war architectural discourse.[44] According to architectural historian Matthew Aitchison, Pevsner's early impact on Townscape – which he referred to as 'visual planning' – was based on the simple idea that 'planning should serve the views it creates'.⁴⁵ Qualifying this scenographic approach, Pevsner argued that conventional planning concerns including 'housing, slum clearance, traffic regulation, etc. [...] are indispensable, but visual planning is also indispensable, and if the whole of a town is in the end not visually pleasing, the town is not worth having'.⁴⁶

Within the pages of the *AR*, Townscape was initially used as an umbrella category to examine the design of railings, kerbs, junctions, verges and margins, street furniture, pavements and other miscellaneous aspects of the urban scene, from the past as well as the present. However, the theory behind the series emphasized the importance of the city as an environment for the complete human being, to be experienced statically and in movement. According to Cullen, this complete human being 'demands more than a picture gallery, he demands the drama that can be released all around him from floor, sky, buildings, trees and levels by the art of arrangement'.⁴⁷ The concept understood the typical town not as a pattern of streets but as 'a *sequence of spaces* created by buildings'.⁴⁸

Townscape depicted these spaces by employing powerful visual rhetoric. As a highly skilled draughtsman, Cullen produced colourful, hand-worked drawings, in which a city's inhabitants are often seen at a distance, in a variety of everyday situations and designed environments. The visual language of the illustrations is also distinct, and many of them reproduce Britain through the lens of a benign form of modernism that was also found on the South Bank during the Festival of Britain (see Figure 3.6). Good townscape designs are often represented with light washes of colour and complete with idealized human situations, and bad townscape designs are represented by darker versions of the existing environment, with monstrous street furniture, cluttered streets and chaotic scenes of traffic and pedestrians colliding. Some illustrations are helpfully labelled 'do' and 'don't', a practice which was typical of the time (see Figure 3.7).⁴⁹ Photography was also central to educating readers on the Townscape model, and black and white photographs of bollards and pedestrians simultaneously capture the banality and mysteriousness of the city in which, as Cullen notes, 'anything could happen or exist, the noble or the sordid, genius or lunacy'.⁵⁰ Like much of the *AR*'s contribution to the street furniture debate, Townscape's language was often poetic; for instance, the ruthlessness and rigidity of modern lighting installations was described as marching through towns and villages 'like a posse of soldier ants'.⁵¹

Townscape reflects a great deal about how the *AR* applied its visual re-education campaign to city planning more generally, and street furniture specifically. In many ways, the imagery produced in Townscape expressed the aesthetic ideals of the magazine, and its focus on the visual qualities of a town resulted in a highly aestheticized expression of post-war urban planning. Yet it also exposes the reality for architects and planners in post-war Britain, in particular the difficulties they faced in preserving the historical fabric of the city alongside encouraging new, more modern development. For Townscape, the question of how to unify these disparate elements, which were widely perceived as not only aesthetically but also ideologically in conflict, was solved by re-presenting the city as a collage.

Figure 3.6 Illustration of an idealized piazza by Gordon Cullen, 'South Bank Translated', the *Architectural Review*, August 1951, Vol. 110, No. 656, 137. Courtesy of Gordon Cullen Estate and RIBA Library Books & Periodicals Collection.

171, don't jolt the rustic harmony by planning urban-looking car parks on the canal side. 172, don't fence off or regiment nature. The canal should fit into the countryside.

173, don't litter the towpath with litter baskets and prim, puritanical benches. Design such things carefully and unobtrusively. 174, don't lay out canal-side tea gardens in this kind of formal, unimaginative, municipal garden style.

Figure 3.7 Drawing of benches and litter bins by Gordon Cullen, 'Special Number on Canals', the *Architectural Review*, July 1949, Vol. 105, No. 107, 61. Courtesy of Gordon Cullen Estate and RIBA Library Books & Periodicals Collection. Gordon Cullen advised readers: 'don't litter the towpath with litter baskets and prim puritanical benches. Design such things carefully and unobtrusively', Townscape, 1949.

However, Townscape reflects a much more radical position than its stylized imagery or surreal photographs of Victorian cast-iron work might otherwise suggest (see Figure 3.8). Perhaps because of its intellectual and aesthetic links to the picturesque, Townscape represents a form of liberty from tyranny. For Pevsner this link between the picturesque and liberty had a profoundly English quality. In 'Picturesque England', a Reith Lecture broadcast by the BBC in 1955, Pevsner cites George Mason in his 1768 *Essay on Design in Gardening* who attributed the invention of landscape gardening in England to the English 'Independency… in matters of taste and in religion and government'.[52] In the same way, Townscape can be equated with liberty; it was certainly an early way in which the *AR* sought to

Figure 3.8 'Townscape: Unconscious Sculpture', the *Architectural Review*, December 1952, Vol. 111, No. 672, 405. RIBA Library Books & Periodicals Collection.

protect public space – and therefore street furniture – from defilement by 'those who decide public matters'.[53] Indeed, its focus on environmental design was intended to reflect the *AR*'s anti-authoritarianism. In this way, the politics of Townscape can be understood as a means of challenging the status quo in post-war Britain. By criticizing the actions of the bureaucrats in charge of city planning, the *AR* tried to position itself outside the centre of power and align itself with the public to serve their interests. But how did the public respond to what were outwardly aesthetic aims?

The magazine's editor J. M. Richards later recalled that many readers quickly became bored with the subject of Townscape and criticized the stereotypes offered as solutions.[54] Such stereotypes were central to the Townscape campaign to re-imagine Britain and thus present a better version. Moreover, although the vision of good streetscape design encouraged by the AR through Townscape may have celebrated variety in urban space and rejected tyranny, its narrow interpretation of how the city ought to be designed was perceived as itself tyrannical. Looking back in 1975, Ian Nairn suggested Townscape's attempt to create an 'ecology of man-made things' was wilfully misconstrued as a fad, and even seen as a counterpoint to the urban forms promoted by American urban theorists Jane Jacobs and Kevin Lynch. According to Nairn, 'Jacobs thinks that townscape is fiddling with visual frills and Gordon Cullen regards the urban grass-roots approach as an impediment to the grand poetic design'.[55] It is difficult to assess whether Cullen prioritized a city's 'frills' over its physical experience by users, but it was certainly true for many at the AR that the quality of the city as a whole could be measured through such elements.

The margin and the centre

However, the AR was not only content with presenting its own version of how the post-war street should look; it also took issue with the efforts of others. In this sense, the AR's self-imposed exile on the margins of taste also created an opportunity for the magazine to assess the taste of other design organizations, particularly those in more powerful positions within the street furniture debate, like the CoID. In a report on industrial design in 1946, the AR characterized the CoID as little more than a 'government department... however able'.[56] Such a comment deliberately carried with it connotations of bureaucracy and conventionality, and the AR underlined its reluctance to leave the issue of design standards to the CoID alone. While the two organizations were markedly different, they often found themselves in conversation with each other. One such conversation occurred in 1951, when the AR published a progress report on the CoID following the Festival of Britain.

The AR's assessment of the CoID's contribution to the Festival of Britain can best be described as tepid. While it had praised the South Bank's street furniture some months earlier, its 'CoID Progress Report' claimed that out-with this category there were 'quite a number of real atrocities on show and a very large number of aesthetically indifferent products'.[57] In order for standards to improve, what was required was 'firm aesthetic guidance', and the AR asked: 'is the CoID hampered in its selectivity by the Board of Trade behind it, naturally used to judging success in terms of figures and especially export figures? One would like to know?'[58] In many ways, this question goes to the root of the relationship between the two organizations, since the AR was essentially concerned about the role of government in setting aesthetic standards. As an arm of government, the CoID effectively set these standards. For the *AR*, they were far too low; rather than being daring, the CoID merely desired to 'keep on the safe side'.[59]

For CoID director Gordon Russell on the other hand, such criticism missed the point. He responded to the *AR*'s 'CoID Progress Report' two months later, pointing out the realities that an organization like the CoID faced, including shortages of material and labour, rising costs, taxes and quotas, and fear of nationalization.[60] According to Russell, many manufacturers were hostile to the CoID and did not understand the importance of design in any case. Working in this environment demanded that the CoID was open to compromise, and Russell admitted, 'I cannot help feeling that when the *Architectural Review* says we have a lack of belief in a high aesthetic standard and have opened the flood-gates, whilst the National Brassfoundry Association complains that selection was far too drastic, we cannot be so far out'.[61] In other words, the *AR*'s aims were unrealistically lofty and industry's were pessimistically low.

What is interesting about this argument is that both the CoID and the *AR* inhabited the same world. *Design* after all was likely to have had the same readership as the *AR*. The argument does therefore have an internalized quality, for the *AR* responded by commending Russell's battle for Good Design 'down in the market place' with its 'appalling realities'.[62] There was, however, it said, a place for the 'ivory-towerish' approach.[63] The *AR*'s ivory tower was otherwise known as the Bride of Denmark pub, and Russell may even have socialized there with *AR* staff.[64] The *AR* added that it was 'in the fortunate position of being free to use any means, however base, to propagate its ideas: *Design*, on the other hand, can never escape the shackles of public responsibility… could it not be a little more adventurous [or] approximate more closely to its fairy godmother Graphis, and play down the paternal uncle, His Majesty's Stationary Office?'[65] Sarcasm aside, the attitude of the *AR* was clear: while it represented independence from government, and high artistic standards, *Design* – and by extension the CoID – remained a government department.

This argument prompted others to contribute, especially those aggrieved parties caught in the crossfire.[66] The National Brassfoundry Association – which had been characterized by Russell as resistant to good design's value – criticized the CoID's dominance, adding that it was

> extremely unlikely that there are no important groups disagreeing with the Council on many matters. We believe that such groups exist but that they are unorganized and inarticulate through (a) being spread out over the country, (b) lack of secretarial help, etc., and (c) lack of cash. An artistic group centred on London backed by public funds and a propaganda magazine is in too strong a position and may very readily become exclusive. Past experience shows us that the best work is produced when there is plenty of articulate opposition.[67]

The *AR* quite clearly represented one such voice of opposition. And yet, the qualities that the National Brassfoundry Association lists as being indicative of an exclusive approach are as relevant to the *AR* as they are to the CoID. There is an irony then, in publishing a warning about the threat of exclusivity in the *AR*.

Questions about the magazine's exclusivity were raised by one of its own writers and photographers, Eric de Maré, the following year. In an open letter to the *AR*, Maré questioned whether its 'exclusively visual propaganda which only a handful of people appreciate can have any noticeable effect on our frightful environment'.[68] The twentieth century, according to Maré, lacked any degree of visual order, and therefore purely aesthetic and architectural agendas were unlikely to improve the environment. Instead, change must be grounded in political and economic ideas of reform, for the 'social pattern as a whole creates the environment and until the aesthetes have the backing of the public they must go on crying in the wilderness without avail'.[69] Maré also speculated on the future of magazines like the *AR*:

> Can we go on sitting in our snug little room with the blinds down playing Chopin quietly to ourselves much longer? The rumbling outside is beginning to drown even for us the music no one else can hear anyway. I implore you at least to fling up the window for a breather and have a look outside – all around and not just down at that fascinating floorscape.[70]

Besides satirizing the *AR*'s preoccupation with drains and cobblestones, Maré also predicted that the new culture emerging after the war was in danger of premature death because it was 'being attended to by clumsy midwives'.[71] True to form, the *AR* responded with a denial of any wrongdoing: 'Mr. de Maré implores us to fling up the window for a breather, which it is our habit to do; not to shout exhortations out of it or make speeches on economics out of it but to look out of it and discuss what we see.'[72] Thus the *AR* presented itself as offering a mirror to society, rather than seeking to make any broader political or economic statements. From this exchange, it is clear that the *AR* represented a more aesthetically driven approach to post-war design debates than other groups. And yet, its disinterested position on the political backdrop to aesthetic decisions was changing. As Maré prophesied, aesthetes were beginning to realize that unless they had the support of the public, their campaigns would be of little value.

Soft power: Negotiation and diplomacy

The impact the *AR* had on the street furniture debate was significant but it was not the only alternative voice to the CoID. Organizations like the Royal Fine Art Commission, the Georgian Group and the Civic Trust also engaged in the debate. These groups often overlapped, not only in terms of their objectives, but also in terms of the people who set them up and even ran them.[73] Such a degree of overlap suggests that the design profession in the post-war period was a relatively intimate – though not always congenial – circle; many of its key figures having been educated together, served on wartime ministries together, or were simply linked through social and family ties.[74]

And yet, while the networks producing, advising and contributing to these different bodies and publications might have looked relatively cosy, the way in which their voices were expressed was significantly different. While the *AR* was a privately financed magazine able to express a variety of often contradictory views, and take a public stand on the issues it felt strongly about, several of the other organizations listed were publicly funded, and therefore had to express themselves through negotiation and diplomacy behind the scenes. This distinction between public and private is important, as it demonstrates the way in which different organizations could or could not raise their voice within the debate about street furniture design, depending on the financial or political powers available to them.

Soft power is a useful lens through which to examine the relations between these different official and semi-official groups. Originally coined by Joseph Nye in an article he published in the journal *Foreign Policy* in 1990, soft power was a concept specific to the Cold War era, and essentially refers to an informal type of power that relies on influence rather than force or legislation.[75] Soft power's application during the post-war period already has some precedent. In Peter York's book *Style Wars*, the British historian A. L. Rowse is credited as having said, 'in the sixties… the *soft* people ran things and now it's time for the *hard* men'.[76] The soft people, Rowse implied, might constitute voluntary groups, or committee members that took decisions on the basis of advice. They might have a working relationship with the state, but might also rely on networks of unelected people. The *hard* men by contrast might also have a relationship with the state, but could equally be characterized as independent or corporate figures able to make direct decisions without consultation, relying less on influence and more on legislative or market forces. While Rowse's comment was made in the context of 1980s Britain – arguably, a period characterized by one particularly hard woman – nevertheless, it retains some value in the context of the 1950s. As Richards once said, the 1950s was a time when 'committees of one kind or another were formed and dissolved'.[77] And though committees in themselves are not necessarily indicative of soft power, their powerful presence in the 1950s – alongside collaborative societies, civic engagement groups, voluntary organizations, and a way of working that was often performed behind the scenes – suggests that soft power is a useful concept in this context.

One of the organizations that can be understood in the light of soft power was the Royal Fine Art Commission (RFAC). Having been appointed under Royal Warrant in 1924, the RFAC's remit was to 'inquire into such questions of public amenity or of artistic importance as may be referred to them from time to time by any of our Departments of State'.[78] In this way, the RFAC was no more distant to government than the CoID. It had two main functions, which were often in conflict: to safeguard Britain's man-made and natural heritage, and to encourage new works.[79] Its powers did not exceed beyond information requests or site visits, and it was only permitted to advise on cases with national significance. According to the *Municipal Journal*, the RFAC was 'able to arrange a *marriage de convenance* between beauty and utility'.[80] Effectively, it provided high-level advice on artistic matters for central and local government and other public bodies, and often advised on cases of artistic controversy.[81] Such high-level advice was mostly supplied by practicing architects, who constituted about half the board, but sculptors, engineers, historians and others interested in aesthetics were equally represented.[82] People like Richards, Betjeman, Kenneth Clark, John Piper, Maxwell Fry, Henry Moore and John Summerson – many of whom also worked on other publications and advised other organizations – were all, at one point, members of the RFAC.[83] They met to discuss a wide range of issues, including the powers of planning authorities, the construction or repair of buildings and bridges and the siting of street furniture.

A similar organization to the RFAC in its use of soft power was the Georgian Group (GG), though in other respects it was a very different organization – being a purely private pressure group. Douglas Goldring originally set it up in 1937 but left shortly after, leaving the group in charge of Lord Derwent, Angus Acworth and Robert Byron. While these people were certainly passionate about Georgian architecture, one of Goldring's friends earlier warned him that 'your Georgian group will develop into an informal club of rich dilettante who have taken up Georgian architecture as a fashionable hobby'.[84] Despite its elite amateur beginnings, the group would eventually accommodate many of the same figures active in the street furniture debate, including Betjeman, Pevsner and Summerson.[85] Initially a sub-group of the Society for the Protection of Ancient Buildings, the group quickly gained enough momentum to function independently and protect not only Georgian architecture but also Georgian environments, including period street furniture.

In order to contribute to the debate on street furniture, both the GG and the RFAC were forced to employ soft power tactics. The GG had no formal power, and largely relied on private networks of influence and association, but the government had, from the outset, built in the soft qualities of the RFAC. When the Ministry of Transport (MoT) made the CoID responsible for the appearance of street furniture in 1952, the RFAC became responsible for the siting of specific objects but only in cases of national public amenity.[86] Inherent in this clause were several ambiguities, after all, how was the RFAC expected to enforce its advice without the support of legislation or any executive powers? And, at what point was street furniture considered a national and not a local public amenity? Just as ambiguous was how the RFAC could advise on what was an appropriate object of street furniture in a specific context, without first addressing the issue of appearance.

These ambiguities weakened the RFAC in several ways. For Richards, it meant that the practice was

> to accept its advice about policies and designs for which the government is responsible, or government permission necessary, only when that advice

happens to accord with the government's convenience. Since the body is appointed by Parliament to advise it, the Government should surely feel obliged either to follow its advice, or if there is a good reason for not doing so, make the reason public.[87]

And Richards cited a second weakness of the RFAC, which was

a habitual reluctance to come out in the open, to announce its disquiet about any proposal at an early enough stage for public opinion to be effective. To rally public opinion has always been the Commission's strongest weapon, but too often it has preferred to negotiate behind the scenes with, I believe, the idea that it should not antagonize the public authorities it has to work with.[88]

Both weaknesses are related, for if the RFAC was unwilling to sour relations with the very public authorities it was set up to monitor, this was possibly due to government routinely ignoring its advice when inconvenient. Moreover, despite the RFAC's role as watchdog for public amenities, the public often remained ignorant when it did represent their interests, because its private way of working did not lend itself well to publicity. The RFAC could try and improve details of a scheme that it fundamentally disapproved of, but in doing so, it inevitably ran the risk of being held responsible for the scheme itself. This left the RFAC in the difficult position of having to caveat every claim it made lest it caused offence, and being liked and respected by no one unless it was convenient for them to do so.

While satirical poems were composed about the pointlessness of Royal Commissions (see Figure 3.9), in fact, its institutional weaknesses were typical of the period. The political context of the 1950s appeared to oscillate in its approach to state control depending on which party was in office, and as a result, the power of cultural and aesthetic bodies like the RFAC was limited. This posed serious challenges for the RFAC in its appointed task concerning the siting of street furniture. Yet, it also had implications for the broader debate. The effect of these ambiguous powers – or soft powers – meant that no organization or design body knew exactly which part of street furniture design was under its control, making any contribution to the debate fraught with challenges, and bringing each group into conflict with the others. To some extent, these overlaps in power merely served to exacerbate the internal debate on street furniture within design circles.

Internal debates

An early example of these internal debates occurred in 1950, when the RFAC commented on the appearance of street furniture in its annual report. At this point, the RFAC was still effectively responsible for approving the design of street furniture, and its stance was that 'aggressive modernistic shapes' in street furniture

Royal Commission

IF you're pestered by critics and hounded by faction
To take some precipitate, positive action
The proper procedure, to take my advice, is
Appoint a Commission and stave off the crisis.
By shelving the matter you daunt opposition
And blunt its impatience by months of attrition,
Replying meanwhile, with a shrug and a smile,
"The matter's referred to a Royal Commission."

A Royal Commission is strictly impartial,
The pros and the cons it will expertly marshal
And one of its principal characteristics
Is getting bogged down in a sea of statistics.
So should you, perhaps, for inaction be chided
An answer to all men is aptly provided;
You simply explain, again and again,
"The Royal Commission has not yet decided."

Let the terms of its reference lack proper precision
That arguments lengthy may hold up decision,
And then, while they fumble with fact and with figure,
The conflict within the Commission grows bigger.
And so, when at last its report is provided,
If clamour for action has still not subsided,
You say with a pout "The matter's in doubt.
The Royal Commission is somewhat divided."

Thus, once a Commission its session commences,
All you have to do is to sit on your fences
No longer in danger of coming a cropper,
For prejudging its findings is highly improper.
When the subject's been held for so long in suspension
That it ceases to call forth debate and dissension,
Announce without fuss "There's no more to discuss.
The Royal Commission's retired on a pension."

If delay quite indefinite be your endeavour,
There's nothing to stop the thing sitting for ever,
Till its members, worn out by their manifold rigours,
Die off, one by one, like the ten little niggers.
Though, shrouded with cobwebs, a sight for compunction,
A few frail survivors may labour with unction,
If someone asked why, they'd sadly reply,
"The Royal Commission's forgotten its function."

GEOFFREY PARSONS

Figure 3.9 Satirical poem about Royal Commissions, in *Punch*, 24 August 1955, 207. Reproduced with permission of Punch Ltd, www.punch.co.uk.

was not desirable, and was indeed worse than classical styles.[89] Such forthright views placed the RFAC in a bind, since if it maintained an active presence in the debate on street furniture – as it was formally expected to do by the MoT – it would inadvertently attract scorn from other voices in the debate. Its comment on the appearance of street furniture inevitably had this effect, not least from the *AR*. In a report the *AR* published on the RFAC the following year, the magazine condemned the 'deplorable' standard of Britain's street furniture, much of which had been approved by the RFAC, and it encouraged the RFAC to publically state that 'no worthy designs at present exist' rather than be associated with substandard designs.[90]

Yet the *AR* did not only condemn the RFAC's approval process, it also fundamentally criticized its methods, particularly its policy of 'getting minor modifications made to unsatisfactory designs by means of careful diplomacy, on the principle no doubt that some improvement is better than none, and that by this means it can retain the co-operation of the offending architects'.[91] The *AR* argued that such a weak policy was counterproductive to the improvement of street furniture, since 'by following a policy of compromise, and by setting out to act as a mere ameliorative agent, [the RFAC] is undermining its own influence'.[92] The *AR* also reminded the advisory body that

> if anyone was in a position to stand up to a Ministry that seeks to put expediency before public amenity it is the RFAC, and, once more, if it had resolutely stuck by its opinions instead of allowing itself to be satisfied with a compromise it would have received so large a measure of support that the Ministry would very likely have been compelled to change its mind.[93]

Yet the *AR* was dismayed to find that the RFAC seemed reluctant to use those powers, leaving the public to fight the battle alone. To emphasize this point, the *AR* reminded the RFAC that it had been established as a public watchdog against a system in which 'accomplished facts are thrust on the public without their previous approval or consent – the reverse of the democratic principle, the aesthetic equivalent of taxation without representation'.[94] The role of the RFAC then was to act on behalf of the public and protect their interests, and unless it did so, it was effectively considered an ally of the forces working against the public. Indeed, as far as the *AR* was concerned, the RFAC increasingly resembled 'the authority by which Authority excuses the aesthetic crimes it commits'.[95] It was, in other words, a rubber-stamp approval used by public bodies 'to camouflage their disasters'.[96]

This argument against the RFAC is useful on several levels, largely because it raises a fundamental question: What was the point of setting up an organization to approve site-specific designs which the critics disliked, which could not advise on local cases that were close to the public's heart, and whose advice was routinely ignored by government and other public bodies, since there was no compulsion to refer street furniture designs to it and, in any case, it had no power to enforce its advice? The point, according to the *AR*, was that the RFAC had *influence*, since it could 'wield much power by the mere fact of publically labelling a wrongly conceived project as contrary to the public interest'.[97] In other words, the RFAC had more influence than a magazine like the *AR*, because of its status as a state-funded body and because of its relationship with numerous high-profile figures. This amounted to serious leverage in the debate. Rather than having no power the RFAC just wasn't using its soft powers to full advantage.

These soft powers were instrumental in shaping the street furniture debate during the 1950s, which explains the *AR*'s frustrated attitude towards the RFAC. Yet this argument also exposes the *AR*'s own perceived role within the street furniture debate – as an aesthetic watchdog, committed to safeguarding artistic standards – as well as its perception of the RFAC as a conciliatory body, able only to preside over mediocrity. No doubt the RFAC would have rejected the *AR*'s characterization, but it goes some way to illustrate the way in which different groups within post-war design circles perceived each other. To some extent, state-funded advisory bodies like the RFAC handicapped magazines like the *AR*, and left the public confused about who was ultimately responsible for maintaining street furniture standards. At the same time, the gulf between the RFAC and the *AR* was superficial. Both Richards and Betjeman were Commissioners for the RFAC during the early 1950s, while simultaneously working for the *AR*.[98] As such, internal debates within design circles can be potentially misleading, because they suggest that these groups were in constant conflict with each other. In fact, despite maintaining independence from each other publically, in private these divisions seem much less distinct, which may explain why the post-war street furniture debate adopted a somewhat artificial quality among the design elite.

The same tension can be discerned between the RFAC and the CoID. Against the ministries, the RFAC and the CoID were privately allies, but publically they had several disagreements. For instance, in its 1952 annual report, the RFAC made a depreciating comment about lamp posts, and the extent to which inappropriate designs were 'particularly noticeable in some of our more attractive country towns'.[99] For Russell, the RFAC was missing the point and in a letter to *The Times*, he pointed out that bad design remained bad regardless of whether it was installed in a beautiful setting since no district deserved badly designed street furniture.[100] What Russell's letter reflects is not only a point about hierarchies of place and the continuation of Good Design discourse, but that using a forum like *The Times* was an important way in which organizations like the CoID – and for that matter, the RFAC – could deploy their soft powers. The *AR*'s report on the RFAC can be seen in the same light, since all of these examples show that the press was used as a way of bringing the debate about design standards – and therefore, street furniture – into the public eye.

Public initiatives

By the early 1950s, organizations like the RFAC began to realize that their influence over those who actually made the decisions on street furniture largely existed in name only. In the majority of cases, neither central nor local government showed any attempt to accept or implement the RFAC's advice, and without executive power, the RFAC's soft powers had limited effect.[101] Despite advising on seventy-five cases involving lighting schemes in 1957, the constraints placed upon the RFAC meant that its influence was often confined to denouncing particular cases where its advice had been overlooked.[102] But criticizing the use of 'tall lamp-posts of inappropriate design' in Whittlesey and Paddington was of little use when such statements were made in its annual reports, a channel that simply did not have a broad enough reach.[103] As a result, organizations like the RFAC began to realize that engaging the public was a far better way of furthering their interests. Encouraging the public to become involved in the street furniture debate and lobby government for higher standards was a much more effective way of fulfilling its obligations to the MoT than seeking to change the minds of those who actually made the decisions on street furniture. Influence remained a key instrument of change, but it was redirected towards the public. Because of this shift, the RFAC was able to become increasingly critical of local authorities, whose actions often prevented the public from participating in design decisions until too late in the process.[104] Evidently, because of the ambiguous nature of the RFAC's remit, and its lack of legislative power, the only way in which the RFAC could effectively extend its interests was by encouraging the public to fight on its behalf.

As members of the public themselves, commissioners of the RFAC were sometimes forced to fight their own battles. One such case was widely publicized in 1957, when establishment figure Professor Sir Albert E. Richardson, past president of the Royal Academy and member of the RFAC, objected to the concrete posts erected outside his eighteenth-century home in Ampthill, Bedfordshire. In an article titled 'Do Britain's Lamp-posts Drive You Mad?' published in *Everybody's Weekly*, Richardson was pictured shaking his umbrella at a particularly objectionable example and quoted as saying: 'Don't call them street lights… call them monstrosities!'[105] As a man who reputedly read only eighteenth-century newspapers, and who deliberately eschewed electricity in his Georgian home, it is arguable Richardson would have railed against modernization of any kind.[106] Despite his efforts, Richardson's protest was unsuccessful and the modern lamps were installed. A plaque was subsequently commissioned commemorating that 'These incongruous lamp posts which detract from the beauty of this historic town were erected by the urban district council against the advice of the Royal Fine Art Commission.'[107]

However, the RFAC was far from being the only organization to encourage the public to fight back. The 1950s was a period characterized by government-funded public initiatives and one of the most significant of these was the Civic Trust. Founded in 1957 by the Minister of Town and Country Planning, Duncan Sandys, the Civic Trust was an independent civic-amenity initiative intended to 'mobilise the energies of all who care about these things and provide a focus for thought and initiative'.[108] According to Richards (who served on Sandys' committee of advisors prior to the CT's formation) it was conceived as 'a permanent organization to support and coordinate the work of local amenity societies and educate the public in matters of planning and conservation'.[109] Funded through industry, the CT was another form of soft power, since it had no executive powers, and was careful not to antagonize the public authorities it worked with. According to the RFAC, the CT's remit where street furniture was concerned was to be tackled through 'propaganda and education'.[110] Yet unlike the RFAC, the CT was also actively engaged in design projects.

The Civic Trust's pilot project for these design ideas was the Magdalen Street scheme completed in May 1959. The project centred upon an ordinary street in Norwich, which the CT's 1960 film *The Story of Magdalen Street* described as 'dingy and down at heel'.[111] The Trust appointed the architect Misha Black as coordinator and design consultant, and together with his colleagues at the Design Research Unit – of which he was a Co-founder – Black produced a manual of operations for revitalizing the street. The manual provided guidance and general design principles, and it focused on clearing the street of excess street furniture and remodelling and rationalizing it where necessary, re-painting the shop fronts according to Black's colour scheme, and redesigning all the visible lettering using thirteen pre-selected typefaces. According to *The Story of Magdalen Street*, the point of the scheme 'was not to impose a dreary uniformity throughout the street but only to establish certain limits of visual good manners, within which the utmost variety could be achieved'.[112] As the accompanying before and after shots indicate, the street was effectively tidied up and redecorated in the nursery colour palette fashionable at the time (see Figure 3.10). The project was well received, however, and drew the praise of several well-known figures including the architect Sir Basil Spence, and even the CoID. *Design* magazine described Magdalen Street as more than just an exhibition; it was 'tangible evidence of an awakening of public consciousness against the mediocrity and muddle that has for so long been accepted as inevitable in our streets'. And the magazine added that such positive results 'cannot but emphasise the failure of local authorities' planning control, with its negative power and aesthetic censorship, to cope with the problem'.[113] The CT's film speculated that Magdalen Street could be 'the beginning of a movement which may well entirely change the appearance of our whole country'.[114]

In some ways, the CT's project, and others of its type that followed, did have an effect on the appearance of Britain, if only for a short while. The style of Magdalen Street gradually seemed less daring or even relevant, and in 1964 Ian Nairn observed that 'pastel colours were applied often cruelly out of touch with the local colour-range, and after five years it looks as jaded and unreal as last year's fashion'.[115] Despite Nairn's criticism, the ultimate point of Magdalen Street was to have a huge impact. Much like all of the CT's endeavours, the exercise proved that 'our surroundings need not be taken for granted. They are man-made, and can be changed if we wish it.'[116] Encouraging the public to take a greater role in the landscape they lived in, and the everyday objects that surrounded them, was a central development during the 1950s. Eventually the activities of organizations like the CT would have a cumulative effect on changing government's perceptions of who had the authority to make design-based decisions. Yet, while organizations like the RFAC and the CT capitalized on public interest in street furniture design, they also actively encouraged the public to become involved in these projects and the broader debate. Since they had no legislative power, influencing the public became the strongest weapon the RFAC and the CT could use to improve standards in street furniture design.

Figure 3.10 Before and after: The Civic Trust's Magdalen Street scheme, 1959. Cover from brochure on the Civic Trust's Magdalen Street scheme. Civic Trust Awards and Roger Cullingham, The Royal Windsor Website and Forum.

Directing public opinion

Throughout the 1950s, the tide of opinion among the design elite was slowly moving towards greater inclusion of the public voice in the debate about street furniture. However, if public opinion mattered – and by the mid-1950s it was increasingly seen to – then the general consensus seemed to be that it would have to be carefully managed. On this basis, many of the design groups that encouraged the public's participation did so by framing the debate and alerting the public to what constituted good and bad street furniture design. They perceived municipal authorities as the chief offenders where bad street furniture was concerned, because of their considerable power to furnish the street combined with a pronounced lack of design awareness or training. As a consequence, the design elite sought to steer the course of the debate, and positioned themselves directly against municipal authorities.

Within the post-war design elite, the *AR* was arguably the first voice to actively try and initiate public action in the street furniture debate, since if the public could be encouraged to participate then it was likely they would lobby for higher standards. The magazine's anti-authoritarianism meant that its efforts initially manifested in attacks on municipal authorities, given their responsibility for buying, installing, maintaining and sometimes even designing street furniture. As such, the *AR* directly contributed to the process by which municipal authorities were labelled philistines and discredited in the debate.

The *AR*'s negative attitude towards municipal authorities began shortly after the end of the war. At first, the magazine merely made comments about their work being 'unimaginative' but it quickly developed into a broader disdain for municipal figures like borough engineers, planners and surveyors, who were perceived as lacking adequate design training but were nonetheless in a position to make design decisions.[117] As a result of their increase in power, the designer was reduced 'to a mere extra, doing "background stuff"'.[118] The *AR* criticized the puritan culture of the town council, in which beauty was something to be scared of and 'everything must be seemly, rigid and controlled'.[119] This approach was described as a sort of 'unnecessary and restrictive buttoning up', in which the liveliness and character of a place was under threat from faceless municipal powers.[120] These municipal powers were to be feared because their taste in street furniture was considered so poor. One expression of this lack of taste became known as municipal rustic, which manifested as small rock gardens in city centres complete with 'rubble walling, crazy paving and thin finicky ironwork' (see Figure 3.11).[121] Found materials like logs and roughly hewn wood were often incorporated as benches. Collectively, the *AR*, the RFAC and the CT deplored municipal rustic, for its contrived sense of rural charm imposed on urban public places.[122] What was particularly objectionable was that the style reflected the taste of anonymous amenities committees, who mistakenly perceived it as an expression of whimsy. The *AR*'s condemnation of municipal rustic reflected an underlying anger about the impact powerful groups were having on the environment more generally, and by 1955 it decided that municipal authorities needed to be educated on the subtleties of urbanity to avoid these errors.[123] The most important example of this was through a 1955 feature called Outrage.

102 Street Furniture Design

unsuitability

7 and 8, two absurd brain-children of the rockery-nook man: a rustic floodlight and a stone strait-jacket for flowers, seen together in 9 with all the rest of the paraphernalia which has recently been lavished on the previously fine entrance to the Royal Military College at Camberley, Surrey. A few yards further down the main road through Camberley, 10 and 11, is a garden which might well have been made from the left-overs of the more pretentious memorial job in 9. It successfully raises a barrier-reef between the road and the public open space alongside it where the local fairs are held.

Figure 3.11 Municipal rustic: an expression of whimsy? Donald Campbell, 'Townscape: Municipal Rustic', the *Architectural Review*, October 1952, Vol. 111, No. 670, 237. RIBA Library Books & Periodicals Collection.

Outrage

Depending on one's interpretation, Outrage was either a special issue of the *AR* or a prophecy of doom (see Figure 3.12). Certainly it was an excellent piece of visual and textual polemic by Ian Nairn and Gordon Cullen, which in no uncertain terms accused local authorities of destroying towns and cities though misplaced interventions, and a lack of sensitivity or care. Such authorities had, according to Nairn, the 'most power and often the least awareness of the visual responsibility

Figure 3.12 Cover, *Outrage* (London: The Architectural Press, 1955). RIBA Library Books & Periodicals Collection.

that should go with it'.¹²⁴ By imposing a 'creeping mildew' of monotonous design upon the whole country, Nairn prophesied that soon 'the end of Southampton will look like the beginning of Carlisle, the parts in between will look like the end of Carlisle or the beginning of Southampton'.¹²⁵ What masqueraded as Improvement,

Figure 3.13 Gordon Cullen's interpretation of the 'unwitting agents treated by their authors as though they were invisible'. Illustration of street furniture by Gordon Cullen, in Ian Nairn, *Outrage* (London: The Architectural Press, 1955), 370.

Progress or Amenity, he said, was in fact subtopia: a state that signalled the 'annihilation of the site, the steamrollering of all individuality of place to one uniform and mediocre pattern'.[126] According to the architect Hugh Casson, who was by that point serving on the *AR*'s editorial board, the concept of subtopia was 'the result of making a universal ideal of the suburban fantasy, taking it from its original context where it was admirable, and applying it to the whole country, where it is horrible'.[127] Through examples of blight as varied as pylons, arterial roads, miles of cable and wiring, ugly lamp posts and inappropriately designed benches – also known as unwitting agents that were 'treated by their authors as though they were invisible' – Outrage blamed local government for essentially making Britain's visual landscape indistinguishable (see Figure 3.13).[128]

Through a series of rhetorical images of British places, Outrage was, according to Casson 'a tourist guide in reverse, picking out the bad, not the good'.[129] And street furniture was a key feature of this inverse guide to Britain. For instance, standardized concrete lamp standards (see Figure 3.14) were blamed for stamping 'any scene in which they appear with their own apathetic pattern and if the scene is fragile, as Warwick is, or having a hard time to stay intact anyway like Blackrod, it disintegrates'.[130] Particular styles were also attacked, particularly municipal rustic, a 'post-war disease' which combined anti-urbanism with pastiche rural, and provided no social or economic advantages. The guilty style was deemed responsible for 'wrecking the environment so than man can everywhere see the projection and image of his own humdrum suburban life: mild lusts, mild fears, mild *everything* – a herbaceous border'.[131] Outrage also identified several specific sites that were particularly poor in terms of street furniture. Bours Hill in Oxford was considered typical of the problem, having framed its skyline between concrete lamp standards.[132] Leamington had shown some ingenuity in 'the careful choice of the wrong lamp standards for the wrong place', and Warwick's lamp standards had a bad case of 'elephantiasis'.[133] Benches in Stafford and Lancashire showed little taste by either the buyer or the manufacturer,[134] and the litter bins in Lakeland 'robs the landscape of spontaneity'.[135] Kendal had only one lamp post in its marketplace, which was described as overpowering, clumsy and callous.[136]

Similar attacks on urban development had been made previously. For instance, in Evelyn Waugh's *Vile Bodies*, one of the characters looks out of an aeroplane window at the landscape below and he sees 'arterial roads dotted with little cars; factories, some of them working, others empty and decaying; a disused canal; some distant hills sown with bungalows; wireless masts and overhead power cables'.[137] Waugh's description bears a startling similarity to Nairn's characterization of subtopia, and it would appear that many in Britain objected to needless industrial development and urban expansion, which was perceived as destroying local identity across the country. At the time when Outrage was published, it is important to remember that many of those who objected would have also fought for their country in the Second World War. Preserving their country – the country they had fought for – would have taken on greater significance. After such a lengthy struggle, the particular and the local were considered too valuable and too vulnerable to lose to municipal carelessness.

Figure 3.14 Diverse range of concrete lamp standards, in Ian Nairn, *Outrage* (London: The Architectural Press, 1955), 373. RIBA Library Books & Periodicals Collection. Standardized concrete lamp standards like these were blamed for stamping 'any scene in which they appear with their own apathetic pattern'.

One can also situate the argument underpinning Outrage in a political as well as an aesthetic context. After all, the *AR* defined Outrage's purpose as drawing the world's attention to 'an offence being committed on the nation which it is no one's business to prevent'.[138] In this sense, the real enemy for the Outrage campaign was the philistine. Outrage blamed both local authorities and the public 'since the public authorities respond to public opinion, the ultimate responsibility rests on the public no [*sic*] the Authority'.[139] Thus in order to draw attention to municipal blight, the *AR* sought to shock because

> unless we are shocked into awareness, the consequences of our visual laissez-faire may make us incapable of distinguishing good from bad and we may be mutated into subhumans without our ever knowing it has happened. It's not just aesthetics and art work: our whole existence as individuals is at stake, just as much as it ever has been from political dictatorship, Left or Right; and in this case the attack is not clearly defined and coming from the other side of the globe, but a miasma rising from the heart of our collective self.[140]

Using an argument that draws heavily upon the rhetoric of political freedom, *Outrage* also reminded readers that

> you *have* eyes to see if you have been exasperated by the lunacies exposed in these pages; if you think that they represent a universal levelling down and greying out; if you think that they should be fought, not accepted. Don't be afraid that you will be just one individual registering dissent. It is *your* country that is being defaced, it belongs to *you*... So use your double birthright – as a freethinking human being and as a Briton lucky enough to be born into a country where the individual voice can still get a hearing.[141]

Such lunacies, according to *Outrage*, could be dealt with very simply. By writing letters and organizing campaigns, the *AR* encouraged its readers to act, for 'in trying to keep intact the identity of your environment you will maintain your own as well'.[142]

While not everyone agreed with Outrage – the *Scotsman* called the *AR* a 'subtopian production' – many readers reacted positively.[143] Many within the MoT were impressed, and even had copies distributed among other ministries.[144] Outrage clearly affirmed the viewpoint of the *AR*, but it also framed the street furniture debate during the 1950s more generally. It did this by placing street furniture in an aesthetic context, in which badly designed or badly sited street furniture constituted a visual crime. It also located the debate in a moral context, whereby bad street furniture was equated as being morally wrong. And lastly, it placed street furniture in a political context, suggesting that those who were responsible for the damage – local authorities – were abusing their power and threatening the freedom of the British people.

Largely as a consequence of the efforts by the design elite, by the mid-1950s municipal authorities began to be considered responsible for unsightly street furniture. Like the letter page of *Design*, the *AR* also published correspondence from its readers, many of whom criticized municipal authorities. One reader accused 'civic authorities' of showing contempt for public space, and a pronounced absence of taste.[145] Another reader from Blackheath complained about the proliferation of rustic benches and 'a veritable forest of poles' that had invaded his community.[146] So if municipal authorities weren't protecting the public's interests, who was?

According to the *AR*, 'a few frustrated intellectuals' were trying to protect the public's interests – a statement that at once distinguishes the *AR* from municipal authorities, as well as making a claim for superior intelligence – not through artistic channels, but by going straight to the municipal authorities themselves.[147] Writing in the *MJ* in 1956, Betjeman proposed a number of ways that municipal authorities could prevent the uses of bad street furniture. According to Betjeman, municipal authorities could invite a local artist to participate in their street furniture committee meetings, and the county planning officer could also become more involved in the siting and design of street furniture.[148] Without the application of such measures, Betjeman warned, public aversion would only increase: 'I foresee the day when local residents associations and amenity bodies will march on their town hall to end the tyranny of officials and local councillors who will keep dragging party politics into aesthetic matters.'[149] Betjeman's proposals not only demonstrate a faith in the planning system, but also the perception that by making decisions on street furniture, municipal authorities were meddling in aesthetics, a subject in which they had no authority. Officials in municipal authorities had no validity as artists, yet that was the role they were performing in furnishing the street. This is a fundamental point within the post-war street furniture debate, and by making it in the context of the *MJ*, Betjeman was trying to take his argument into an arena where those who actually made the decisions for shaping the street might hear it.

In fact, the process by which design decisions were made by government agencies began to dominate the street furniture debate around this time, and the *AR* published several features on planning and the way in which its machinery was routinely bypassed.[150] The *AR* clearly believed that the views of the design elite ought to have a far greater bearing on decisions relating to design, than the views of those who lacked the proper knowledge, i.e. municipal authorities. And yet, municipal authorities were freely elected representatives of the public – the same group that Outrage was directed towards. So was the *AR* guilty of representing private concerns as public ones in its campaign for public justice? Just who was the real tyrant? David Solkin's book *Painting for Money* depicts a cultural landscape in eighteenth-century Britain that is remarkably similar to post-war Britain, in which 'people of quality' – i.e. those privileged social groups at the upper tier of the class hierarchy – tended to define themselves as connoisseurs so as to further their own interests.[151] In a similar way, magazines like the *AR* were able to appropriate the intellectual and cultural high ground by representing themselves as the authority of connoisseurship. By criticizing the ways in which decisions could be made by municipal authorities without any degree of openness or transparency, the *AR* sought to shore up its privileged position.

However, the *AR* and the other interlocking professional design alliances discussed throughout this chapter were also powerful, and sought to extend their influence upon the government, the public and each other. These elite alliances clearly sought to represent their own aesthetic interests in the street furniture debate, but equally, they often presented their campaigns in altruistic terms, which presents something of a paradox. For while magazines like the *AR* and other design organizations like the Civic Trust, the Georgian Group and the Royal Fine Art Commission sought to capitalize on public interest in street furniture design, they were also simultaneously reluctant to give up their privileged position as advisors and interpreters. Yet as the next chapter will discuss, surely if you encourage the public to speak up, you also have to listen to them?

Notes

1 J.M. Richards, *Memoirs of an Unjust Fella: An Autobiography* (London: Weidenfeld and Nicholson, 1980), 91; The *AR*, 'AR History'. Available online: http://www.architectural-review.com/story.aspx?storyCode=8603298 (accessed 30 July 2015).
2 Ibid.
3 John Betjeman, *Ghastly Good Taste: Or the Depressing Story of the Rise and Fall of English Architecture* (London: Anthony Blond Ltd, 1970. First published by Chapman and Hall Ltd, 1933); Richards, *Memoirs of an Unjust Fella*, 122.
4 'The Second Half Century', the *AR*, January 1947, 21.
5 See Betjeman, *Ghastly Good Taste*, 111.
6 'The Second Half Century', 22–3.
7 Pick, The Art of the Street, 1.
8 'The Second Half Century', 25.
9 Ibid.
10 Ibid.
11 The *AR*, Vol. 79, 1936, 151–4. See also Harris, *Romantic Moderns*, 92.
12 'The Second Half Century', 24.
13 Ibid., 23–4.
14 Ibid., 25.
15 Ibid., 26.
16 Ibid., 25.
17 'The Submerged Third', the *AR*, August 1948, Vol. 104, No. 620, 50.
18 Ibid.
19 Ibid.
20 The *AR*, Vol. 85, 1939, 229–46.
21 Harris, *Romantic Moderns*, 53.
22 Ibid. See also Angus Calder and Dorothy Sheridan, *Speak for Yourself: A Mass Observation Anthology* (Oxford: Oxford University Press, 1985).
23 Harris, *Romantic Moderns*, 58.
24 'Townscape', the *AR*, December 1949, Vol. 105, No. 636, 354.
25 Ibid.
26 Ibid., 371.
27 Andrew Hammer, 'Townscape: Programme Sculpture', the *AR*, April 1951, Vol. 109, No. 652, 255.

28 Reyner Banham, 'Object Lesson', the *AR*, June 1954, Vol. 115, No. 690, 403.
29 Ian Nairn, 'Townscape', the *AR*, April 1958, Vol. 123, No. 735, 280.
30 See Rosalind Krauss, *L'Amour Fou* (New York: Abbeville Press, 1985); Andre Breton, *Nadja* (New York: Grove Press, 1994. First published 1928); Robert Elwall, *Photography Takes Command* (London: RIBA Heinz Gallery, 1994).
31 Kenneth Browne, 'Trim: The Treatment of Junctions, Verges and Margins', the *AR*, February 1953, Vol. 112, No. 674, 106.
32 Peter Varney, 'Miscellany – Survey of Street Lighting', the *AR*, July 1951, Vol. 110, No. 655, 51.
33 Ibid., 54.
34 'Townscape: Outdoor Publicity', the *AR*, May 1949, Vol. 105, No. 629, 248.
35 Ibid.
36 Ibid. 249.
37 'Lettering', the *AR*, January 1952, Vol. 111, No. 661, 59.
38 Ibid.
39 Peter Lowden, 'Correspondence', the *AR*, January 1952, Vol. 111, No. 661, 64.
40 Ibid.
41 Editors response, ibid.
42 C. Forshoe, 'Street Furniture: History of the Bollard', the *AR*, September 1953, Vol. 112, No. 681, 191; Varney, 'Miscellany – Survey of Street Lighting', 54; 'Marginalia: Litter in the Parks', the *AR*, October 1955, Vol. 118, No. 706, 211.
43 Pevsner in Aitchison, *Visual Planning and the Picturesque*, 177. See also Uvedale Price, An Essay on the Picturesque (1794).
44 Christopher Hussey's book *The Picturesque: Studies in a Point of View* (London: G.P. Putnam & Sons, 1927) was particularly influential.
45 Aitchison, *Visual Planning and the Picturesque*, 20.
46 Nikolaus Pevsner, 'Townscape – Address at the Annual Meeting of the Council for Visual Education', *Journal of the Institute of Registered Architects*, Vol. 10 (1955): 41, in ibid., 20.
47 Gordon Cullen, *Townscape* (London: The Architectural Press, 1961), 28.
48 Ibid., 46.
49 'Special Number on Canals', the *AR*, July 1949, Vol. 105, No. 107, 61.
50 Cullen, *Townscape*, 51.
51 Ibid., 144.
52 George Mason, 'Essay on Design in Gardening, 1768', in *The Englishness of English Art: An Expanded and Annotated Version of the Reith Lectures Broadcast in October and November 1955*, ed. Nikolaus Pevsner (London: The Architectural Press, 1956), 166.
53 Gordon Cullen, 'Townscape: Common Ground', the *AR*, March 1952, Vol. 111, No. 663, 183.
54 Richards, *Memoirs of an Unjust Fella*, 191.
55 Ian Nairn, 'Outrage 20 Years After', The *AR*, 1975, Vol. 158, No. 946, 329.
56 'Industrial Design Special Number', the *AR*, October 1946, 92.
57 'Street Furniture', the *AR*, August 1951, Vol. 110, No. 656, 119–20; CoID Progress Report, the *AR*, December 1951, Vol. 110, No. 660, 349.
58 Ibid.
59 Ibid., 351–2.
60 Gordon Russell, 'CoID Progress Report: The Director Replies', the *AR*, February 1952, Vol. 111, No. 662, 74.

61 Ibid., 75.
62 Editors reply, ibid.
63 Ibid.
64 See Richard J. Williams, *The Anxious City* (London: Routledge, 2004), 31–4.
65 Editors reply, 'CoID Progress Report: The Director Replies', the *AR*, February 1952, Vol. 111, No. 662, 75.
66 David Pye, 'Correspondence', the *AR*, February 1952, Vol. 111, No. 662, 134.
67 'Correspondence', ibid., 422.
68 Eric de Maré, 'Correspondence', the *AR*, April 1953, Vol. 112, No. 675, 273.
69 Ibid.
70 Ibid.
71 Ibid., 274.
72 Ibid.
73 The lines of division between these groups – both between themselves, and in relation to central government – were ambiguous. J. M. Richards, for instance, edited the *AR*, as well as sitting on the street furniture committees of the RFAC and the CoID. John Betjeman was associated with the *AR*, as well as sitting on the board of the GG and the RFAC. The CT operated its own independent schemes for revitalizing streets, as well as managing the *AR*'s Counter Attack Bureau, a service provided by the *AR* for the public to complain about municipal design.
74 Richards' autobiography *Memoirs of an Unjust Fella* gives a strong sense of the professional and personal links that defined the design elite at the time. See also the RFAC, *15th Annual Report 1957– 1958*, 4, 720.6041.
75 Joseph S. Nye Jr., 'Soft Power', *Foreign Policy*, No. 80, Autumn 1990, 153–71.
76 Peter York, *Style Wars* (London: Sidgwick and Jackson Limited, 1980), 8.
77 Richards, *Memoirs of an Unjust Fella*, 230.
78 The RFAC, *9th Annual Report 1948–1949* (London, July 1950), 4, 720.6041.
79 Ibid., 5.
80 The *MJ*, 25 June 1954, Vol. 62, 1406.
81 See the RFAC, *19th Annual Report September 1962-December 1965* (London, April 1966), 3, MoDA Ref. 720.6041.
82 Ibid., 7–8.
83 John Summerson, for instance, had also served as the assistant editor of the *Architect and Building News*, and for a time was Richard's opposite number. In Richards, *Memoirs of an Unjust Fella*, 90.
84 Harris, *Romantic Moderns*, 71–3. Harris also notes that the Georgian revival was 'precisely the opposite of Little Englandism: it was an investigation of England's cultural relations with Europe and an effort to promote an audaciously international version of Englishness'.
85 Ibid., 128. The GG, About/ History. Available online: http://www.georgiangroup.org.uk/docs/about/index.php (accessed 30 July 2015). For Pevsner, however, Britain was 'too glued to genuine Georgian – or imitation Georgian' – see Pevsner, 'At Aspen in Colorado', 1953, in *The Aspen Papers: Twenty Years of Design Theory from the International Design Conference in Aspen*, ed. Reyner Banham (London: Pall Mall Press, 1974), 15.
86 The CoID, *8th Annual Report 1952–53*, 9; and Woodham, *The Industrial Designer and the Public*, 84.
87 Richards, *Memoirs of an Unjust Fella*, 243.
88 Ibid.

89 The RFAC, *9th Annual Report 1948 and 1949* (London, July 1950), 13, 720.6041.
90 'The Royal Fine Art Commission', the *AR*, April 1951, Vol. 109, No. 652, 206.
91 Ibid., 205.
92 Ibid., 206.
93 Ibid.
94 Ibid., 207.
95 Ibid.
96 'Royal Fine Art Commission', the *AR*, October 1954, Vol. 116, No. 694, 212.
97 'The Royal Fine Art Commission', the *AR*, April 1951, Vol. 109, No. 652, 207.
98 The RFAC, *10th Annual Report 1950 and 1951* (London, November 1952); the RFAC, *11th Annual Report 1952* (London, July 1953), MoDA Ref. 720.6041.
99 The RFAC, *10th Annual Report 1950 and 1951* (London, November 1952), 6–7, MoDA Ref. 720.6041.
100 Gordon Russell, 'Letter to the Editor', *The Times*, 24 June 1952.
101 In 1957, the RFAC questioned why the MoT was so reluctant to invite its opinion, or indeed any other aesthetically motivated body. It claimed that designs for the new traffic signs adopted by the ministry were prepared by a committee 'on which those interested in the general appearance of street furniture were not represented'. See *14th Annual Report of the RFAC – 1955 and 1956* (London, February 1957), 15, 720.6041. Moreover, records held in the National Archives show that the RFAC was regularly forced to reject street furniture cases because of their local qualities. Signage in Christleton was one example, and grit bins in Chelsea was another. See Royal Fine Art Commission, 1952–71. 'Discussions on Design of Street Furniture', BP 2/279.
102 The RFAC, *14th Annual Report 1955 and 1956* (London, February 1957), 13, 720.6041.
103 The RFAC, *13th Annual Report 1954* (London, April 1955), 5, in ibid.
104 The RFAC, *14th Annual Report – 1955 and 1956* (London, February 1957), 14, in ibid.
105 Alexander Barrie, 'Do Britain's Lamp-posts Drive You Mad?' *Everybody's Weekly*, 16 November 1957. For more information on Richardson's involvements with lamp posts, see Simon Cornwell's website on the topic. Available online: http://www.simoncornwell.com/lighting/install/cambridge/rc/index.htm (accessed 31 July 2015).
106 Glendinning, *The Conservation Movement*, 315.
107 For more information on Sir Albert Richardson's campaign against modern lamp posts, see Ampthill Images. Available online: http://www.ampthillimages.com/Media/SirARichardson-Gall./pages/Streetlights%201957%2003.html (accessed 30 July 2015).
108 Duncan Sandys, 'Comment: Ten Years of Civic Action', *Design*, No. 224, August 1967, 20.
109 Richards, *Memoirs of an Unjust Fella*, 244.
110 The RFAC, *15th Annual Report 1957* (London, June 1958), 12, MoDA Ref. 720.6041.
111 *The Story of Magdalen Street*, 1960, sponsored by the Civic Trust, directed by Pamela Wilcox Bower, East Anglian Film Archive. Available online: http://www.eafa.org.uk/catalogue/304 (accessed 30 July 2015).
112 Ibid.
113 Peter Whitworth, 'Street Revitalised', *Design*, No. 130, October 1959, 35.

114 *The Story of Magdalen Street*, 1960, sponsored by the Civic Trust, directed by Pamela Wilcox Bower, East Anglian Film Archive. Available online: http://www.eafa.org.uk/catalogue/304 (accessed 30 July 2015).
115 Ian Nairn, 'Norwich: Regional Capital,' in *Nairn's Towns*, introduced, edited and updated by Owen Hatherley (London: Notting Hill Editions, 2003. Originally published 1967), 222.
116 The Civic Trust, *Pride of Place: A Manual for Those Wishing to Improve Their Surroundings* (London: Civic Trust, 1972), 12.
117 'Special Number on Canals', the *AR*, July 1949, Vol. 105, No. 107, 61.
118 Gordon Cullen, 'Focus on Floor', the *AR*, January 1952, Vol. 111, No. 661, 33.
119 Eric de Maré, 'Buttoning Up', the *AR*, April 1952, Vol. 111, No. 664, 233.
120 Ibid. 235.
121 The RFAC, *11th Annual Report – 1952* (London, July 1953), 5, 720.6041.
122 Ibid., Donald Campbell, 'Townscape: Municipal Rustic', the *AR*, October 1952, Vol. 111, No. 670, 285.
123 Ibid., 290.
124 Ian Nairn, *Outrage* (London: The Architectural Press, 1955), 363. Originally published in the *AR*, June 1955, Vol. 117, No. 702.
125 Ibid., 365.
126 Ibid., 371.
127 Letter to RFAC by Hugh Casson, 24 June 1955, 1, loose in Royal Fine Art Commission, 'Discussions on the Design of Street Furniture', N.A. Cat. Ref.: BP 2/279.
128 Nairn, *Outrage*, 367–71.
129 Letter to RFAC by Hugh Casson, 24 June 1955, 1, loose in Royal Fine Art Commission, 'Discussions on the Design of Street Furniture', BP 2/279.
130 Nairn, *Outrage*, 372.
131 Ibid., 386.
132 Ibid., 403.
133 Ibid., 411.
134 Ibid., 416/420.
135 Ibid., 436.
136 Ibid., 431.
137 Evelyn Waugh, *Vile Bodies*, 169, cited in Harris, *Romantic Moderns*, 175.
138 Letter to RFAC by Hugh Casson, 24 June 1955, 1, loose in Royal Fine Art Commission, 'Discussions on the Design of Street Furniture', BP 2/279.
139 Ibid.
140 Nairn, *Outrage*, 372.
141 Ibid., 451.
142 Ibid., 452.
143 Marginalia: 'Outrage and After', the *AR*, September 1955, Vol. 118, No. 705, 141; 'Correspondence', the *AR*, October 1955, Vol. 118, No. 706, 211.
144 Memo on the issue of street lighting and the RFAC's powers, sent by H. Gillender, 15 February 1957, to Mr. Lovell, in Ministry of Transport, 'Highways Engineering: Registered Files. Street Lighting. Design of Lamp Standards: Including Painting and Guidance by Royal Fine Art Commission'. MT 95/210.
145 'Correspondence', the *AR*, January 1955, Vol. 117, No. 697, 82.
146 'Blackheath Then and Now', Correspondence, the *AR*, October 1956, Vol. 120, No. 717, 212.

147 Marginalia: 'Outrage and After'.
148 John Betjeman, 'Design of Street Furniture', the *MJ*, 9 November 1956, Vol. 64, 2673. This viewpoint was shared by members of the public – see Joan Evans, 'Matters of Taste', *The Times*, 10 October 1957, 11.
149 Ibid.
150 R. Furneaux Jordan, 'London County Council', the *AR*, November 1956, Vol. 120, No. 718, 303.
151 David Solkin, *Painting for Money* (New Haven, CT and London: Yale University Press, 1993), 16.

Chapter 4

MUNICIPAL VANDALISM: TYRANNY, CONFRONTATION AND RESISTANCE

While many of the decisions that shaped post-war street furniture were made away from the public gaze in private local government committee meetings – at which few of those attending were trained in matters of design – central government were also actively involved. This chapter examines the exchanges between them to reveal a more nuanced picture of how the debate was actually enacted, and the presence of internal conflicts about official taste, snobbery and class.

Government's direct involvement in the design of street furniture began in 1949, when the Ministry of Transport hosted two important meetings on the subject. The first took place in February 1949 and concerned lamp columns; however, the second meeting in July of that year was more significant. The Royal Fine Art Commission and the Council of Industrial Design had petitioned the MoT to convene an informal private discussion on the design of street furniture. Privacy was stressed due to the delicate nature of the debate, and around fourteen interested bodies participated from other government ministries, local government and industry, as well as the design organizations that jointly hosted the meeting. The meeting had been called for a number of reasons, not least the perception that wartime damage provided an unexpected opportunity for renewal. The Festival of Britain, scheduled to take place in 1951, was another incentive, and the RFAC and the CoID hoped that some progress on street furniture could be made within that two-year window. However, while the post-war physical and cultural environment might have been ready for such substantial changes, the economic context was less permissive. Rationing was still in place and materials like steel were strictly controlled. As such, the objective of the meeting was not to encourage 'large-scale scrapping of existing equipment' but simply to start early thinking on the subject.[1]

Despite suggesting that their objectives were relatively benign, the RFAC and the CoID opened the meeting by warning those present that insufficient progress was being made in street furniture design.[2] It is telling that at this early meeting, design required definition, and the RFAC and the CoID described it as 'that choice of form or colour, which, after meeting purely functional demands, gives an article its final appearance'.[3] Design was clearly equated with appearance, and both organizations argued 'there is in every case an aesthetic element, even if it is only in the choice of a particular curve for a lighting bracket or the precise proportions for a sand-bin; it is with this "extra" that we are here primarily concerned'.[4] That the meeting would focus on this 'extra' element is extraordinary, largely because of its ambiguity. Being able to 'study the situation more closely', the RFAC and the CoID were 'perturbed' by contemporary street furniture, much of which they said looked as though 'a large collection of miscellaneous objects had been dropped from a great height and left where they happened to fall'.[5] Ill-considered colours, unsatisfactory forms and lack of spatial relationship between objects were considered largely to blame, the causes of which ranged from a 'general uncertainty of taste and poverty of invention', to an increased demand for public services and therefore street furniture, and the multiplicity of authorities responsible.[6] Both the RFAC and the CoID reasoned that the importance of individual items of street furniture was 'comparatively insignificant', but that the complete effect was important to address because the uneducated were unable to distinguish exactly which element of the street was to blame. This placed, they said 'a special obligation on those responsible for the design of street furniture; they cannot rely on public opinion to analyse their efforts properly and tell them whether they have done well or badly'.[7] Clearly, all those present at the meeting were in some direct or indirect way responsible for street furniture, whether through producing, approving, funding or merely installing it. The public were conspicuous by their absence; the implication being that as the 'uneducated' they would be unable to make any valuable contribution to the debate.

One of those present was Leonard Howitt, the city architect of Manchester and representative of the Association of Municipal Corporations. Howitt challenged what he perceived as a tendency by the RFAC and the CoID to dictate a sensitive issue like taste from above, and he contended that 'such an attitude would no doubt meet with objection from the Association of Municipal Corporations, and in any event it is questionable whether compulsion should be exercised in matters of taste'.[8] Pre-empting the reaction by other local authorities across the country, Howitt added that 'equally objectionable would be… the control of street furniture in any national body', and that 'in such matters there should be complete freedom of choice by the Local Authority'.[9] According to Howitt, badly designed or shoddy street furniture was not the fault of local authorities, but manufacturers.[10] Other local government representatives joined Howitt in questioning the speed by which sufficient improvements could be made to street furniture in advance of the Festival of Britain. According to Mr Swallow of the Urban District Councils Association, not only were 'Local Authorities too preoccupied with more urgent matters to send people to meetings on this subject' but they also 'would not have any time to do anything before the 1951 exhibition'.[11] Mr Woolnough from the Rural District Councils Association concurred, and asked that 'Local Authorities be left to do it their own way'.[12]

For the RFAC and the CoID, the position presented by local government at this meeting risked producing a stalemate in the debate. It was pride, they supposed, that prevented local government from allowing others to comment or criticize their street furniture.[13] Yet this attitude also had an impact upon their own position: after all, how could they hope to exert influence over a group that openly resisted outside interference? To accept that local government was fully competent in its approach to street furniture would have undermined the meeting, as well as the foundations of the RFAC and the CoID's involvement in the debate more generally. At the very least, local government needed to acknowledge that street furniture design could be improved. And yet despite these unresolved issues and doubts about its workability, the outcome of the meeting was that a small committee should be established, representing multiple interests and agendas.[14] This small committee can be understood as the first of its kind after the war, in which a broad range of representatives – with the exception of the public – joined together to discuss the design of street furniture.

Lobbying after the meeting

In the months after the meeting, the design groups present sought more informal ways to pursue their agenda. For its part, the RFAC identified the principal obstacle to bettering street furniture design as local government's resistance to 'compulsion in matters of taste', and its contention that 'any necessary coordination for the purpose of combining designs harmoniously should be local'.[15] To circumvent this, the RFAC privately considered challenging the 1947 Town Planning Act, which exempted street furniture owing to an idea that 'it would be better to leave them to be coordinated by local consultation than to overburden the planning authorities with the task of controlling them'.[16] An alternative proposal was to remind the ministries of their power in this matter, given that the Act provided 'a valuable opportunity for guiding design in consultation with bodies on the aesthetic side'.[17] They also continued to apply indirect pressure to government. For instance, in advance of Betjeman's attack on street lighting in *The Times* discussed earlier, the RFAC privately advised him on his argument, and was even given the opportunity to correct any errors and reinforce certain arguments prior to publication.[18] Such an arrangement suggests that despite its official status, the RFAC clandestinely acted alongside Betjeman in his attack on modern street furniture. This was a further means of lobbying government and rousing public interest in the debate using a more public forum.

Like the RFAC, the newly established CoID also privately lobbied government, and presented itself as a useful ally in the fight against bad street furniture design. In December 1949, Gordon Russell wrote privately to J. R. Willis, the Minister of Transport to inform him of the CoID's valuable skills. According to Russell, local government's unhelpful attitude meant that the CoID and the RFAC could perform a useful role in liaising with manufacturers, a relationship the CoID was already establishing through its work on the Festival of Britain.[19] He also added that in the case of street lighting, 'we have already found that many of the larger manufacturers producing excellent lighting units are extremely worried about the inability of the user authorities to select the appropriate column and equipment'.[20] That user authorities, i.e. local authorities, might be unable to identify and therefore purchase good street furniture design, was a clear rejection from manufacturers of their responsibility. For their part, the CoID and the RFAC appeared to lay the blame squarely at the feet of those purchasing bad design and Russell's letter emphasized this point to Willis, perhaps in an effort to convince him to act.

Other design bodies also sought to influence government on street furniture around this time. For example, in 1951 Lord Rosse of the Georgian Group wrote to Hugh Dalton – who was by then working at the Ministry of Local Government and Planning – to ask for his support in the group's campaign against unsightly lamp posts. According to Lord Rosse, 'the effectiveness of planning control and measures for the preservation of buildings of special architectural interest are going to be gravely impaired if lamp standards, which are perhaps the most conspicuous of street furniture are to be erected by reference solely to considerations which take no account either of planning or of aesthetics'.[21] And Lord Rosse petitioned Dalton to issue a directive to local authorities drawing their attention to the importance of ensuring that lighting schemes relate to the character of a place. As a former president of the Board of Trade and an enthusiastic supporter of modern design, Dalton had considerable influence on matters of this kind, and possessed strong views on the subject of street furniture. Eventually, after several drafts which he rejected as being inconceivably pompous and complacent, Dalton responded to Lord Rosse but admitted that 'I feel that this is one of those matters where we should get much better results by educating local councils to a higher standard of taste. This is not being left to chance.'[22] Clearly, government believed that it would be better for local authorities to deal with the matter voluntarily rather than by regulation. However, Dalton's reassurance that the matter was not being left to chance was a direct reference to the newly formed joint committee on street furniture.

The street furniture booklet

Despite the initial difficulties, doubts and reservations, the ad hoc committee eventually agreed to publish a street furniture booklet. This booklet would act, the committee hoped, as an explanatory text for engineers and planners in local authorities, and subtly educate them on standards of taste in the process, without actually forcing them to change their methods. As the RFAC claimed shortly after the initial meeting, 'it seems better to aim at digging channels of effective but informal cooperation in relation to actual requirements as they arise or have to be planned for than to create further formal machinery that may accomplish little or nothing of real use'.[23] From the outset then, it is clear that neither the committee nor the booklet had any underlying force and could only hope to induce informal cooperation from local authorities.

The CoID was asked by the committee to prepare the booklet – subject to approval – and its first attempt reflects the organization's attitude to local authorities. It defined the problem of street furniture as a municipal one because 'visitors from tidier countries must often leave with the impression of a gargantuan municipal hoarder, reluctant like his domestic counterpart, to discard anything that might conceivably "come in"'.[24] Blaming local authorities for displaying a psychological sickness in their attitude to street furniture was perhaps a less than ideal way to begin a booklet devised for local authorities. Yet the CoID continued in this vein by warning that to place the responsibility for street furniture into the custody of the community was dangerous, because once 'something is everyone's business, it becomes no-one's business'.[25] Good street furniture design was presented as being important not just for its aesthetic values, but for the preservation of a nation's values. Such values were being eroded by the actions of local authorities, which had created a 'petrified forest of concrete standards towering above a tangled undergrowth of bollards and litter bins'.[26] Therefore, the objective of the booklet was defined as educating local authorities on Good Design, which 'implies a sympathy with its background. But to attempt to answer this as some have done by disguising petrol stations as thatched cottages and bus shelters as half timbered summer houses has only one logical sequel – to dress every country bobby in knee-breeches and make a posthorn standard equipment on every rural bus route.'[27] Rather than nostalgically return to the past – or even worse, a contrived appropriation of rusticity – the CoID used the booklet to promote Good Design.

Yet the first draft was not a success. Even the RFAC – a supposed ally of the CoID on design matters – objected to it on several levels. One commissioner, the British art historian John Summerson, responded by asking:

> For whom is this prepared? If for secondary school children it is satisfactory. If for local authorities it is too whimsical, too arty, too general and lacking in relevance of method… As it stands, the book seems to be completely useless except as popular propaganda. At no point does it go to the root of the matter or assist in a practical way. There is, besides, too much play with the PAST. A Georgian bollard may be all right but any fool can see that it is not 'elegant'. And early Victorian pictures seem to teach a very doubtful lesson.[28]

Summerson's reservations about the booklet largely concern its lack of practical application and excessively artistic approach, yet the tone in which he delivers his view is blunt. Summerson's attitude was shared by J. M. Richards, who advised the RFAC on how to convey Summerson's remarks to the CoID. Responding to a letter the RFAC had drafted, Richards said:

> I am not so happy. I think this is a case where, even at the cost of causing despondency in the CoID, the Commission ought to be outspoken. We all agreed – I did – most emphatically with John Summerson's forthright condemnation of the whole tone and conception of the booklet – and, although I realize that the report he gave to the Commission could not be passed on to Gordon Russell as it stood, I feel that your letter should be just as critical…your second paragraph, though obviously intended to soften the blow, in fact gives the impression that the Commission did not dislike the booklet and merely had minor criticisms to make. I think that instead of that very diplomatic sentence, we should take the bull by the horns and say outright that the Commission did not feel that the booklet was at all the sort of thing that was required.[29]

Such exchanges show the strength of opinion within the joint committee about street furniture design and on how it ought to be represented in the booklet, as well as the divisions within the group. Taking into account Richards' suggestions – but not necessarily his direct approach – the RFAC eventually wrote to the CoID with the view that 'we do not feel that it is on the right lines in its present form'.[30] It also recommended that the CoID considered the local authority perspective and what their real requirements might be, and even proposed some ways of restructuring the booklet according to municipal departments, e.g. Highways and Parks.

As a result of these comments, the CoID produced a second draft in 1952. The response from the RFAC, however, remained critical. While commissioners such as Lionel Brett and the sculptor Henry Moore reluctantly gave their approval without necessarily supporting the booklet, others like the architect and town planner Frederick Gibberd claimed that 'the approach tends to be rather unreal and rather artistic' and not at all valuable as a handbook of technical advice for local and highway authorities; indeed, he felt as if he was 'being talked down to'.[31] Art historian Professor Geoffrey Webb argued that 'I don't much like the "scout master" tone of some of the text', and he warned that there was 'too much insistence perhaps on the need to run to the Commission on every occasion'.[32] And the sculptor Charles Wheeler accepted that while the need for this booklet was urgent, it did not fulfil its objectives to 'supply the help it is intended to give'.[33] Following the doubts of its commissioners, the RFAC wrote again to the CoID proposing that, without relying upon examples from abroad or from the past, the booklet ought to answer practical questions for borough engineers and highway committees over, 'what current designs are considered good, whether they have official approval, whether they comply with regulations and where they are obtainable'.[34]

Through the various drafts of these letters to the CoID from other design bodies like the RFAC, it is possible to see that articulations of the debate varied according to how public the channel of communication was. The individuals involved clearly possessed strong opinions about street furniture, and were prepared to voice them privately. These letters show that there were significant differences in approach, and by 1952 the RFAC started to distance itself from the booklet. But what was central government's reaction?

Government reaction

The Ministry of Transport and the Ministry for Housing and Local Government (MHLG) shared the RFAC's attitude towards the booklet, and felt that the CoID should 'take full responsibility for publication' – both in terms of cost and message.[35] As far as the MHLG was concerned, the booklet was 'an urgent necessity', but it privately doubted whether the MoT or the Treasury would fund the booklet or consider it as too much of a luxury.[36] Clearly, there were divisions within government about the booklet, and whose responsibility it was. Indeed, in an internal memo from the MHLG, one civil servant warned the deputy secretary that,

> I would suggest that we, as a Department, should be a bit careful about getting too deeply involved in what is a matter of very great controversy and might lead us far afield. That does not mean that we should sit back: I think our province is to stimulate and do what we can to support and help the CID [CoID] in their endeavours.[37]

To some extent, this private opinion confirms the distant attitude of government to the whole debate, but it was by no means representative of the entire ministry. Handwritten below this memo is a response from the deputy secretary, stating that, 'I don't at all want to be too careful about getting too deeply involved. The whole subject seems to me of very great importance to civic and moral amenity and I think that we might well take a leading part (when Transport are plainly prepared to do so) in a campaign for education and improvement.'[38]

The disagreement within the MHLG clearly caused sufficient alarm because others then sought to diffuse it. Another civil servant, Miss W. M. Fox, responded with her view that,

> I would like, if I may, to say how heartily I agree about the need to improve the design of street furniture generally and with the view that we ought to take at least a leading part, if not the lead, in any campaign for improvement. I have it very much on my conscience, particularly when one sees some of the frightful lamp standards one sees about, that most street furniture is permitted local authority development.[39]

Fox appears to have approached the disagreement with the interests of the ministry at heart. She reminded the deputy secretary that 'we have a much better defense against attack if we are ourselves helping in the educational process' of improving street furniture, and moreover that, 'I am sure that to spend some money in attempting to educate local authorities and the public generally is likely to produce better and cheaper results than would follow if we felt obliged as a result of the present mess to go back on the permitted classes, and to require express application to be made for new street furniture'.[40] Fox's comment reveals why government was so resistant to being more active in the debate, a resistance that seems driven by economics. In the light of these potential costs, Fox sought to clarify the level of support the ministry could offer, suggesting that, 'as to involving ourselves deeply I think there is a distinction to be drawn between getting involved in a campaign for better street furniture and identifying ourselves with any particular designs, or schools of design'.[41] For the ministry, it was increasingly clear that any support for the CoID-produced booklet would only invite questions about centralized taste. Thus in order to avoid any serious risk – financial or otherwise – all the ministry could do was ensure that expert technical advice was available to each local authority to help guide them towards making the 'right' decisions concerning street furniture themselves.

This example is useful because it illustrates post-war government's hesitancy about contributing too much to the street furniture debate, as well as the unofficial position of some of its civil servants. Clearly, some did want to contribute more to the debate, and considered it to be a moral duty. Others resisted on financial grounds, but also because of the potential risk the controversial issue of taste could have upon the credibility of the government. In 1953, Willis, the minister of transport, wrote to the CoID with his concerns that the booklet was turning into propaganda 'to educate public taste than a guide to the technical officers of local authorities on the selection and placing of street furniture'.[42] Evidently, the MoT expected the booklet to be the latter, and was reluctant to participate in any efforts to influence taste.

Government's suspicions about the agenda of organizations like the RFAC and the CoID had been circulating for some time. For instance, during the Festival of Britain, some officials characterized the CoID's involvement as showing little practical sense for economic realities, and more interested in appearance.[43] The RFAC faced similar accusations. In 1950, A. E. N. Taylor from the MoT wrote to the RFAC with concerns at the way it was behaving towards the street lighting industry on lantern design, in which he said, 'I think we all agree that this attention to aesthetic design is a good thing and should be encouraged, particularly as for the present the approach from the manufacturers is a voluntary one'.[44] However, having met with industry representatives, Taylor relayed to the RFAC his impression that, 'they were getting a little disheartened as, amongst other things, they felt that insufficient attention was being paid to the advisability of compromise owing to the present financial conditions'.[45] Taylor also added that a realistic attitude ought to be made compatible with the RFAC's artistic values. Such artistic intransigence also placed the MoT in a difficult position. During a meeting on the subject of concrete lighting standards in 1951, the MoT acknowledged that its authority would be compromised if it were to 'refuse to agree to lighting schemes which… were required for safety purposes because the schemes were objected to on aesthetic grounds'.[46] Thus, while recognizing the value of artistic advice, clearly the priorities of the MoT were more practical in nature.

It was in this practical sense that the MoT hoped the street furniture booklet would make a positive contribution, so that it could at least 'set people thinking about the subject and might help to form a public opinion which would influence Local Authorities'.[47] Others within the MHLG were more anxious about to whom the booklet was directed. Internal correspondence reveals that some within the MHLG believed that, 'partly it must be the manufacturers and engineers… but should it also be the engineer and the man who ought to judge, in placing his orders whether a particular design is appropriate for the place in which he wants to use it?'[48] It was largely these unresolved issues that led to government dissatisfaction with the booklet, indeed at one point, the MHLG even considered publishing its own advice for engineers to complement the CoID's guidance. This was not financially possible however, and instead the MHLG urged the MoT to consider the extent to which 'they can and will exercise control' over the booklet, i.e. to keep the artistic tendencies of the design organizations in check.[49]

By 1953, the ad hoc committee's deliberations were beginning to frustrate those other parties involved in the debate. Unsatisfied with Dalton's assurances in 1951 that the improvement of street furniture would not be left to chance, Lord Rosse from the Georgian Group petitioned Dalton's replacement, Harold MacMillan, for his help. Using the same argument he adopted towards Dalton, Lord Rosse pointed out that local authorities seemed more concerned with 'comparative cost and efficiency' than with 'the aesthetic considerations involved' with street furniture.[50] While MacMillan may have shared Lord Rosse's dislike of what he later described as 'the unsightly gibbets which have been put up in what seem to be quite unsuitable places', he could not promise any more than Dalton could.[51] He also claimed that it would only be through the influence of groups like the GG, rather than direct government control, that progress could be made especially when the matter required the reconciliation of several interests, including finance, road safety and aesthetics. MacMillan's rejection clearly articulates the soft power role that the Georgian Group – but to some extent, even the Council of Industrial Design, the Royal Fine Art Commission and the Civic Trust – were both expected and forced to perform.[52]

During the early 1950s the GG held several meetings on street furniture, at which local government was blamed for the damage it was allegedly causing to the urban environment. In his address to one meeting in February 1954, Betjeman warned the audience that it was the ordinary 'dim' places in England that would be ruined with inappropriate street furniture if nothing were done (see Figure 4.1). For it was in such places, according to Betjeman, that

> the Engineer was seldom intelligent or enlightened enough to seek advice from CoID, RFAC or the amenity societies. He took the course of least intellectual effort and chose the cheapest standard from the catalogue of, say 'Concrete Utilities' which satisfied Engineering requirements – more particularly if it was passed by the 'Royal Fine Art Commission'. It was useless to expect such men to consider the aesthetic aspects or the suitability of standards to the street scene.[53]

Betjeman's dislike of local authority engineers and their choice of lamp standards is expressed here through their alleged lack of aesthetic education, their distance from the intellectual hub of cities, and less directly, their class. Collectively, these factors amounted to a perceived lack of taste. The CoID – whose officers attended the meeting – concurred with Betjeman's condemnation of the local authority engineer, adding that the CoID would seek to impress upon the ministries 'the involvement of planning officers who were clearly much better able to consider the aesthetic aspect'.[54] MacMillan also attended the meeting, and he reiterated the government's position that planning permission should not be required for the installation of every lamp post, largely because of the burden it would place on the planning machine, but also because he believed the authorities entrusted with this responsibility ought to be capable of doing the job properly.[55]

By 1953 the booklet still wasn't considered good enough for government to sponsor or fund, and no other organization's help was forthcoming either.[56] Thus after almost four years of development, Russell was forced to write to the MoT

124   *Street Furniture Design*

Figure 4.1 An example of inappropriate street furniture in the ordinary 'dim' places in England – in this case, Morecambe. Concrete Utilities Ltd., 'Modern Lamp Columns', List 38, 1946, 16. CU Phosco lighting Ltd.

to state that the booklet would be abandoned, and the material reworked into a feature in *Design* magazine.[57] It is unclear what further actions the committee took, or whether it even met again, but both the MoT and the MHLG continued their discussions on how best to improve street furniture, especially lighting.[58] This unsuccessful four-year project to produce guidance on street furniture exposes a number of important realities within the debate, most obviously between the aesthetic anxiety expressed by the more artistically minded joint committee members, and the resistance expressed by both central and local government over aesthetic interference in what was for them, a practical matter. This official struggle over what street furniture should look like and who should decide was largely informed by arguments to do with power, education and taste. But one important voice was missing from these discussions: the public.

The anger of the untrained

While official bodies blamed one another over how best to improve the standard of street furniture design, public debate on the subject was increasing. Indeed, even before the booklet on street furniture was officially abandoned, disagreements over street furniture were unfolding in streets across the country. As the previous chapters have demonstrated, letters were regularly published in design and architecture magazines complaining about particular street furniture designs, and the design organizations involved were well aware of the public's anger. But by the early 1950s, the public also started directly confronting government ministries and local authorities, demanding action and better street furniture.

One early confrontation took place in Highgate in 1953, following a letter of complaint from Lady Norah Ritson to the borough engineer at St Pancras Council, Mr Bainbridge.[59] The complaint concerned the new lighting scheme outside Ritson's home – a scheduled Ancient monument – in Highgate Village. According to Lady Ritson, the introduction of concrete neon lighting standards had no place in 'one of the oldest and most unspoiled parts of London', and she added that the standards were 'needlessly grotesque, the design is poor, the colour ugly, and the light they throw is atrocious, making every human face seem sub-human. This is a grave defect, and against public policy, in a village place frequented by courting couples.'[60] Lady Ritson's objection to the colouring of lighting and its adverse effects on the pallor of pedestrians – particularly courting couples – was a common complaint, and will be addressed again later. Lady Ritson's further objection that the height of the lighting scheme 'makes attempts to sleep a fantasy. One either has air and an impossible light, or no air and darkness' reinforces the negative social perceptions of modernization at this time.[61] And, according to Lady Ritson, the lack of other protests was because 'the public have been bludgeoned into apathy'.[62] Unfortunately, no photographic evidence of the offending concrete lamp posts in Highgate has survived. However, an advertisement by Concrete Utilities Ltd depicts another installation by St Pancras Council, which gives an idea of the taste of Mr Bainbridge, the borough engineer responsible (see Figure 4.2).

Lady Ritson's letter represents the resistance to modern street furniture from the top levels of British society. Her title, the status of her home, as well as her reference to public policy, suggests an awareness of effective strategies to use towards government and a high level of education. Not content with merely involving the borough engineer, Lady Ritson also wrote to the Ministry of Housing and Local Government and relayed her horror upon discovering that, after speaking with Mr Bainbridge, St Pancras Council were not obliged to consult any other authority in the upgrade of council lighting except the MoT and the

Figure 4.2 Advertisement by Concrete Utilities Ltd, 1953. CU Phosco Lighting Ltd. Lighting installation by St Pancras Council, Concrete Utilities Ltd advertisement.

Commissioner of Police.[63] In this letter, Lady Ritson claimed that, 'I find it very difficult to believe that the general public who value the historic and aesthetic amenities of this country are aware that these matters can be settled by a local council who have often no knowledge, no interest in, and no desire to preserve, beautiful irreplaceable historic places'.⁶⁴ Sharing the disdain that countless others had expressed before her for the insensitivities of local government, Lady Ritson suggested that an architect ought to be consulted before such changes took place, given the matter involved 'the preservation of something so important to the background and fabric of our country'.⁶⁵

Internal correspondence within the MHLG reveals the extent to which opinion on how best to respond was divided. One civil servant privately declared that 'my sympathies are entirely with Lady Ritson, but hard cases do not make good law'.⁶⁶ This particular individual also conceded that given advice on the matter already existed, the 'tragedy is that borough engineers and the local authorities seem unable or unwilling to take advantage of it'.⁶⁷ Yet rather than seeking to alter policy, the MHLG's advice seems to have been consistent: for 'the authorities concerned to be awakened to their responsibilities, and become better educated in doing the job'.⁶⁸ Several draft letters circulated around the MHLG, and suggestions varied from advising Lady Ritson to 'redirect her attack to the Metropolitan Borough Council and build up local agitation in support', to somewhat patronizingly reminding her that 'I know you would agree how important local government really is'.⁶⁹ What was consistently clear, however, was the ministry's opinion that it could not 'pull the chestnuts out of the fire', nor 'properly intervene' in the matter.⁷⁰ The explanations given for its lack of direct involvement is attributed to the need for local government to take responsibility for these issues because 'the tendency to shift the point of decision to higher and more remote authorities is bad for local government and peculiarly bad where the question at issue is essentially one of taste'.⁷¹ Evidently, the ministry's anxiety stemmed from this issue of taste, and it was at pains to communicate to Lady Ritson that it was busy 'sponsoring the use of good design' but that 'good advice has an unfortunate way of not making much impression on the people it is meant to benefit', an allusion perhaps to the street furniture booklet discussed earlier.⁷²

What is striking, however, is that, while publicly justifying its inability to intervene, the MHLG was simultaneously willing to offer its support to Lady Ritson's campaign privately, by encouraging her to 'keep pegging away at the Council and try to stir up interest on the part of the members'.⁷³ Some within the MHLG objected to the official line that was to be taken, and wished to adopt a more direct approach. One civil servant confided to a colleague that,

> I do not feel willing to write the letter proposed to Lady Ritson. I share her feeling that considering the things we do interfere with we might well take a more active part over street furniture… why can't we – jointly with Ministry of Transport – publicly express horror at the hideous erections and call attention to whatever it is that CID [CoID] have done – and generally make a stir?⁷⁴

There were seemingly very good reasons why the ministry could not 'make a stir', based on economics and the controversial nature of the topic, but also because it would undermine relations between local and central government.

Eventually the MHLG did send a friendly reply to 'Norah'; however, the message was broadly the same as that expressed in earlier drafts, i.e. that really nothing could be done, and the minister reasoned that increased centralization was not the answer: 'there is far too much control and regulation and form filling in the world, and if one has a system of local government one really ought to let the Local Authorities be responsible for matters of local importance'.[75] Entitling local authorities to make these decisions without central supervision, the minister added, would ensure improvements in the quality of local government.[76] He did, however, agree with Ritson that 'the heavy concrete stands in Highgate Village are disastrous', but proposed that 'a body independent of government' might be better placed to deal with such matters given that 'government pronouncements on aesthetics are not always successful'.[77] The minister's only advice was to tread 'a long and weary road' and basically: 'keep at it. If only more members of the public would create a stir about the aesthetic atrocities perpetrated or permitted by public authorities, we should really make progress'.[78] Thus the MHLG's official position was for protesters to simply focus on arousing public feeling by vigorously campaigning. The language used in the minister's letter to Lady Ritson is surprisingly candid, though whether it would have expressed itself in such terms to local authorities is rather less likely. While the controversy over lighting in Highgate village achieved very little, especially for Lady Ritson, it illustrates the degree to which opinion within the MHLG was split on how to address the public's anger over modern street furniture.

'Concrete gibbets' in Greenwich

A further controversy over street lighting occurred in Greenwich in June 1956. The dispute began when a resident of the area – J. A. C. Platts – wrote to the RFAC asking for its help to preserve the Crooms Hill area in Greenwich. According to Platts, the area was under threat from Greenwich Council, whose installation of large concrete lamp posts was, he said, 'turning this beautiful road into a subtopian by-pass'.[79] The RFAC agreed to take the case on, and wrote to Harold Whetstone, the Town Clerk of Greenwich Council reminding him of the importance of architectural setting when using particular lamps, and requesting that work be temporarily suspended until a meeting could be held and a resolution found.[80] Whetstone responded by claiming that 'the Council has special regard to the aesthetic appearance of the columns to be used' and that both the CoID and the RFAC had in fact approved the concrete Revo columns in question (see Figure 4.3).[81]

This revelation placed the CoID and the RFAC in an embarrassing position, since the local authority had effectively acted in accordance with their guidelines. Nonetheless, the public remained unsatisfied and argued that the lighting standards made Greenwich look like 'a prisoners-of-war compound'.[82] Clearly, approved street furniture was just as likely to incite public protest as objects that had been rejected. Some years earlier, the RFAC had predicted that cases like this might occur, but the issue remained unresolved.[83] This inherent weakness

Municipal Vandalism 129

Figure 4.3 Revo concrete lamp post, Greenwich, in 'Crooms Hill: Opposition to Design of Lamp Standards'. The National Archives. Old and new: Swan-neck concrete Revo lamp post in Greenwich in the foreground, an older model in the background.

emphasizes the fact that opinion on what constituted good street furniture design fluctuated and was even split across different parties. Platts also noted that 'the Blackheath Society, having found out by accident that the lighting was to be changed, wrote to the Council offering their help in the selection of suitable standards. They received a reply stating that their offer could not be accepted as the meeting at which their letter was read was the meeting at which the standards were chosen', and as a result Greenwich Council rigidly refused to alter its plans.[84] It acknowledged, however, that since residents primarily objected to the use of concrete, it was prepared to install steel lamp posts if others contributed to the cost. At this point, the RFAC appealed to the MHLG to intervene.[85] It must also have written to the Royal Commission on Historical Monuments (RCHM) as a letter was returned with the RCHM's view that 'Greenwich Borough Council are rock bottom out of a rock bun and their official Mr. Clinch [the borough engineer] is about on the same degraded level.'[86] Following the RFAC's appeal, the MHLG wrote to Greenwich Council to say that it shared the view of the RFAC – that the lamp posts should be of steel and not of concrete – and that Greenwich Council was the financially responsible party as the area was an outstanding architectural masterpiece.[87] Indeed, according to the MHLG, 'the scheme adopted should be as unobtrusive as possible'.[88] But what constituted an unobtrusive scheme?

For groups like the CoID and the RFAC, an unobtrusive lighting scheme meant steel standards, though many disputed this interpretation.[89] In a letter to the MoT in 1956, the Stanton Ironworks Company complained that 'everything hinges on the word "obtrusive", as I feel that some people might consider that, in certain circumstances and depending upon the type, a concrete column is less obtrusive than a steel column' (see Figure 4.4).[90] And as the voice of local authorities, the *MJ* was equally dubious about the unobtrusive qualities of steel because 'the fallacy of the case for steel is that it no more marries with old and picturesque property than does any other medium. Any form of modern street lighting fails to conform with by-gone periods.'[91] This view was supported by Royal Saint Marylebone Metropolitan Borough Council in 1957, which stated that 'modern equipment – street lighting – cannot be made to harmonise with a background a century or more in age unless by bogus "olde world" treatment'.[92] From the perspective of many groups outside of the design elite, the decision to favour steel over concrete was based on little more than visual preference irrespective of whether one was more or less obtrusive than the other. In any case, where this question of obtrusiveness was concerned, the opposite was also true. One of the main reasons why concrete became so central to the majority of street furniture protests was because of its perceived ability to erase local difference: appearing everywhere and making everywhere look the same.[93] This disorientating effect emerged as one of the key issues within the whole debate, but it also exposes a fundamental irony: despite its alleged inconspicuousness, modern street furniture was highly visible since it looked considerably different from pre-war designs and often bore very little stylistic relationship to the context in which it was situated. Thus objects that were designed to be ignored were simultaneously expected to be seen.

Municipal Vandalism 131

Figure 4.4 Column designed by David Mellor – an example of the unobtrusive steel designs favoured by the Council of Industrial Design. David Mellor, tubular steel lighting column designed for Abacus, 1955. David Mellor Design.

Government was equally divided over concrete lamp posts, and according to a MHLG memo in 1953, 'Transport seems to think there is nothing wrong with them.'[94] The MoT's position probably had less to do with taste, and more to do with economic constraints, since the MoT remained responsible for releasing steel for use in lamp posts and lanterns at a time of considerable shortage. Much of Britain's steel at that time was being exported to restore the country's finances, and accommodating design organization's aesthetic preference for steel over concrete was not a priority. It was a subject that caused considerable friction between the MoT and the MHLG.[95] Nevertheless, such difficulties did not, according to the MHLG 'excuse some of the dreadful designs which were adopted'.[96] And by 1953 restrictions upon steel were slowly being relaxed, leading the MHLG to conclude that 'there seems to be no reason why these horrors should continue'.[97] The subject clearly aroused strong feeling within the MHLG because one of its civil servants, Mr Beaufoy, proposed issuing a 'circular to local authorities encouraging them to do something better than the dreadful concrete gibbets which we all abhor'.[98] The expression 'concrete gibbets' appears to have been a popular one within government, and Beaufoy also added, 'if somebody is prepared to allot enough steel for a purity campaign, then it seems to me for the Minister of Transport to tell his people that, in future – no gibbets! No doubt, however, manufacturers have hundreds and perhaps thousands of them in store and whether he would be prepared to make a stand, I do not know'.[99] Beaufoy's comment reveals the extent to which the MHLG and the MoT differed in their approach to street furniture, and even the variable tastes of government. But it also exposes one of the stark realities within the debate, which the public might not have understood or even been aware of. Concrete lamp posts were considerably cheaper than steel lamp posts, and did not involve additional MoT permission. Moreover, if manufacturers did have excess stock of 'concrete gibbets', the MoT could hardly prevent them from selling that stock on aesthetic grounds, because doing so would have inevitably led to accusations of a centralized taste-making campaign.

It was against this background that the case in Greenwich unfolded, much to the annoyance of all concerned. Having applied some pressure to Greenwich Council, the MHLG received a clear rebuttal.[100] Since no other body was prepared to supplement the cost of steel lights, the minister wrote to the RFAC to inform it that Greenwich Council was 'adhering to their decision not to budge unless we (or you) paid the difference in capital cost'.[101] Evidently the minister decided not to oppose Greenwich Council – despite having the powers to do so – since he added in his letter to the RFAC that he was 'sorry that this has not ended happily'.[102] In the months after this exchange, various other parties tried to apply pressure on Greenwich Council – including Betjeman – but the RFAC were forced to acknowledge that, where the concrete lamps in Greenwich were concerned, 'we are not in a position to insist'.[103] In such a situation, the absence of legislative powers was brought into stark relief.

Community action in Blackheath

Another protest against Greenwich Council surfaced shortly after, though on this occasion the result was slightly different. In 1959, the Council extended its re-lighting scheme across Blackheath Park prompting community protests.

According to Ian Hay Davison, a former resident of Blackheath and instigator of the protests, the area was originally lit by 'charming Victorian gas lamps' until the Council decided to replace them with ugly curved concrete standards with 'question-mark' lantern fittings – the same as those erected in Crooms Hill (Figure 4.3). Davison's wife Morny had worked for the CoID's street furniture committee, and like many other residents, was incensed at Greenwich Council's decision. Perhaps because of these connections, the CoID was keen to promote the story and publically criticized what it called 'clumsy concrete standards' with 'pimple lanterns'.[104] The controversy was also reported by *The Daily Telegraph*, which noted that the replacement design was RFAC-approved, causing embarrassment and placing additional strain on the relationship between the CoID, the RFAC and Greenwich Council.[105] While Greenwich Council described the replacement lamps as 'graceful, modern and efficient', residents considered them to be 'fat, ugly and out-of-date'.[106] However, despite protests by Blackheath's residents, as well as by the RFAC and the CoID, Greenwich Council explained it could not justify spending public money to purchase new lights, so the residents decided to take matters into their own hands.

Led by the Davisons, who lived in Blackheath Park's Span estate – a 1960s development, which itself was not particularly popular with neighbours who preferred the traditional Regency houses that had previously occupied the site – the Blackheath Park Lighting Fund was established in 1960. After canvassing local opinion, the Fund petitioned Greenwich Council and eventually raised £300 to have the lamps replaced by a more attractive design. At least half of this sum was donated by Leslie Bilsby, the developer of the estate, but as Davison later recounted: 'We kept Leslie Bilsby's contribution of £150 a secret so as not to offend our other supporters to whom the dreaded Span was anathema: he was not amused.'[107] In a letter sent out to residents, Blackheath Park Lighting Fund described the new lamps – which had been approved by the CoID and had won one of the Design Centre's 'Design of the Year' Awards in 1959 – as being manufactured by Atlas and made up of a 'slender aluminium column with an unbreakable Perspex lantern' (see Figure 4.5).[108] The Fund encouraged residents to contribute to the cost and share fully 'in helping to preserve the amenities of this delightful road'.

While the success of the campaign demonstrated, according to Davison, 'that people do care about even such apparently pedestrian matters as street lights and that even the Borough Council is not always right!', Greenwich Council refused to admit defeat.[109] The Council's Works Committee was reported in *The Kentish Mercury* as saying, 'we are not prepared to admit that from an aesthetic view the lantern and column chosen by the residents is in any way superior to the council's standard fitting'.[110] For its part, the CoID continued to promote the example, not just because the replacement choice of lantern validated its own recommendations about modern design, but also because of Davidson's attitude to municipal authorities.[111] For the CoID, the whole exercise had proved that 'constructive criticism can pay dividends if handled with tact, diplomacy and patience' – the very approach the CoID had cultivated since its formation.[112]

Figure 4.5 Blackheath lighting – preferred lamp post design. Courtesy of Ian Hay Davison. Winner of a 'Design of the Year' Award in 1959.

Both examples in Greenwich expose the inherent weaknesses of the official design approval system: the first example because it illustrates the CoID's position out-with the borders of public taste, and the second because it illustrates the confusion generated by such a complex system. Yet they also reveal the power of local government to ignore external pressure, even from central government. The only reason the public won the argument in Blackheath was because they were financially able and willing to cover the cost of replacement lamp posts. What this story also shows is the limits of the RFAC's soft power, indeed, it is difficult to know the extent to which any impact was actually exerted by the RFAC in its clandestine dealings in either of these controversies behind the scenes. Yet not all lighting schemes ended like this, and there were in fact occasions when government did intervene.

One rare example of government intervention was reported in the *MJ* in the same year as the dispute in Greenwich. In 1956 a disagreement over aesthetics broke out between Eton College and Buckinghamshire District Council, which sought to install modern lamp standards in the vicinity of the college. After rejecting both the concrete and painted steel lamps proposed by the District Council, Eton College invited the RFAC to mediate.[113] According to the *MJ* the RFAC was quoted as saying that 'the appearance of Eton was of national as well as local concern', and it suggested that additional care ought to be taken to consider the surroundings of the college before installing what were alleged to be inappropriate lamp standards.[114] When the District Council rejected the RFAC's recommendations and tried to proceed with its original plans, Eton College asked the MHLG to intervene. Following this appeal, the MHLG awarded the College an exemption from national regulations on lighting standards, forcing the District Council to retreat.

The government clearly had the power to intervene in the street furniture debate when it desired to, despite its claims to have no authority on the matter. Ministerial intervention could be arbitrary, but the government often acted against the introduction of modern street furniture, at least in certain circumstances. For instance, Cabinet minutes from 1962 reveal that the use of concrete opposite Westminster Abbey was deliberately prevented because it 'may look shoddy'.[115] And in 1964, Victorian lamp-standards were protected so as not to 'detract from the character of two streets which contributed to the beauty of the St James Park area'.[116] All three examples indicate that government tended to intervene in areas that its own members were likely to frequent, which raises serious questions about who modernism was meant for.

'15-foot spectres' in Chelsea

Though the previous examples might indicate the prevalence of double standards on the part of government, there are plenty of caveats to such a claim. For instance, in 1960 the modernization of lamp posts in Chelsea provoked considerable public anger. *Country Life*, *Design* and the *AR* all took an interest in the case, as did the *London Evening Standard* which published a report by stage designer Oliver Messel about his 'considerable consternation over the unsightly new lamp posts which are being put all over Chelsea to replace the extremely attractive old ones [which have] great character and charm' (see Figure 4.6).[117] Besides publically drawing attention to this issue, Messel also privately wrote to the Office of Works (OoW) and the

Figure 4.6 Lamp posts in Chelsea, in 'Columns in Context', *Design*, February 1960, No. 134, 36. Design Council Archive, University of Brighton Design Archives. New lamps in Chelsea: The Borough Council's installation is pictured in the foreground on the left, the older model can be seen in the background. On the right, *Design*'s preference was temporarily erected (and taken down again) to show that 'a modern column is the most appropriate solution in an old street'.

MHLG, to inform them that Kensington Borough Council had purchased 'huge quantities of hideous lamp posts to replace all the old ones in Kensington', and that by doing so, numerous small residential streets of considerable architectural merit would be spoiled.[118] For both ministries, the issue was ultimately a planning problem; however, the OoW conceded that 'the demolition of lamp-posts does not require planning consent, and although the erection of new ones does, there is a blanket exemption in force'.[119] While the exemption could be withdrawn, the OoW stated that after considerable analysis in the wake of the *AR*'s campaign against the spread of subtopia, it had decided that 'nothing very useful could be done about it'.[120]

Records show that the ministries communicated between themselves on whether they ought to protect lamp posts by listing or scheduling them under the Ancient Monuments Acts, or Section 30 of the Town and Country Planning Act. In a letter to the MHLG, permanent secretary for the OoW, John Hope, wrote: 'I understand that legally, there is no objection to this, and indeed you have listed a lamppost and I have scheduled a pillar-box. It is clear however, that this is not the most appropriate way to deal with this problem, and I imagine that somewhere amongst your armoury of planning powers, you have the right weapon.'[121]

Unfortunately, the MHLG was unwilling to use these apparent powers, and its minister, Henry Brooke, replied that,

> usually the reason why people complain about the loss of old lamp-posts is that they dislike the new ones put in their place. It seems to me that the best way of tackling this problem is to make sure that the new ones are well-designed and that their design fits the surroundings. A lot has been done and is being done to bring this about.[122]

In this respect, Brooke could have been referring to the collective work of the CoID and the RFAC, as well as the Civic Trust. It was their work, he proposed, that was 'more likely to bring about useful results than the direct exercise of planning powers'.[123] Indeed, the main aim for the MHLG seems to have been to encourage local authorities 'to realise for themselves what kinds of lamp-post are suitable in different settings. It has been very encouraging to see in recent years how several offending councils have been vigorously set upon by their own ratepayers'.[124] The position of the ministers was later conveyed in a letter to Oliver Messel, in which direct ministerial intervention was said to be much less effective than local action.[125]

The CoID took a different approach, preferring to shame the Borough Council responsible. Since its installation went against the advice of the CoID, *Design* reported that the implication of such 'nostalgic yearnings' for such outdated products was a rejection of 'progress'.[126] It also stated that, 'unless the sorry lesson of Chelsea is quickly comprehended, this pathetic concession to the past may yet be inflicted on residents of other elegant London boroughs'.[127] To prove the argument, the CoID erected a temporary replacement, to illustrate that modernism was not the problem; the problem was the specific lamp chosen by the authorities.

For the *AR*, the case merely reflected the arrogance of local authorities. According to author Derek Barton, badly designed lamp posts were not just 'an affront to the eye' but also an affront to a public who were 'seldom informed or consulted about them'.[128] The lamp posts in Chelsea had prompted considerable discussion – they were described in Parliament as '15-ft. spectres' and 'replicas of dustbins' – and Barton reported that the problem 'aptly illustrates a general threat to good design'.[129] Barton clearly articulated his campaign using the discourse of Good Design, but he also situated it in a political context, in which the issue was 'one of those delicately balanced situations between governors and governed which abound in British democracy'.[130] He gave the examples of several London councils which had experimented with different methods of involving ratepayers in their decisions, and cited Chelsea Borough Council as the least inclusive.[131] Chelsea, according to Barton, 'has chosen its new lamp-posts with an absolute minimum of publicity and has then gone half-heartedly and disingenuously through some of the motions of giving the citizens a chance to criticize without, it would seem, the least intention of allowing criticisms to bear any fruit'.[132] Rather than invite participation on matters of such great community importance, Barton claimed that council meetings were 'virtually proceedings for rubber stamping decisions reached in secret by committees'.[133] The implication here is that committees were known for reaching decisions by mysterious and often questionable methods – an interpretation which was borne out by Greenwich Council and the letter from the Blackheath Society cited previously. In addition, Barton criticized the borough engineer, 'who, judging by the tone and style of his correspondence, is of the authoritarian variety'.[134] According to Barton, the power wielded by local authorities was disproportionate to that of the citizen, and their methods were undemocratic.[135] That the complete modernization of Chelsea's lighting was more expensive than merely converting the existing lamps to electricity was attributed to pure regimentalism.[136] And in his concluding comments, Barton summarized by stating that 'as long as the provision of street lighting is considered primarily as a road engineering matter, English towns and boroughs will continue to be defaced by inappropriate street lamps in the name of efficiency and "cheerfulness" by councillors without the aesthetic judgment to stand up to the advice of technicians'.[137] Barton's comments reveal the degree to which councillors were perceived as lacking aesthetic sensitivity, and borough engineers were technicians who bullied their councils into retreat.

Revivalism and regret

The street lighting controversies discussed so far illustrate the increasingly public nature of these disputes, and the extent that local authorities could ignore outside advice unless forced to do so by government or by financial incentive. However, they also show that throughout the 1950s and early 1960s, many members of the public fought to protect the historic objects they believed added character to the street. The *MJ* reported several examples in which the public registered their regret at the renewal of their town's street furniture. In 1955, residents of Shrewsbury were reported to have mourned the departure of old street water conduits largely because of their indirect function as hand warmers.[138] And on some occasions other uses were found for obsolete street furniture. For example, in 1956 a local contractor in Bradford bought his local authorities' old police boxes and sold them on as garden huts and tool sheds.[139] Others adopted a much more confrontational approach. For instance, in 1956 the sculptor Arnold Machin asked his wife to padlock him to a Victorian gas lamp on 'the Villas' – his Victorian estate in Stoke-on-Trent – as part of his attempt to resist its removal by the local authority (see Figure 4.7).[140] As reported in *The Daily Mail*, while workmen hired to fit the electric replacement looked on, Machin and his wife 'defied subtopia' by reading *The Seven Lamps of Architecture* by Ruskin while shielding themselves from the sun with an umbrella.[141] The police eventually arrived and despite Machin's status as a Royal Academician and designer of Britain's postage stamps depicting HM the Queen, his bid to protect the lamp failed and the new lamps were finally installed. Nonetheless, a compromise was reached: the gas lamp in question was re-installed in Machin's garden. According to Machin's nephew, the irony is that 'the Villas' was declared a conservation zone some years later and the 'modern' concrete lamp posts were all replaced with replica cast iron lamps.[142]

Municipal Vandalism 139

Figure 4.7 Mr and Mrs Arnold Machin standing next to an ornamental lamp post in Stoke-on-Trent. Courtesy of *The Sentinel*. Mr Machin was chained around this post in 1956.

That historic or period styles of street furniture were worth keeping was a view that eventually even local authorities began to support. In 1959 Old Bosham Parish Council rejected its own modern street lighting installation for being too ugly.[143] And when Chipping Camden erected a pilot scheme of electric street lamps in 1960 and asked residents to vote on their preference, they voted overwhelmingly in favour of gas lamps.[144] Even more industrial places adopted this approach – including Belfast, which sought to retain its period light fittings – and some modern housing schemes adopted a similar model.[145] In 1962 the development corporation of Merthyr Tydfil installed a period water fountain in one of its schemes on the basis that it would 'add just that touch of originality and tradition needed to associate the modern scheme with the past of the old town'.[146] And in Brighton in 1964, decorative lanterns were commissioned for the seafront without public protest.

The CoID, however, continued to campaign for modern street furniture design, allegedly on the public's behalf, disparaging any efforts to retain historic styles as regressive. In 1962, *Design* discovered London County Council's plans to re-light the riverside walk along the South Bank, and purchase thirty-five replicas of the 1860 Victorian dolphin-style lamp posts originally designed by Vuillamy.[147] *Design* criticized what it regarded as an expensive folly, which would 'fill with gloom the hearts of all those who associate the Festival of Britain site with the first great upsurge of modern design in this country since the war'.[148] It continued,

> No doubt the LCC has reasons for this choice, but what seems incredible is the report that it is unwilling to consult either the Civic Trust or the Royal Fine Arts Commission on a matter of such considerable public interest. Even more strange, in view of the fact that the CoID's open air street furniture exhibition has stood next to County Hall for two years, is that no-one thought it worthwhile consulting the Council's street furniture panel.[149]

That a body as significant for the capital as the LCC could forego CoID advice on street furniture suggests that the CoID had considerably less influence than it imagined. Furthermore, any alarm expressed by the CoID about the project had little or no effect upon the LCC's decision. By the end of 1962, the LCC's chief engineer, architect and valuer published a joint report on the proposed scheme, and justified it on the basis that dolphin-style lamps would help retain a sense of continuity on the riverwalk.[150] While some within the LCC questioned the substantial financial cost of the lamps, and others questioned whether they would look 'out of place in front of the modern buildings of the south bank', such concerns were dismissed and the proposed plan went ahead.[151] *The Times* explained that though 'John Ruskin in a celebrated diatribe assailed them from the functional point of view that gas did not come from fishes' tails, there can be little doubt that a liking for ornament, in this severely utilitarian age remains unsubdued'.[152] Where once local authorities were generally considered to be supporters of modernization, by the 1960s and onwards many were in fact supportive of retaining or commissioning period (and often decorative) street furniture – a move that manufacturers supported. One aspect of the debate remained constant, however: local authorities could continue to make design decisions virtually single-handedly, which meant they were consistently held responsible for poor standards.

In some ways it is hardly surprising local authorities attracted such scorn. They were the biggest developer in the country at the time, and had the most responsibility for street furniture, in addition to a host of other duties. During the 1950s, local authorities across Britain were increasingly challenged over their lighting schemes, and lighting engineers in turn responded by becoming much more vocal about their critics and the arbitrary nature of the criticism.[153] Thus, in an effort to diffuse what was becoming an increasingly hostile situation, the *MJ* began to publish extensively on the subject. Writing in 1954, the *MJ* called on local government to avoid creating 'an architectural style which is too often unrelated to the actual site', and while designing 'specials' was impracticable, the most appropriate design was presented as being 'an elegant modest column'.[154] In this respect, the CoID and the *MJ* appeared to be united. However, local authorities often had their own idiosyncratic ideas about what constituted well-designed street furniture.

The CoID tended to advise local authorities that well-designed street furniture was unobtrusive. Thus a well-designed litter bin not only held litter but also concealed it.[155] Scarborough's Health Committee had other ideas, and the *MJ* reported in 1955 that it had painted all of Scarborough's litter bins cream instead of green, on the basis that green litter bins attached to lamp posts were 'drab and offer no incentive to people to use them'.[156] Windsor Council was equally resistant to unobtrusive litter bins, and in 1958 painted its litter bins red and yellow to make them stand out more.[157] Similarly, Whickham Urban District Council painted 130 of its litter bins in 'gay pastel shades' in 1962, but was forced to bow to pressure from Durham County Council which refused to grant planning permission to fit Whickham's newly painted litter bins to lamp posts unless they were repainted grey.[158] In Carrickfergus, County Antrim in 1961, litter bins painted in Ireland's national colours were repeatedly targeted by 'local patriots', who threw the bins into the sea until they were finally installed outside of the town hall.[159] And it wasn't just litter bins that proved contentious. In 1956 Prudhoe District Council enforced a cream doorstep rule when some housewives tried to paint their doorsteps red, so as not to 'upset the colour scheme'.[160] In 1957, the Dover Works Committee painted its signs yellow – despite protests from the local art school – reasoning that 'this design hits you right between the eyes. It will be excellent publicity for Dover'.[161] These examples not only illustrate the way that local authorities resisted outside interference, but also the complexities of local government. Even within a relatively small area, it was possible to have different authorities making different decisions about design.

Inevitably, given its readership, the *MJ* was quick to defend the design decisions of local authorities. The magazine argued in 1952 that such decisions were made on the basis of little more than intuition or even instinct, in that the difference between a good or bad design was that 'you get quite an active feeling of pleasure from the one and a feeling of general discomfort from the other'.[162] Nevertheless, unqualified instincts were routinely conflated with taste, and for the *MJ* at least, 'local planning authorities, despite anything their critics might say to the contrary, generally show innate good taste'.[163] For critics like Richardson, this couldn't be farther from the truth, and taste was an issue that local authorities simply did not understand.[164] Others, like the architect Peter Shepheard, suggested that taste had nothing to do with poor street furniture. Such objects were merely the 'municipal after-thoughts' of an overburdened borough engineer, since 'nobody commits ugliness on purpose'.[165] While several others agreed with Shepheard's observation, the level of anger directed at local authorities was nonetheless increasing.

'The greatest vandals of all time'

The *AR*'s Outrage campaign in 1955 heightened the intensity of the debate, and several local authority figures wrote to the magazine to defend their colleagues. One reader – a planning officer for the Isle of Ely County Council – complained that 'unhappily many of the things that Outrage condemns are outside the control of planning authorities'.[166] This was the point, according to the *AR*, for all too often 'planning machinery is completely bi-passed [sic] – not even overridden' so that carte blanche is instead given to each government department 'and to anything that has a flower bed in it'.[167]

Another forum for this debate occurred in the letter pages of the *MJ*. The first of these letters was sent by a well-known geographer and government advisor Laurence Dudley Stamp in 1956, who sympathized with Ian Nairn's characterization of the municipal engineer as a 'despoiler of Britain'.[168] Nairn, according to Dudley Stamp, had shown 'the incredible jumble of incongruous developments of all sorts which, spreading like a rash over the whole country, were eliminating not only the beauty created by centuries of loving care and thought but even the little touches of regional differentiation'.[169] Indeed, Dudley Stamp added that the municipal engineer was more responsible than any other individual for this blight, because with 'bigger and better bulldozers, noisier and nastier pneumatic drills, unlimited supplies of cement and numerous nauseating new materials' combined with his 'expert knowledge', the municipal engineer had an unfair advantage over the other committee members on his council.[170] This power, combined with the engineer's supposed lack of training in art, architecture, the local history and regional geography of Britain, or even local geology, biology and history, placed the engineer in a dangerous position able to 'destroy – it may be unwittingly – all traces of the past which have made this country what it is'. As such, 'the municipal engineer of today is in the unhappy position of being at least potentially one of the greatest vandals of all time'.[171]

Dudley Stamp's letter lit a fuse within the debate, and in the following issue of the *MJ* Edinburgh's city engineer, W. P. Haldane questioned the justice in Stamp's argument. Rather than blame the engineer – who only had the interests of the ratepayer at heart – Haldane argued that Dudley Stamp ought to consider the engineer as an ally in the fight against 'municipal vandalism' since 'so often when attempts are made by municipal engineers to apply restraint the cry of "harsh bureaucracy" is raised – raised successfully by the developers'.[172] Another reader based in Kent echoed Haldane's view, suggesting that while Dudley Stamp's view had become fashionable, it showed 'a complete lack of knowledge of engineering works, and worse still, a dismaying regimentation of ideas'.[173] Rather than blame the municipal engineer, such 'horrors of subtopia' were 'thrust upon them by the CoID, or perhaps the Fine Art Commission'.[174] The argument continued until the end of 1956, drawing letters from a range of organizations, including East Suffolk and Norfolk River Board and the CoID.[175] In January 1957, the city surveyor of Manchester joined the row, and questioned the need for 'a dreary monotony of street furniture' and claimed that 'there is ample scope for individuality in the design for lamp-posts, guard rails, litter baskets and all other items which go to make the street scene'.[176]

Others took the view that the issue was lost on a visually blind public. One reader in Durham asked, 'at the risk of being considered cynical I might ask who cares? Professor Stamp evidently cares… I care, a lot of other people care, but a far larger number of people do not care what a thing looks like as long as it is cheap enough, it works, and it is outside somebody else's front door.'[177] Such a view on the antipathy of the British citizen where aesthetics was concerned would harmonize with John Gloag's view of Britain as being aesthetically illiterate, discussed earlier. Sir John Rothenstein, Tate Gallery director, also shared this view, believing that 'people generally remained curiously blind to how things looked'.[178] Yet it was precisely this attitude which the CoID railed against. This particular Durham reader defended the training of engineers, but argued that if it was possible to instil in the engineer a sense of his responsibility in designing the environment then, 'the engineer can be a substantial ally in preventing the disfiguration of the country provided he gets some support and does not have the edge to his keenness so blunted that eventually he tires of the whole thing, slumps in his chair and says bitterly to an uncaring world "if that's what you want – well have it!"'[179] An earlier commentator from Kent then rejoined the fray to complain that,

> What to me is objectionable is the current fashion of assuming that all borough engineers are complete morons in this controversial subject of what is good taste (of discrimination, call it what you will) and what is not. In these matters of balancing functional efficiency, economy and appearance, there are no divisions of black and white but many shades of grey.[180]

These letters provide a rare insight into how local government engineers, planners and surveyors – the people actually responsible for street furniture on the ground – reacted to their negative portrayal by the press. For some years, they had been well aware that organizations like the CoID and the RFAC regularly criticized their apparent lack of aesthetic education and poor taste. By the mid-1950s, however, many had discovered their voice and were prepared to fight back.

Protecting the interests of the ratepayer

Soon after Outrage was published, local authorities became far less passive when dealing with their critics. And, as the *MJ*'s remit was to represent the interests of local authorities, it often became the means though which those critics were reproached. Thus in the aftermath of *Outrage*, the *MJ* reported that

> the fierce critics particularly, would often do well to acquaint themselves with all the factors before rushing into destructive criticism and also to realize that the Committee responsible for public lighting consists of conscientious, public spirited citizens who have the general wellbeing of the whole community at heart in their difficult task of providing adequate lighting within what can be called, at best, a meagre budget.[181]

The *MJ* also questioned the substance to some complaints, citing one example where a man complained about a street light's effect on his prize-winning chrysanthemums, and another where a woman suspected the light of providing those with evil intent to spy on her.[182] Such complaints were made not about the aesthetic qualities of the lamps but the light itself. Indeed, such was the confidence in the work of local authorities that the *MJ* felt able to describe the tall concrete column as 'a modern achievement', and announce that, 'without wishing to seem immodest or boastful or be accused of being complacent we can in the country say that there is little doubt that the general standard of street lighting in Great Britain today, whilst no means as high as all concerned would desire, will bear comparison with that anywhere in the world'.[183] Such confidence was allegedly owing to the skills of British manufacturers, as well as the temperament of the British public and the British climate.

Different criteria for judging street furniture design might explain why disputes between the design profession and local government often became so heated. Many on the municipal side believed that specialist design committees only cared about 'the appearance of columns during the daylight hours! That and nothing else.'[184] For some local authorities, street lighting was intended to 'pierce the gloom and to make British people and cities gay, exciting and glamorous'.[185] Others paid careful attention to the effect on lipstick. In 1958 Norwich City Council was reported to have considered the effect of different types of street lighting on women's make-up before choosing their new installation; poems were even written in response.[186] As one delegate at a 1961 municipal lighting conference explained: 'the pedestrian had usually completed a heavy day at work and was entitled to consideration in walking out with a companion whose features and dress should be seen in reasonable or even complimentary colour rendering. She should not appear to be dressed in drab material and having yellow or colourless features.'[187] The delegate warned that though the advice given by bodies such as the CoID and the RFAC was valuable: 'surely the moral uplift of appreciative colour distinction at night is at least of equal aesthetic value'.[188]

There is no evidence to suggest that design organizations from the period were remotely concerned with street lighting's effect on lipstick or working men's need for well-lit females, but it further serves to demonstrate the different ways that street furniture could be judged.

For the *MJ* the biggest threat to local authorities delivering well-designed street furniture was the obsessive 'crank'.[189] These amateur enthusiasts were often self-appointed critics, whose objective was merely to 'publicly castigate engineers and surveyors, impugning their professional capacity, starting from the assumption that, being public servants they are bereft of any artistic appreciation'.[190] The *MJ* called for the voice of the municipal officer to finally be heard outside of the committee room because 'the critics are getting publicity out of all proportion to their case or merits'. Indeed, the article informs its local government readers that 'the time has come to fight back, to analyse and appraise their case and who that it is essentially phoney, that these alleged classic traditionalists are about as important as Aunt Matilda laying down the law on a dock dispute'.[191] What form this fight would take was not elaborated upon, but the report did question the foundations of these critics, or 'opinionated busybodies' as arbiters of national taste. Their criticism – or 'carefully calculated thrown-off brilliancy' – could, according to the *MJ*, 'quickly destroy the long deliberations of a council committee'.[192] It also defended the 'anonymous and far from colourful public officer', whose expert but drab accounts were less newsworthy than the 'public invective and eye-catching simile' written by public figures.[193] Despite this, the *MJ* warned against giving into pressure from these critics because 'we must be extremely careful that sentiment and artistic trends do not entirely dictate policy – the functional aspects of design must receive much, if not most, consideration.'[194] Expressing a view that would have been greeted with considerable sympathy across local government, the *MJ* claimed that, 'the uninfluenced and unfettered decision of a council is the more likely to commend itself to those who pay the bill'.[195]

The references here are easy to relate to the *AR* and *Design* – both of which represented a position described in the *MJ* as 'long haired "art-for art's-sakers"' – and it shows the debate in action.[196] Yet what this article also demonstrates is the use of the same arguments that were used in *Outrage*: aesthetic, moral and political. As government predicted – given its reticence about engaging too deeply in the debate – local authorities interpreted interference as a negation of its 'democratic control'.[197] For the *MJ*, local government was 'one of the strongest bulwarks against a dictator state', and it only had the interests of the community at heart.[198] The first consideration of the lighting engineer, for instance, was the performance of his installation and his duty to ratepayers, who were unlikely to appreciate expensive, experimental schemes. Moreover, lighting remained 'of the town, for the town, to serve and contribute to the appearance of the town'.[199] The point made by the *MJ* is clear: as elected officials we act in the interests of the ratepayers, and not the interests of the design elite – a view which street furniture manufacturers capitalized on in their advertising campaigns (see Figure 4.8).

Figure 4.8 Advertisement by Concrete Utilities Ltd, 1956. CU Phosco Lighting Ltd. The argument used in this advertisement 'by Concrete Utilities Ltd (1956)' is dependent upon ideas of technological progress, and the notion that local authorities should act in the best interests of their ratepayers.

Counter-Attack

Yet such assurances did not satisfy everyone. The *Architectural Review* remained just as frustrated as ever with local government's continued destruction of the landscape, and as a result, the *AR* published 'Counter-Attack' in December 1956, as a sequel to Outrage published a year earlier.[200] Picking up many of the same themes, author Ian Nairn used Counter-Attack to criticize the continuous sprawl of subtopia, which he defined as a 'mindless juggernaut, a mixture of ministerial inertia, the megalomania of public bodies, the petty squabbles of local authorities and the sheeplike acceptance by all of out-of-date theories constructed to apply to nineteenth-century industrialism and now codified into a set of inflexible byelaws'.[201] Such levels of inertia had, according to Nairn, 'dulled the efforts of the very people who ought to be thinking and working hardest – not the planning officers, but the committees that control them and the ministries above them. It is easy for them to represent as public apathy what is in fact public hopelessness.'[202] Consequently, Counter Attack presented a plan of action, arming the public 'with arguments against the wrong way and examples of the right way of doing things'.

The advice provided by Counter Attack can broadly be understood as centring on planning, but it also extended to street furniture design. For instance, while horizontal objects were considered to flow and blend with the landscape, Nairn advised the public that 'erecting a vertical automatically means that man is interrupting the landscape to say something'.[203] Nairn also helpfully arranged street furniture into categories according to the most appropriate context. For example, in the category of seating, monumental types were considered suitable for metropolitan settings; neat, mass-produced types were considered suitable for towns, sophisticated and dainty seating was suitable for 'arcadian' landscapes, and rough and workmanlike seating was suitable for the countryside.[204] Wild landscapes were reported to have no need for seating and Nairn directed readers to 'sit on the landscape'. The same model was applied to shelters and railings (see Figure 4.9), and readers were advised that metropolitan settings should extend walls instead of railings, or use only monumental designs; 'light and deft, never shouting' railings were to be used in towns; arcadia would use 'simple and subtle or neat/parklike' designs, and countryside settings would use horizontal types, that were 'rough and firm'.[205] Nairn's advice on lamp standards was that they be 'crisp and small or make them thin – really thin'.[206] The tone of Counter-Attack implies that any deviation from these principles by municipal authorities simply meant that they were not committed to Good Design. In such an event, the reader – as a member of the public and a ratepayer – could legitimately protest. However, the argument adopted demonstrates the *AR*'s emerging alliance with the public. For the first time, the design elite and the public were broadly united against a common enemy: local authorities.

Figure 4.9 Ian Nairn, The Shelter, 'Counter-Attack', the *Architectural Review*, December 1956, Vol. 120, No. 719, 373. RIBA Library Books & Periodicals Collection.

The guidelines Nairn set out in Counter-Attack owe a considerable debt to the discourse of Good Design for the way in which improvement is defined in binary terms of right and wrong. While intended to be helpful, it also reflects a somewhat paternalistic attitude, in which the public was to be schooled by experts. Even at the time, this attitude was satirized (see Figure 4.10). *Punch*

Municipal Vandalism 149

Figure 4.10 'Counter Outrage', *Punch*, 13 February 1957, 248. Reproduced with permission of Punch Ltd, www.punch.co.uk.

magazine argued that the magazine's idealized landscape did not include enough genuine amenities to meet the needs of 'plain, ordinary folk', or 'kiddies, doggies, old folk and cripples'.[207] Instead, *Punch* produced its own version called 'Counter Outrage', which pretended to give municipal authorities an opportunity to respond, while simultaneously mocking the 'slightly sterile' landscape recommended by the CoID and the 'Men of the Trees'. For the *AR*, it was a scene where local authorities would 'whitewash each other and everything else in sight'.[208]

Despite the propensity for satire, Counter-Attack was considered so successful that it became a regular series, providing a forum for readers to publically denounce municipal authorities. Public opinion had reached new levels of dissatisfaction with the visual crimes routinely committed by the 'new oligarchy of government departments'.[209] Such crimes were committed 'either by local government departments being their own planning authorities, or by central government departments being outside planning all together'.[210] A laissez-faire attitude in government was perceived as ultimately responsible, for it allowed local government to behave 'like a ludicrous cut-rate edition of national politics… resulting in amenity becoming a minor political counter'.[211]

Off the back of Counter-Attack, the *AR* set up the Counter Attack Bureau in June 1957, which was developed in association with *The Observer* until 1959, at which point responsibility transferred to the Civic Trust, though it continued to be published in the *AR*.[212] The Bureau offered a free service for readers, who could write in with specific cases of the visual crimes committed by municipal authorities, and in return the Bureau promised that 'each case will be followed through to the end, prodding and nagging local or national authorities for months on end if necessary'.[213] Publishing the progress of these cases was meant to illustrate that 'outrage is continuing unabated, despite attempts to pooh-pooh the whole idea by those most concerned'.[214] And while the *AR* acknowledged that the Bureau could not guarantee success, it aimed at the very least, to 'give the outrager a good run for his outrage'.[215] It also conceded that the Bureau's advice would not necessarily be in line with what the public desired, but that 'it will always be genuine and never influenced by a "party line", implicit or expressed'.[216] Moreover, given the limited influence the public had over municipal authorities, the *AR* claimed, 'it is high time to open the drawbridge and let them back in again; if the bureau can help to do that it will have fulfilled its purpose'.[217] And, as a final warning to municipal authorities, the *AR* inverted the language from George Orwell's *1984* to declare that 'Little Brother is watching you back again'.[218]

The Bureau dealt with several cases involving street furniture. For instance, in 1957 it reported on a case involving concrete lamps in Abingdon which were eventually replaced with steel after the RFAC was invited to mediate (see Figure 4.11).[219] In another example, the authorities overseeing Bushey, Herts and Banstead were criticized for ignoring public pressure over their non-CoID-approved lamp posts.[220] In Roehampton, the borough engineer who deliberately specified swan-neck lamp standards was derided for his poor taste.[221] The street furniture recommended by the borough of Southwark for the LCC's 1958 Elephant and Castle scheme created a scene the *AR* described as 'downright squalor' and 'sickening'.[222] And St Marylebone Council was criticized for denigrating their opponents as 'regency bucks'.[223]

The language used by the Bureau reflects a highly class-conscious society, in which hierarchies are constantly being defined. Much like the *1984* reference, the public is routinely referred to as 'minions', who are pitted against municipal authorities, otherwise known as the 'High-ups'.[224] Clearly, the series was not just about visual crimes, but about class and the struggle for power: the power of local

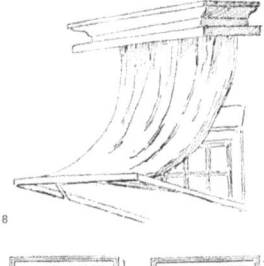
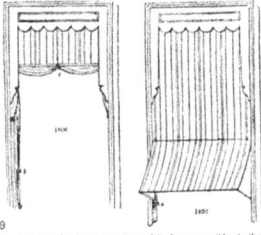

Figure 4.11 The gallant fight against ugly posts and inappropriate flowerbeds. 'Counter-Attack', the *Architectural Review*, June 1958, Vol. 123, No. 737, 422. RIBA Library Books & Periodicals Collection.

government to make design decisions, despite their allegedly bad taste; the power of central government whose laissez-faire attitude effectively sanctioned these crimes; and the perceived lack of power by the *AR* to do anything about it. Central government's argument was that getting involved would only be harmful because it would 'rob the freely elected Local Authorities of their present discretion [and] interfere with individual freedom'.[225] For the *AR*, however, local authorities were in fact 'the worst present-day offenders against individual freedom'.[226] And it added that 'with local authorities acting as many of them do at present, rigorous planning cannot give the citizen less freedom, because in these matters he has none already; and it might at least assure him of a fair hearing. The whole planning system is a gift to any local Napoleon'.[227] The alternative, according to the *AR*, would be difficult and complex, but it was better, they said, than 'Tin-pot Fascism, which is where we are drifting at the moment – and not through too much central planning, but through too much power in the wrong hands through the muddled application of a mixture of control and *laissez-faire*'.[228] This point about control reflects the inherent contradictions within the post-war political landscape, but if the wrong hands implied municipal authorities, then whose were the right hands?

The right hands, as the previous chapter identified, belonged to the design professionals, who believed themselves as having appropriated the culturally superior higher ground. However, the argument by local government concerning its democratic rights to make design decisions appears to have solidified. When one reader of the *AR* complained about the redevelopment of Russell Square in 1961 – which he said was under attack by 'municipal schizophrenia' – Holborn Borough Council fought back.[229] According to the chairman of Holborn's Highways and Works committee, C. F. Burke: 'Mr. Hall is anxious to preserve what he describes as a lost spaciousness, loneliness, freedom, but maybe these characteristics could only be equated with the use of the square by the few as against the great numbers of the general public that have shown their appreciation of the present scheme in the most practical way – by its use'.[230] Holborn Borough Council plainly sought to justify its improvements by reverting to the issue of access, and thus of class and privilege. At a time when British society was struggling to come to terms with the enormous changes affecting its traditional hierarchical model, local government was keen to align itself with 'the people'. But did the people know what they wanted, and if they did, was it 'Good Design'?

As this chapter has shown, the relations between the different bodies involved in the post-war street furniture debate were characterized by a lack of consensus. As demonstrated by the efforts to produce a booklet on street furniture, the variety of controversies over street lighting, and local governmental fallout after Outrage, opinion was split in both local and central government, as well as within the public body and the design elite. But was it just the appearance of street furniture that aroused such a passionate debate? Or was it ideas like taste, authority, and the role of the state? The next and final chapter will pick up these themes and show how street furniture provided a forum to challenge the very notion of Good Design during the 1960s and 1970s.

Notes

1   Design of Street Furniture: Notes of a Meeting Held at Ministry of Transport, 8 July 1949, 1, loose in Royal Fine Art Commission, 'Street Furniture. Design: Correspondence and Minutes'. BP 2/127.

2 Memo on street furniture design, submitted by the RFAC and the CoID to a conference of departments and organizations interested at the Ministry of Transport, 8 July 1949, 1, loose in ibid.
3 Ibid.
4 Ibid.
5 Ibid., 2–3.
6 Ibid., 2.
7 Ibid.
8 Leonard Howitt, 'Design of Street Furniture', statement to conference at Ministry of Transport, 8 July 1949, 1, loose in ibid.
9 Ibid.
10 Ibid., 2.
11 Design of Street Furniture: Notes of a Meeting Held at Ministry of Transport, 8 July 1949, 1, loose in ibid.
12 Ibid., 4.
13 Letter from Haswell Miller [RFAC Scottish Committee] to Godfrey Samuel [RFAC] 29 May 1950, loose in ibid.
14 The committee included the RFAC, the CoID, Urban District Councils Association, Rural District Councils association, Association of Municipal Corporations, County Councils Association, LCC, Ministry of Town and Country Planning, MoT, and the MHLG.
15 'Design of Street Furniture', 7 October 1949, 4, loose in Royal Fine Art Commission, 'Street Furniture. Design: Correspondence and Minutes'. BP 2/127..
16 Ibid.
17 Ibid.
18 'Street Furniture' [memo on a private lunch with Mr Lees-Milne], 22 May 1950, loose in ibid.
19 Letter from Gordon Russell to J. R. Willis, MoT, 8 December 1949, 1, loose in ibid.
20 Ibid.
21 'Street Lighting', letter from Lord Rosse of the GG to Hugh Dalton, Minister of Local Government and Planning, 24 May 1951, loose in Ministry of Housing and Local Government, 'Street Lighting: General Questions and Correspondence on Design Amenity and Aesthetics'. HLG 51/847.
22 Draft reply to Lord Rosse from Ministry of Local Government and Planning, with amendments written in red ink by Hugh Dalton, 16 June 1951, [Signed by HD 17 June 1951], loose in ibid; Reply to Earl of Rosse from Hugh Dalton, Ministry of Local Government and Planning, 28 June 1951, loose in ibid.
23 'Design of Street Furniture', 7 October 1949, 5, loose in Royal Fine Art Commission, 'Street Furniture. Design: Correspondence and Minutes'. BP 2/127.
24 Typescript of Street Furniture Booklet, 1, loose in ibid.
25 Ibid., 3.
26 Ibid., 1.
27 Ibid., 3.
28 Mr. John Summerson's notes on the draft booklet on Street Furniture prepared by the CoID, October 1951, loose in ibid.
29 Letter to Godfrey Samuel [RFAC] from J.M. Richards, 16 October 1951' loose in ibid.
30 Letter to Gordon Russell from Godfrey Samuel [RFAC], 23rd October 1951' loose in ibid.
31 Draft Booklet on Street Furniture – Comments by members of RFAC; May–July 1952' loose in ibid.
32 Ibid.

33 Ibid.
34 Letter to Gordon Russell from Godfrey Samuel [RFAC], 12 July 1952, loose in ibid.
35 Street Furniture, internal letter to Deputy Secretary, 19th March 1953, from Mr Beaufoy, 1, loose in Ministry of Housing and Local Government, 'Street Lighting: General Questions and Correspondence on Design Amenity and Aesthetics'. HLG 51/847.
36 Ibid., 2.
37 Ibid., 2–3.
38 Ibid., 3.
39 Letter from Miss WM Fox to the Deputy Secretary, 24 August 1951, loose in ibid.
40 Ibid.
41 Ibid.
42 Letter to Paul Reilly, 30 March 1953 from J. R. Willis, loose in Royal Fine Art Commission, 1952–71. 'Discussions on Design of Street Furniture'. BP 2/279.
43 See joint statement for the press by the LCC and the Council of the Festival of Britain 3, in 'Lansbury Housing Sites 1-5', and 'Letter to Cyril Walter, Director of Housing and Valuer, from G Barry loose in London County Council, 'Lansbury Housing sites 1-5'. CL HSG 2 31.
44 Letter from AEN Taylor [MoT] to Godfrey Samuel [RFAC] 4 January 1950, 1, in Ministry of Transport, 'Highways Engineering: Registered Files. Street Lighting. Design of Lamp Standards: Including Painting and Guidance by Royal Fine Art Commission'. MT 95/210.
45 Ibid., 2.
46 'Design of Street Lighting Units in Towns and Villages of Artistic Interest', minutes from a meeting held on 19 December 1951 on the issue of concrete lighting standards, in ibid.
47 Letter to Paul Reilly 30 March 1953 from JR Willis, loose in Royal Fine Art Commission, 1952–71. 'Discussions on Design of Street Furniture'. BP 2/279.
48 Internal correspondence to Mr Phillips from Mr Waddell, 12 November 1953, loose in Ministry of Housing and Local Government, 'Street Lighting: General Questions and Correspondence on Design Amenity and Aesthetics'. HLG 51/847.
49 Ibid.
50 Copy of a letter dated November 27 1953 to the Rt. Hon. Harold MacMillan from Lord Rosse, loose in Royal Fine Art Commission, 'Discussions on Design of Street Furniture'. BP 2/279.
51 Copy of a letter dated 22 December 1953 to Lord Rosse from Mr. Harold MacMillan, loose in ibid.
52 See conference on 'The Street Scene' held by GG at Cheltenham, 23–26 March, 1953, loose in ibid; Annual Report of the GG cited in the *MJ*, 9 July 1954, Vol. 62, 1569.
53 'Street Lighting: Note of a Meeting held on Tuesday 16 February 1954 by the Georgian Group', 1, loose in Royal Fine Art Commission, 'Discussions on Design of Street Furniture'. BP 2/279.
54 Ibid., 5.
55 Ibid., 2.
56 Even the *MJ* refused to help launch the booklet. See correspondence to Mr Phillips from Mr Waddell, 8 October 1953, and correspondence to Mr Phillips from Mr Beaufoy, 26 October 1953, 2, loose in Ministry of Housing and Local Government, 'Street Lighting: General Questions and Correspondence on Design Amenity and Aesthetics'. HLG 51/847.

57 Letter from Gordon Russell to Mr. J. R. Willis, MoT, 30 March 1954, loose in ibid.
58 Letter from Mr. S. W. C. Phillips, MHLG, to Mr. Willis, MoT, 30 April 1954, 1, loose in ibid.
59 Letter to Mr. Bainbridge from N. Ritson, Highgate 14 August 1953, loose in ibid.
60 Ibid.
61 Ibid.
62 Ibid.
63 Letter to the secretary of the MHLG, from Lady Ritson, Highgate 22 August 1953, loose in ibid.
64 Ibid.
65 Ibid.
66 Memo to Mr Waddell, 25 September 1953, loose in ibid.
67 Ibid.
68 Ibid.
69 Draft letter to Lady Ritson, no date, loose in ibid.
70 Ibid.
71 Draft letter to Lady Ritson (no.2), no date, loose in ibid.
72 Ibid.
73 Ibid.
74 Internal correspondence, 8 October 1953, to Mr Phillips from Mr Waddell, loose in ibid.
75 Letter to Lady Ritson, 22 October 1953, from A. Sharp, 1, loose in ibid.
76 Ibid.
77 Ibid., 2.
78 Ibid.
79 Letter from J. A. C. Platts to the RFAC, 28 June 1956, loose in Royal Fine Art Commission, 'Crooms Hill: Opposition to Design of Lamp Standards', BP 2/103.
80 Extract from minutes of the 341st meeting of the RFAC held on 11 July 1956, loose in ibid; Letter to Harold Whetstone, the Town Clerk of Greenwich, from Godfrey Samuel, RFAC, 7 July 1956, ibid.
81 Letter from Harold Whetstone, the Town Clerk, Greenwich to Godfrey Samuel, the RFAC, 23 July 1956, loose in ibid.
82 Letter from J. A. C. Platts to the RFAC, 14 September 1956, loose in ibid.
83 During the approval process for lighting columns, the RFAC raised the objection that 'fashions change and designs approved by the Commission many years ago might not be passed by them today', in minutes of a meeting held on 5 March 1951 by the MoT, signed by JRW, in Ministry of Transport, 'Highways Engineering: Registered Files. Street Lighting. Design of Lamp Standards: Including Painting and Guidance by Royal Fine Art Commission', MT 95/210.
84 Letter from J. A. C. Platts to the RFAC, 14 September 1956, loose in Royal Fine Art Commission, 'Crooms Hill: Opposition to Design of Lamp Standards', BP 2/103.
85 Letter from Godfrey Samuel, the RFAC, to the Secretary of the MHLG, 22 February 1957, loose in ibid.
86 Letter to Godfrey Samuel from the Royal Commission on Historical Monuments, 27 March 1957, loose in ibid.
87 Letter to the Town Clerk, Metropolitan Borough of Greenwich 15 April 1957, from R. Brain, MHLG, loose in ibid.
88 Ibid.

89 For instance, while the GG expressed its preference for steel – see 'Annual Report of the Georgian Group' cited in the *MJ*, 9 July 1954, Vol. 62, 1569 – readers of the *AR* doubted its advantages over concrete. See P. Michael Thomas, the *AR*, September 1955, Vol. 118, No. 705, 142.
90 Letter from L. Rawlins, Stanton Ironworks Company Limited to D. Williams at the MoT, 22 February 1956, loose in Ministry of Transport, 'Highways Engineering: Registered Files. Street Lighting. Design of Lamp Standards: Including Painting and Guidance by Royal Fine Art Commission', MT 95/210.
91 'Self Appointed Expert Is the Curse of Local Government', the *MJ*, 26 April 1957, Vol. 65, 887.
92 The *MJ*, 27 September 1957, Vol. 65, 2031.
93 See Adrian Forty, *Concrete and Culture: A Material History* (London: Reaktion, 2012).
94 'Street Furniture', internal letter to Deputy Secretary, 19 March 1953, from Mr Beaufoy, 2, loose in Ministry of Housing and Local Government, 'Street Lighting: General Questions and Correspondence on Design Amenity and Aesthetics'. HLG 51/847.
95 According to Beaufoy: 'As you know, we had quite a battle to keep the concrete standards out of the High Street at Canterbury and to get Transport to release about 3-tons of steel as an alternative', loose in ibid.
96 Internal correspondence to Mr Phillips from Mr Beaufoy, 26 October 1953, loose in ibid.
97 'Street Furniture', internal letter to Deputy Secretary, 19 March 1953, from Mr Beaufoy, 2, loose in ibid.
98 Internal correspondence, 26 October 1953, to Mr Phillips from Mr Beaufoy, loose in ibid.
99 Ibid.
100 Extract from minutes of 378th meeting of the RFAC, 9 December 1959, loose in Royal Fine Art Commission, 'Crooms Hill: Opposition to Design of Lamp Standards', BP 2/103.
101 Letter from H. F. Summers [MHLG] to Godfrey Samuel [RFAC] 10 May 1957, loose in ibid.
102 Ibid.
103 Letter to Mr Oakley, 29 November 1957, from Godfrey Samuel [RFAC] loose in ibid.
104 Peter Whitworth, 'Street Furniture', *The Times Review of Industry*, 11 October 1962, in Council of Industrial Design. 'Street Furniture: Articles and Lectures'. Box 220 (1432.15 Part III).
105 The *Daily Telegraph*, 8 December 1959. For further details on the communication between these groups after the *Daily Telegraph* report, see 'Telephone Message One: From Peter Whitworth (CoID), 8 December 1959, Subject: Street Lighting, Blackheath', 2, loose in Royal Fine Art Commission, 'Crooms Hill: Opposition to Design of Lamp Standards', BP 2/103.
106 'Council's Lamp Standards Will Come Down – Residents Pay For and Put Up Type They Like', *The Kentish Mercury*, 29 July 1960.
107 Email correspondence with Ian Hay Davison.
108 Blackheath Park Lighting Fund, letter to residents (Ian Hay Davison Personal Collection).
109 Letter to Mr Bilsby, 3 March 1962 from Ian Hay Davison, in ibid.

110 'Council's Lamp Standards Will Come Down – Residents Pay For and Put Up Type They Like', *The Kentish Mercury*, 29 July 1960.
111 Paul Reilly, *Lamp Post Feature: Notes Sent to Lord Snowdon (Confidential)*, 19 March 1962, in Council of Industrial Design. 'Street Furniture: Articles and Lectures'. Box 220 (1432.15 Part III).
112 Whitworth, 'Street Furniture', ibid.
113 The RFAC, *14th Annual Report – 1955 and 1956*, (London: February 1957), 13.
114 'Eton Street Lighting Is Not Just a Local Authority Matter', the *MJ*, 14 September 1956, Vol. 64, 2115–17.
115 'Topic Three on Agenda: Government Building: Broad Sanctuary', minutes of meeting, 6 March 1962, in CAB 195/20 0045.
116 'Cabinet Conclusions of a Meeting Held at 10 Downing Street on the 25th June 1964', 3–4, CAB 128/38 0047.
117 See *Design*, No. 134, February 1960, 34; 'Oliver Messel Puts the Case Against Those Chelsea Lamps', the *Evening Standard*, 25 May 1960, 20, loose in Office of Works, Ancient Monuments and Historic Buildings: Registered Files. General. Proposed Scheduling of Old Lampposts and other 'Street Furniture', WORK 14/2302.
118 Letter from Oliver Messel to John Hope MP, 9 June 1960, re. Chelsea Lamp posts, loose in ibid.
119 Letter from Mr N. Digney, 1 July 1960, loose in ibid.
120 Ibid.
121 Letter from John Hope MP to Mr Henry Brooke [MHLG], 7 July 1960, loose in ibid
122 Letter from Mr Henry Brooke [MHLG] to John Hope MP, 4 August 1960 loose in ibid.
123 Ibid., 2.
124 Ibid.
125 Letter to Oliver Messel from John Hope, MP, 15 September 1960 loose in ibid.
126 *Design*, No. 134, February 1960, 34.
127 Ibid.
128 Derek Barton, 'New Lamps in Old Streets', the *AR*, June 1960, 411, loose in Ministry of Transport, 'Ministry of Transport and Successors, Highways Management and Services Division: Registered Files. Street Lighting. Council of Industrial Design: Design of Street Lighting Equipment', MT 109/132.
129 Ibid., 411–15.
130 Ibid., 412.
131 According to Barton, 'the Marylebone Borough Council… went to the length of putting up three different types of lamp outside the Town Hall and inviting citizens to ballot for their choice (as it turned out, the preference was for the most expensive)' in ibid.
132 Ibid.
133 Ibid.
134 Ibid.
135 Ibid., 415.
136 Ibid., 416.
137 Ibid.
138 The *MJ*, 2 December 1955, Vol. 63, 3269.
139 'People and Places', the *MJ*, 1 June 1956, Vol. 64, 1245.
140 Ian Nairn, *Counter Attack against Subtopia* (London: The AP, 1957), 407
141 'Mr Machin Accepts a Lamp-post (Curlicues and All). His Wife Chains Him to It to Defy Subtopia'. *The Daily Mail*, 12 July 1956.

142 Correspondence with Dominic Newton, March 2015. See *Artist of an Icon: The Memoirs of Arnold Machin by A. Machin* (Guildford and Kings Lynn: Biddles, 2002). For more information, see The Machin Arts Foundation. Available online: http://www.machin-arts-foundation.org.uk/ (accessed 31 July 2015).
143 The *MJ*, 29 May 1959, Vol. 67, 1466.
144 This may not be surprising given the Arts and Crafts legacy of the area, see the *MJ*, 16 December 1960, Vol. 68, 3993.
145 The *MJ*, 26 October 1962, Vol. 70.
146 The *MJ*, 16 November 1962, Vol. 70, 3536.
147 'LCC General Purposes Committee Papers and Minutes October–December 1962', 378.
148 *Design*, No. 169, January 1962, 27.
149 Ibid.
150 Joint Report by Chief Engineer, Architect and Valuer to Council, LCC: South Bank Development, Minute 6542. 11 November 1962 Presented to Council on 22 October 1962', 1, in 'LCC General Purposes Committee Papers and Minutes October-December 1962'.
151 Concurrent report 17 October 1962 by the Comptroller of the Council Frank Holland, Minute 6542. 11 November 1962 Presented to Council on 22 October 1962, 1, in 'LCC General Purposes Committee Papers and Minutes October–December 1962'; Point No.13 By Mr Sebag-Montefiore of the Chairman of the General Purposes Committee [Freda Corbet], 13 November 1962, in 'LCC Minutes and Records 1962', 838.
152 'Art and the Lamp-post', *The Times*, 27 November 1962, 11.
153 'Landscape Architecture in County Development Plan', the *MJ*, 7 March 1952, Vol. 60, 495; 'APLE Conference', the *MJ*, 17 September 1954, Vol. 62, 2213.
154 Ibid., 2215.
155 'Exhibition Marks a Step Forward in Design of Litter Bins', the *MJ*, 14 October 1960, Vol. 68, 3198.
156 'Drab Litter Bins', the *MJ*, 16 September 1955, Vol. 63, 2480.
157 The *MJ*, 6 June 1958, Vol. 66, 1374.
158 'In Defiance of a Colour Bar by Durham County Council', the *MJ*, 6 April 1962, Vol. 70, 990.
159 'That Controversial Litter Bin', the *MJ*, 15 September 1961, Vol. 69, 2937.
160 The *MJ*, 12 October 1956, Vol. 64, 2379.
161 The *MJ*, 15 February 1957, Vol. 65, 324.
162 'Landscape Architecture in County Development Plan', the *MJ*, 7 March 1952, Vol. 60, 495.
163 'Good Taste in Planning', the *MJ*, 30 December 1955, Vol. 63, 3469.
164 Prof. A. E. Richardson, 'The Rebuilding of London', the *MJ*, 2 July 1955, Vol. 63, 2057.
165 Peter Shepheard, 'Landscape in the Town', the *MJ*, 22 July 1955, Vol. 63, 1981–2.
166 'Correspondence', the *AR*, December 1955, Vol. 118, No. 708, 352.
167 Ibid.
168 L. Dudley Stamp, 'Municipal Engineer a "Despoiler of Britain"', letter, the *MJ*, 30 November 1956, Vol. 64, 2823.
169 Ibid.
170 Ibid.
171 Ibid.

172 W. P. Haldane, 'Subtopia, "Engineer Is Not the Culprit"', letter, the *MJ*, 7 December 1956, Vol. 64, 2869.
173 Ibid.
174 Ibid.
175 K. E. Cotton, 'Letter to the Editor', the *MJ*, 14 December 1956, Vol. 64, 2923; Mr Williams, 'Letter to the Editor', the *MJ*, 28 December 1956, Vol. 64.
176 R. Nicholas, 'Letter to the Editor: "Individualism in Street Furniture"', the *MJ*, 4 January 1957, Vol. 65, 10.
177 A. C. Wildsmith, ibid.
178 The *MJ*, 2 April 1965, Vol. 73, 1162.
179 A. C. Wildsmith, 'Letter to the Editor', the *MJ*, 4 January 1957, Vol. 65, 10.
180 H. D. Hargreaves, ibid.
181 'Public Lighting', the *MJ*, 8 March 1957, Vol. 65, 503.
182 Ibid.
183 Ibid.
184 'Self Appointed Expert Is the Curse of Local Government', the *MJ*, 26 April 1957, Vol. 65, 887.
185 'More Lights Needed to Make Cities Gayer', the *MJ*, 19 March 1965, Vol. 73, 956.
186 'Shedding More Light on a Lipstick Problem', the *MJ*, 10 April 1959, Vol. 67.
187 'APLE Conference', the *MJ*, 6 October 1961, Vol. 69, 3208.
188 Ibid.
189 Hugh Casson, 'Defence against Subtopia', the *MJ*, 4 May 1956, Vol. 64, 995.
190 'Self Appointed Expert Is the Curse of Local Government', the *MJ*, 26 April 1957, Vol. 65, 887.
191 Ibid.
192 Ibid.
193 Ibid.
194 'Public Lighting', the *MJ*, 8 March 1957, Vol. 65, 503.
195 'Self Appointed Expert Is the Curse of Local Government', the *MJ*, 26 April 1957, Vol. 65, 887.
196 'Value of Experience in Street Light Planning', the *MJ*, 25 September 1959, Vol. 67, 2647.
197 'Self Appointed Expert Is the Curse of Local Government', the *MJ*, 26 April 1957, Vol. 65, 887.
198 'Notebook', the *MJ*, 11 October 1957, Vol. 65, 2147.
199 'Value of Experience in Street Light Planning', the *MJ*, 25 September 1959, Vol. 67, 2647.
200 Ian Nairn, 'Counter-Attack', the *AR*, December 1956, Vol. 120, No. 179.
201 Ibid., 351.
202 Ibid., 353.
203 Ibid., 357.
204 Ibid., 365.
205 Ibid.
206 Ibid., 393.
207 'Counter Outrage', *Punch*, 13 February 1957, 246.
208 Marginalia, the *AR*, April 1957, Vol. 121, No. 723, 221.
209 'Counter-Attack: The Next Stage in the Fight against Subtopia', the *AR*, June 1957, Vol. 121, No. 725, 405.
210 Ibid.

211 Ibid., 406.
212 Ibid., 407; 'Counter-Attack', the *AR*, August–September 1959, Vol. 125, No. 751, 135.
213 'Counter-Attack', the *AR*, June 1957, Vol. 121, No. 725, 407.
214 'Counter-Attack', the *AR*, April 1957, Vol. 121, No. 723, 273.
215 'Counter-Attack', the *AR*, June 1957, Vol. 121, No. 725, 407.
216 Ibid.
217 Ibid.
218 Ibid.
219 'Counter Attack', the *AR*, July 1957, Vol. 122, No. 726, 78.
220 'Counter-Attack', the *AR*, June 1958, Vol. 123, No. 737, 422–3.
221 'Counter-Attack', the *AR*, November 1957, Vol. 122, No. 730, 347.
222 'Object Lesson – Townscape', the *AR*, July 1958, Vol. 124, No. 738, 43–6.
223 'Counter-Attack', the *AR*, November 1957, Vol. 122, No. 730, 348.
224 'Counter-Attack', the *AR*, June 1957, Vol. 121, No. 725, 451.
225 'Counter-Attack', the *AR*, February 1958, Vol. 123, No. 733, 141.
226 Ibid.
227 Ibid.
228 Ibid.
229 'Correspondence', the *AR*, October 1961, Vol. 130, No. 776, 226.
230 'Correspondence', the *AR*, December 1961, Vol. 130, No. 778, 374.

Chapter 5

BEYOND GOOD DESIGN: A PERIOD OF TRANSFORMATION, 1960-1974

In a confidential letter to Lord Snowdon in 1962, Paul Reilly advised him on his new appointment as member of the Council of Industrial Design. Since part of the job involved engaging with street furniture, Reilly considered it wise to warn Snowdon that 'practically no two artists, painters, sculptors, architects or planners seem to agree on this subject'.[1] The design of street furniture was certainly divisive. Indeed, by the 1960s some members of the CoID suggested it had merely become 'fashionable' to protest about street furniture, and all that was needed to incite such a reaction was 'for an official body to erect or remove something from a public place'.[2] Others perceived the criticism of street furniture as having become a 'sport' in which works committees and engineers were baited by 'eminent architects, aged actors and journalists alike', and 'the excitement of blooding one or other of the contestants has tended to eclipse the real problem'.[3] But what was the 'real' problem?

To understand the progression of the debate, it is vital to locate the period historically. By the early 1960s, Britain was in the middle of a transformation. Though it might not have felt like it for those living outside major cities, it is a widely accepted view of the period in question.[4] This transformation was, according to historian Arthur Marwick, experienced largely in terms of opportunities and freedoms, in which individuality, diversity, equality and prosperity sat alongside wider access to education, housing and health care.[5] Yet it was also expressed through design – not just stylistically, but also the way in which design was understood and discussed. Increasingly, the very concept of Good Design and those who promoted it were criticized. Modernism was beginning to fall out of professional and popular favour and as the government's official voice on design, much of this criticism was levelled at the CoID. Such criticism was part of a wider campaign to recognize the voice of the consumer and represent his/her interests. It was led by magazines like *Which?* and the *Shoppers Guide*, whose independent tests on the performance of British products illuminated the inconsistencies within the CoID's own evaluation procedures. As a result of these tests, the CoID was perceived by some to be complicit in a farcical evaluation process at the public's expense.[6]

The subsequent commentary about the CoID's inconsistent evaluation criteria reveals the extent to which questions about Good Design and taste dominated the debate during the 1960s. While some journalists, like Kenneth J. Robinson in *The Spectator*, defended the CoID and claimed that 'those of us who try to preach about good design being practical have to take a lot on trust (after all we can't afford to set up elaborate testing laboratories),'[7] others took a firmer line. Fellow *Spectator* critic Katharine Whitehorn castigated the CoID for its inconsistencies – reflected, she said, in the Design Awards – and she recalled that her 'timid questions about practicality were received with a vague surprise'.[8] Whitehorn also perceived the designs on display for the Design Awards as too tasteful, too elegant and attractive. They were, according to Whitehorn, 'all right and proper, sane and fine. But perhaps somewhere there is an ecstatic lunatic commissioning something absolutely preposterous that will knock these eighteen into an agreeable, pleasing and appropriate cocked hat.'[9] Whitehorn's perception of the CoID as representing a rigid understanding of modern design was even shared out-with the right-of-centre context of *The Spectator*. Indeed two years earlier at a Society of Industrial Artists event, the left-leaning poet Stephen Spender made a speech criticizing the CoID's narrow interpretation of modernism, in which functionalism translated into 'bareness, simplicity, squareness or roundness, solidity, seriousness'.[10] A perception was growing that the CoID was being strangled by its own restrictive understanding of taste, and that dullness was winning out over genuinely imaginative and novel form.

Even members of the public increasingly saw good taste as something to be wary of. In response to Whitehorn, a reader from Cambridge observed that, 'Deadly good taste and design for design's sake, with too little regard for practical use, seem to me to be the main pitfalls into which organizations like the CoID are likely to fall'.[11] Unwilling to let such perceptions go unchecked, the CoID responded quickly with a firm but deftly phrased defence of its approach.[12] Reilly replied: 'It is surely premature for Mrs. Scurfield's attack on "deadly good taste" while good design is still so scarce a commodity, but if ... she equates "deadly good taste" with "styling" and "gimmicky sales-boosting ideas", then I am with her all the way, though "deadly bad taste" might have been a better description.'[13] That Reilly chose to defend the integrity of the CoID from attack by a member of the public not only emphasizes the influence of *The Spectator* but also the fragility of the CoID's authority.

Invariably the CoID rebuked its critics through *Design*. Functional efficiency was not the only criterion of value, *Design* reported in May 1961, and neither should appearance be considered 'a dirty word', since good appearance only meant that standardization, safety and consumer needs 'have been brought together in a sensible and logical way'.[14] Though much of this discussion was directed towards consumer goods, street furniture was also expected to convey such qualities. One litter bin in particular was celebrated in that year's Design Centre Awards for being 'attractive to look at ... easy to clean [and] ideal for crowded pedestrian ways'; however, it is hard to imagine a less practical object of street furniture (see Figure 5.1).[15] Perhaps as a result of objects like this, *Design* was repeatedly forced to readdress the question of appearance in 1961. On one occasion, *Design* responded to the hypothetical concerns of a manufacturer who complained about the degree of criticism his product received, and it reported that,

Figure 5.1 'Town Number One' cylindrical litter bin: Not only a Design Centre Award winner but also attractive and 'ideal for crowded pedestrian ways'. Designed by Derek Goad and John Ricks for G. A. Harvey & Co. (London) Ltd, a 1961 CoID Design Centre Award winner. Design Council Archive, University of Brighton Design Archives.

"surely it would be better", they say, "to explain what is good about the good things and what is bad about the bad". There is of course much good sense in these comments. But there is also a degree of misunderstanding of our motives... We believe there are valid reasons for choosing the most interesting *looking* designs for analysis... our intention is less to provide a guide to what is best on the market than to suggest, through a close study of individual products, what are the things that really matter in design.[16]

The implication is that only a select group of professionals with superior taste could define the things that really mattered in design. It was an attitude which was increasingly rejected by others, including Robinson who had earlier observed that 'some people really like to make design sound as complex as possible', and he poured scorn on the notion that design required 'a special understanding'.[17]

Reyner Banham and questions of taste

While intervention by the design profession to improve the public's taste or impose a particular aesthetic upon Britain might have been tolerated in the immediate aftermath of the war, by the early 1960s there were signs of a growing distrust towards experts and professionalism more generally. These interventions, however subtle, became increasingly unwelcome, and challenges from members of the public were quickly supported by challenges from those within the design profession.

Reyner Banham had been a long-standing critic of the CoID, and his views illustrate this wider sense of distrust. When writing for the *New Statesman* in 1960, Banham rejected the CoID's fixation on slogans like 'a good design is forever', as well as the boy-scout language it used, which he described as 'campfire jargon' with its references to 'sock-pulling-up' operations.[18] He also accused it of being fundamentally patronizing, particularly when products proved popular, which the CoID perceived as 'playing down to the lowest common denominator of public taste'.[19] Such a conflation of populism and bad taste was at the core of Banham's objection to the CoID, for whom 'the old standardized and unquestioned public school pink-propositions that all common taste is bad and all commercialism is evil appear to need some revision'.[20] He also asked 'how can you condemn public taste as "low" without adopting a position of snobbery intolerable in a Liberal let alone a Socialist?'[21] The issue clearly centred on the principle of democracy, and Banham observed that 'the concept of good design as a form of aesthetic charity done on the labouring poor from a great height is incompatible with democracy as I see it'.[22]

While little of Banham's argument specifically refers to street furniture, it goes straight to the heart of a debate in which discussions of lamp posts and parking meters reflected increasing anxiety about exactly whose taste was informing the design of Britain's streets. As the previous chapters have shown, Good Design – i.e. modernism – after the war was associated with reconstruction and economic progress, but it was also linked to what design historian Stephen Hayward has called an 'elitist taste culture'.[23] The relationship between Good Design and taste has already been established, but for Banham, it reeked of snobbery. The following year Banham published another article in the *New Statesman* about the CoID's methods of assessment. According to Banham, the CoID was aware that they had 'some lemons on the books', but were unable to act because of two fatal institutional flaws.[24] The first flaw was attributed to the CoID's literal interpretation of the slogan 'form follows function', but the second flaw was legislative. Government, according to Banham, had created 'a conscience without limbs, able to worry but not to act, and like other impotent consciences it has festered'.[25] As a result, 'the Council suffers from persecution mania…a ponderous internal censorship; automatic assumption of moral right to support ("After all, old man, we're all on the same side really") and the usual civil service neurosis'.[26] Banham's observation echoes a point made earlier likening the CoID to a government department, but it also shows his sensitivity towards the CoID's moral agenda. Banham wondered whether improving the nation's taste was a morally sound objective, and he doubted whether it was 'a fit occupation for grown men any how – at any rate, not if "taste" is interpreted in the narrowest middle-class sense that the Council understands'.[27]

Banham's concern about the moral and class-based agenda of the CoID was reflected in the debate around street furniture. Much of the discussion about what street furniture should look like and who was responsible was couched in terms of education, taste and proximity to the marketplace – all of which are implicitly class-based. And for the CoID, modern street furniture not only expressed the values of Good Design, but was also a means of improving the public's taste. Such an attitude eventually came to be seen as patronizing since it was based on the distinct perception that middle-class taste was ultimately preferable to the taste of the general public. Banham's concern was shared by a number of other influential figures at this time. In 1962 Misha Black criticized the CoID in *Motif* for adopting 'a position of moral self-righteousness no different from that of the sermonizing total abstainer'.[28] For Black, anyone who deliberately sat outside popular taste assumed 'that his taste, his appreciation of what forms properly reflect his period, is more righteous, or at least more sensitive, than that of the public for which he is working', which effectively amounted to a moral judgement upon society.[29] Such views were representative of a growing sense of scepticism about standards of taste and the distance those who promoted it maintained from wider society.

The anxiety expressed by the likes of Banham and Black about cultural leadership and its democratic implications eventually reached government. In her 1965 white paper, *A Policy for the Arts: The First Steps*, Arts Minister Jennie Lee sought to clarify government's position on cultural leadership by announcing that, 'the relationship between artist and state in modern democratic community is not easily defined. No one would wish state patronage to dictate taste or in any way restrict the liberty of even the most unorthodox and experimental of artists.'[30] Such a claim extended to ensuring high standards in many aspects of British life, not least its urban surroundings and landscape. According to Lee, it was only by ensuring the central place of the arts in everyday life that Britain could regard herself as a civilized community, and she credited the work of the CoID in this regard, and welcomed the organization's efforts to encourage good industrial design.[31] However, the paper also stated:

> No democratic government would seek to impose controls on all the things that contribute to our environment and affect our senses. But abuses can be spotted and tackled, high standards encouraged… It is partly a question of bridging the gap between what have come to be called the "higher" forms of entertainment and the traditional sources… and to challenge the fact that a gap exists. In the world of jazz the process has already happened: highbrow and lowbrow have met.[32]

Lee's white paper reflects a sense that, by the mid-1960s, state-funded organizations like the CoID were being encouraged to reflect a wider range of interests, voices, tastes and interpretations, so as to represent the full breadth of cultural practice in Britain. But how could an organization committed to raising standards of taste fulfil these expectations?

Once the sacred bond between Good Design and good taste was perceived to be negotiable, the CoID was forced to reconsider its remit. The value-laden binary distinctions that had formed the central spine of the CoID – between good and bad, old and new, modern and old-fashioned, enlightened and unenlightened, progressive and reactionary – had undergone considerable stress. What had begun as a question about consumer protection had gradually extended into whether it was possible to measure the qualities of any product, or indeed define Good Design at all. As a consequence the CoID underwent a period of transition during the mid-1960s. Writing in the *MJ* in 1967, CoID officer David Davies defined well-designed street furniture as 'no different from that of other articles with industrial design content: fitness of purpose, proper use of materials, and of course, good appearance'.[33] That same year, however, *Design* acknowledged that Good Design was beginning to appear authoritarian, sterile, 'middle-aged and middle class', and it attributed this reaction to the 'anything goes' attitude of swinging London.[34] Such was the pressure upon the CoID that it was forced to acknowledge that 'good design is not a constant but a variable', a concession which essentially undermines the whole concept.[35]

What was much harder for the CoID to accept was the suggestion that there was no moral basis to Good Design. Since its formation, the CoID had promoted the idea that Good Design could be used as a social tool to improve people's environments and therefore their lives, a position seen as increasingly untenable by the 1960s. Invariably, Banham led the chorus of this criticism. Alongside the architect Henry Dreyfuss, Banham criticized the perceived relationship between morality and style at the International Design Conference in Aspen in November 1966. In line with previous statements, Banham rejected the idea that an object could reflect the morality of its author as demonstrably false, claiming that 'the glitter of a morally sound style does not guarantee a stainless reputation to the product in use'.[36] Such a direct rejection of modernism's inherent morality also rejected the original terms of Good Design.

Yet Banham's speech at Aspen went much further than just criticizing the theory underpinning modern design. He also made the link between the actions of post-war design reformers, and their counterparts in the nineteenth-century. Looking back, Banham proposed that men like Ruskin and Morris were responsible for the 'British tradition of worrying about the state of design', which had led to one of the most misunderstood notions in cultural history: the concept of moral improvement through design.[37] According to Banham, this concept was both 'one of the great intellectual resources of our times … [and] also one of its most powerful sources of confusion'.[38] And it led designers to go to 'camp meetings in the mountains to be told what's right and what's wrong' – a reference to Aspen no doubt – which represented an attempt on the part of the design profession 'to keep itself morally pure by public self-examination'.[39] Such self-examination, according to Banham, was allegedly wasted because of the self-regarding nature of the design profession, which elevated 'the demands of private conscience'.[40] To support this point, Banham returned to Morris and his followers who, he said,

> believed the only good product was one that brought pleasure to its producer. You will hear this proposition usually in the guarded and inverted form that mass production is evil because it brings no pleasure to the worker, but which ever way you phrase it, the whole conception is anti-social and perverse. No more in design than in dentistry can society accept that the first responsibility of its servants is to please themselves.[41]

Banham's analysis goes right to the central tension within post-war debates about Good Design – which he called the 'evil backside on the face of public concern' – in which design was simultaneously used to improve standards for the public good, and also conform to what a select group of people believed to be good. For Banham, this approach was deliberate, because it reinforced 'the belief that design is a thankless task [which] definitely appeals to the martyr complex that design has inherited from its artistic forbears'.[42] Moreover, 'being out of step was a guarantee to their consciences that they were in the right, for design is also part of the great progressive do-gooder complex of ideas based upon the proposition that the majority is always wrong, that the public must be led, cajoled, sticked and garroted onward and upward'.[43] The picture painted by Banham is a familiar one, in which the public was routinely depicted as unable to identify Good Design without the help of experienced design professionals.

While issued in his characteristically combative style, Banham's comments bring a set of ideas about design together. His awareness of the relationship between nineteenth-century design debates and twentieth-century Good Design discourse provides an interpretation of why design reformers used the idea of morality to justify what was essentially taste. The concept of moral improvement through design not only discredits existing design – which might be quite popular – and therefore positions the reformer at a distance from the public, but it also elevates the status of the task to a higher plane. The result is generally self-righteousness on the part of the reformer, and hostility from everyone else.

'The Challenge of Pop'

Largely as a result of attitudes like Banham's – a man who was fighting Good Design from within – the CoID was forced to acknowledge that its attempts to educate the British public on Good Design, and thus improve its taste, were not working. As early as August 1965, *Design* conceded that 'one thing is certain and that is that design education conducted as an exercise in how to acquire good taste is doomed'.[44] Perhaps in recognition of this, Reilly published 'The Challenge of Pop' in the *AR* in 1967. Reilly's article is an important articulation of the CoID's understanding of Good Design at the end of the 1960s since, while he admonished the CoID for encouraging sober designs when sobriety was out of step with the period, many of his arguments remained well within the framework of Good Design discourse. Even his decision to publish in the *AR* suggests a desire to speak to like-minded people (or 'a band of strolling aesthetes' according to Banham).[45] Reilly spoke of the temptation 'to swim with the tide', and in doing so, divided popular and elite culture, much like Pugin had done a century earlier.[46] He also spoke of his regret that 'a consensus of informed, unostentatious, almost neutral solutions' no longer dominated design culture.[47] Such seemly values, he said, were criticized by the 'trades' for being 'clinical, hygienic, aseptic and so *avant garde* as to be out of touch with the market place'.[48] In this way, Reilly reinforces the view that commercial culture was regressive, unseemly and contrary to Good Design – another position that has considerable precedent.

However, 'The Challenge of Pop' is also full of contradictions. For instance, Reilly noted the shift from permanent universal values to an

> acceptance that design may be valid at a given time for a given purpose to a given group of people in a given set of circumstances, but that outside those limits it may not be valid at all; and conversely there may be contemporaneous but quite dissimilar solutions that can still be equally defensible for different groups – mini skirt for the teenager, something less divulging for the matron; painted paper furniture for the young, teak or rosewood for the ageing – and all equally of their times and all equally susceptible of evaluation by a selection committee.[49]

Clearly, while willing to accept the validity of interpretation, Reilly felt compelled to maintain the authority of the committee as ultimate evaluator. In his efforts to remind the *AR*'s readers that the CoID was 'unashamedly adventurous and obviously interested by, if not itself the initiator of, current trends', he characterized its committees as defined by 'colour and pattern, even of gaiety and festivity' (an interpretation that may not have been widely shared).[50] Indeed, Reilly professed his belief that the value of the CoID's committees had only increased as a result of Carnaby Street, because there was an ever-greater need for 'compass and helm than was apparent in the world they have replaced'.[51] Reilly's comments are extraordinary, particularly the suggestion that Carnaby Street inadvertently created more committees. For Reilly, however, this placed the CoID at the centre of design culture again 'even if the things of which we are at the centre seem to be in conflict with much of the doctrine handed down to us'.[52] Reilly continued, 'it is, though, just because so many established canons and received ideas seem to crumple in face of the kinky flamboyance of this permissive, precocious, commercially successful popular culture that extra care must be taken to examine each twist and turn afresh'.[53] That 'extra care' could only be provided by the CoID, whose discipline, and 'common sense in the midst of nonsense', would continually seek the truth and 'sift the contributors from the charlatans when confronted with the challenge of pop'.[54]

Reilly's article is symptomatic of a major rethink among the CoID, which was quickly losing its authority as a taste-maker. By March 1968, however, the organization at least appeared to accept that in order to safeguard its future, some of its established doctrines would need to be revised. In 'Cold Rice Pudding and Revisionism', written by the artist Christopher Cornford for *Design*, the narrow view of Good Design was described as puritan and mean.[55] Cornford identified a paradox within the 'design establishment', which he said was 'common to all situations where something like a revolution has been achieved, whereby the one-time pioneers, without losing their ... sense of being the avant-garde, have now transmuted into elder statesmen, and conceivably in some cases into inadvertent reactionaries'.[56] While the CoID now qualified as reactionaries, Cornford attributed this status to the influence of figures associated with the Bauhaus, which had imposed upon Britain the narrow view that there could only be one ideal interpretation of Good Design. This interpretation was a platonic ideal which had led British design to a sterile dead-end, and reminded Cornford of 'cold rice pudding. It is plain, nutritious, highminded and off-white'.[57] That Good Design could be likened to a bland milk pudding, typical of school lunches across the country, reflects the extent of the turnaround forced upon the CoID by the new social, cultural and political context it found itself in. Cornford's observation was that contemporary society's appetite for being force fed a monotonous diet of Good Design – a 'clean uncluttered modern look' which was essentially based on making an object look tidy – was waning, and its desire to experiment with richer and more exotic design styles was in turn increasing.[58] But did this spell the end of Good Design? And how did these changes affect the country's street furniture?

Standardization and aesthetic monotony

While popular taste during the 1960s embraced individualism and diversity, there was simultaneously an official acceptance of standardized production in state-funded design projects. Thus even while government was rejecting cultural leadership and urging organizations like the CoID to reflect a broader range of tastes, it was at the same time making design decisions on behalf of the nation. Signage, public lettering, postboxes and traffic lights were all affected by these national design projects during the 1960s. These ubiquitous objects relied on a broad set of ideas out-with the doctrine of Good Design to give them shape, including modernization, functionalism and standardization, as well as methods like systems design and ergonomics.

Standardization is a key theme within post-war design debates. Standardized methods of production had played a major role in the state's wartime economy, and continued to be important after the war, much to the amusement of *Punch* which mocked it as a craze.[59] But standardization also heavily influenced the design of street furniture, and it had several advantages in this context. After all, if the design of street furniture could be standardized, mass-produced and installed across the country, then it would not only increase efficiency and reduce production costs, but also act as a visual cipher of modernity, and help combat the visual anarchy or urban clutter that many abhorred. Despite these apparent advantages, complaints about the standardization of street furniture began as early as 1950 and the RFAC frequently received letters expressing apprehension about the subject.[60] The threat of standardized street lighting was even discussed in government and in 1952 the Minister of Transport responded to questions in the House of Commons by rejecting any evidence that 'differing types of street lighting cause confusion or that to standardize them would necessarily improve efficiency in lighting'.[61] London, another MP observed, possessed an 'extraordinary variety of lighting' and that 'uniformity has a great deal to be said for it'.[62] Cabinet took a different view, and according to the Transport minister, 'I would say that there are disadvantages in absolute standardization because streets are quite different – the colour of building materials and the height of buildings are different'.[63] Clearly at this point, the topic of standardization was seen to be acceptable in the context of illumination alone, but not in the context of the design itself. Standardizing technology was one thing; standardizing the appearance of technology was another.

In 1952 standardization and uniformity were often conflated to mean the same thing. Both were used negatively, and even today, there are regular reports in the press that present standardization as a threat to individuality.[64] In 1952, the *MJ* recognized the need to distinguish between the two expressions, particularly given the importance of street furniture to local authorities. It distinguished between 'uniformity of type and standardization of performance', clarifying that 'uniformity in almost any sphere is something to be discouraged', yet standardization by contrast was to be admired.[65]

The CoID remained committed to promoting standardized street furniture, since it offered a way to extend the rational values of Good Design over the British landscape.[66] However, standardization was routinely linked to a further term: monotony, which was offensive to many people. Much of the anxiety about modern street furniture was linked to a perception that the seemingly repetitive, boring, monotonous qualities of such objects would threaten the visual character and identity of the country. For many people in post-war Britain, a landscape in which all street furniture looked the same regardless of context and where idiosyncrasies were systematically removed was a truly frightening prospect. This fear could be understood as a desire to protect the diversity of Britain – seen in terms of its culture, environment and design vernacular – but it could also be attributed to ideas about Britain as an island characterized by eccentricity, individualism and separatism. Alternatively, fears about monotony might be linked to ideas of foreignness in which modern street furniture design represented the unchecked power of the state, which in turn was seen as threatening the democratic rights of British people.

This was certainly the view held by John Betjeman, for whom modern street furniture was an expression of tyranny. Partly because of his earlier efforts, Betjeman emerged as a sort of figurehead for the protection of local architectural and cultural heritage, and he was often invited to participate in local campaigns. Following one such invitation, from a resident of Lyme Regis about the town's 'beastly' new lamp posts, Betjeman replied:

> It is just the sort of town that could not stand them, since the skyline is so important there and the streets are so narrow... you were right to say that Lyme is not a standard town. But Town clerks are all standard men and so are the pettifogging Borough Surveyors who erect these concrete lamp standards. You have been subjected to the usual tyranny.[67]

Standard in this case is clearly meant as an insult, but it is important to remember that those who were responsible for street furniture on the ground – local authorities – were democratically elected to represent the interests of their communities. Though people like Betjeman might have objected to their methods and taste, local authorities were not tyrants, and could (in theory at least) be held to account for their actions.

As a result of these perceptions and anxiety over terms like standardization, uniformity and monotony, the debate shifted to accommodate an alternative expression – coordination – which was presented in the *AR* at least, as being the principal goal in street furniture design. Street furniture that was not coordinated was intractable and disrupting to the coherence of the streetscape, and merely contributed to the 'litter of unrelated, generally ill-designed junk with which our streets are festooned'.[68] Yet the problem with street furniture was considered almost impossible to solve when authority for the design of the street – and the numerous objects of street furniture – was so fragmented. In recognition of this problem, the state began to take a much more direct approach towards the design of Britain's street furniture.

Standardized road signs

There are several important examples of street furniture having been standardized on a national scale during the late 1950s–1960s, and because of their reach, such projects made an enormous contribution to the look of Britain. One of the earliest of these projects concerned the road signing system. Up until 1955 Britain's roads had included a diverse variety of road signs, despite some effort to provide official guidance in 1933.[69] However, after the war renewed interest and investment in transport led many to believe that Britain's signing system was old fashioned, too wordy, inconspicuous and easy to misinterpret, and thus dangerous. Consequently, in 1957 the Ministry of Transport established the Advisory Committee on Traffic Signs for Motorways, known as the Anderson Committee after its chairman Sir Colin Anderson. The objective of the Anderson Committee was to address the problem of signage for the Preston Bypass in Lancashire (the forerunner of the motorway system) then under construction.[70] Graphic designer Richard 'Jock' Kinneir was appointed as design consultant to the committee, in partnership with his former student Margaret Calvert. Since the new road would accommodate speeds of up to 70mph and was free of intersections, the primary objective of the committee was to develop a more legible and safer set of signs (see Figure 5.2). After a series of experiments, the Anderson Committee published its recommendations in 1962, which included a white-on-blue colour scheme for the signs, a much

Figure 5.2 Blue road sign model made by Jock Kinneir and Margaret Calvert for a presentation to the Worboys Committee, Ministry of Transport circa 1962. Courtesy of St Bride Foundation.

larger scale, extensive use of pictograms, a new typeface (later known as Transport) and mixed-case sans serif lettering. The MoT happily accepted the committee's recommendations for the new road and the Preston Bypass scheme was widely considered a success.

Out-with motorways, however, the rest of Britain's road signage remained as disorganized as ever, with local authorities like Oxford completely ignoring advice on best practice and producing their own idiosyncratic designs.[71] Many began to wonder if in fact the new signing system should be extended across the entire road network, and in 1961 Parliament appointed the Worboys Committee for All Purpose Roads to consider this very idea. Working together with the Anderson Committee, the police and the Road Research Laboratory, the Worboys Committee conducted a major review into the suitability of different road signing systems in Europe and America, and published its recommendations in 1964. The final set of designs, which drew heavily on the earlier Anderson system and conformed to European standards, were endorsed by the Ministry of Transport in 1965.[72]

Having worked alongside Kinneir for both phases of the road signing project, Calvert is well placed to reflect on how the signs were actually designed. In an interview with Rick Poyner in 2004, Calvert insisted that 'style never came into it. You were driving towards the absolute essence.'[73] Many of the design decisions were driven by practical realities. The appearance of the signs was reduced to maximize communication and minimize cost, and steel was chosen on the basis of economy since it could be recycled and sold for a good price. Calvert also claims that both she and Kinneir deliberately sought to position their designs outside of the framework of good taste, which for Calvert 'meant death ... conventional, boredom, safety. It lacked personality. It was a three-piece suite in olive green.'[74]

However, the designers did not take design decisions alone. According to Calvert the decision to extend the signs across all roads was made by civil servant T. G. Usborne, who worked as chairman of the working party for the Worboys Committee.[75] Final designs also needed the approval of the committee, and many of their members were highly aesthetically conscious. For a start, both the Anderson and Worboys committees represented a familiar group of people: Worboys acted as CoID chairman, and Hugh Casson acted as chairman for the RFAC and was associated with the *AR*. Other committee members included J. M. Richards, editor of the *AR*, the street furniture designer Jack Howe, who, like Jock Kinneir, was often recommended by the CoID, and Noel Carrington, who was a member of the DIA. The overlap between the same figures on similarly high profile design projects reinforces the notion that those responsible for design decisions were drawn from a relatively small pool. They also had a preference for how the signs should look. Casson allegedly impressed upon Kinneir his preference that the signs ought to be 'as dark as old dinner jackets', despite the fact that Kinneir wished them to be lighter in tone (see Figure 5.3).[76] Casson's expression reflects the class dimensions of the period, and his involvement shows that the committees didn't merely approve but also participated in design decisions, not entirely transparently.

Figure 5.3 Green road sign model made by Jock Kinneir and Margaret Calvert for a presentation to the Worboys Committee, Ministry of Transport circa 1962. Courtesy of St Bride Foundation.

There were objections, however. Even before the Preston Bypass had been officially opened, *The Times* printed a letter from the typographer and stonecutter David Kindersley, who was appalled at the new signs, particularly the use of sans serif lower case lettering. Kindersley wrote letters to the Minister of Transport and to Carrington, begging them to save the country 'from mistakes which I am sure we would all be regretting and finding irremediable within a generation'.[77] For slightly different reasons, members of the public also had reservations. In a letter to *Design* in 1961, W. P. Jaspert recognized the need for improved standards in signposting,

> But there is also a considerable danger in too much good design and design planning. Part of the attraction of English towns ... lies in the happy disorder ... in the streets, many of which would otherwise be very drab indeed. When one returns from abroad where endless grey streets depress the clean

town scene... Most contemporary architecture is so plain in any case that it needs hiding behind posters and signboards. Many of the new shopping streets here and abroad show that too much art direction and insistence on uncluttered buildings produce a degree of standardization which makes for extreme dullness.[78]

Jaspert's argument draws on a widely shared preference for idiosyncrasy and eccentricity in Britain, and an anxiety about standardization's relationship to monotony, and therefore dullness. For his part, Kindersley proposed an alternative alphabet design in an effort to convince the ministry, which was smaller in scale and used upper case serif lettering. Readability tests conducted by the Road Research Laboratory showed that Kindersley's design was marginally more legible at speed than the Kinneir Calvert system. Feeling vindicated, Kinderley wrote to the Minister of Transport, Ernest Marples, urging him to make use of the new research, since 'the present boards mar the landscape and their huge backsides are extremely ugly'.[79] However, any hopes he might have entertained for a fresh start were too late. The MoT rejected Kindersley's design for looking too traditional. They clearly wanted a more modern look, one that was less parochial and more European in outlook. The decision to push the Kinneir Calvert design through against professional advice has been seen by some as politically motivated, and even at the time it was considered to have been an aesthetic choice.[80] Nevertheless, despite Kindersley's predictions, the signs have endured to the present day, and been adopted in many countries worldwide. The typeface Transport is even currently used by the British government's online platform, and is regarded as the official handwriting of Britain.[81]

Letterboxes and traffic lights

Other significant standardization projects during this period involved the industrial designer David Mellor. The first one occurred in 1966 when Mellor was commissioned by the General Post Office to design a new letterbox. He seemed the obvious candidate for such a project since he had already been designing lighting equipment, bollards and bus shelters for the firm Abacus since 1954. Mellor was, according to former rector of the Royal College of Art, Christopher Frayling, a 'pioneering industrial designer with an emphasis on the industrial', and also one of the 'most go-ahead members of a design establishment still dominated by tweed suits and committees who liked bracing walks in the Cotswolds'.[82] Postmaster-General Anthony Wedgwood Benn (the late Tony Benn) believed that the original design that had remained relatively unchanged since 1879 could be improved, and the brief provided by the GPO specified flexibility, ease of operation and ease of maintenance – all qualities that centred on the organization's experience of the box. As Labour minister and a modernizer, Benn had argued in 1964 that 'the most distinguishing characteristic of a vigorous society is one in which the future is more real and important than the past'.[83] And in the context of the letterbox,

Figure 5.4 Pillarbox designed by David Mellor for the Post Office, 1966. Courtesy of David Mellor Design.

Mellor would put this argument into practice. His modern, rectangular design (see Figure 5.4) was perceived by many within the GPO as being much better for holding angular letters than a round or oval box, and would, in turn, bring the organization into line with other nationwide attempts to modernize. While the cost of Mellor's F-type letterbox was expected to be more expensive to produce than the cylindrical cast iron design, the GPO expected to easily retrieve those costs through increased efficiency.[84]

Yet attempts to impose a uniform style of street furniture upon Britain prompted considerable public criticism, and Mellor's F-type letterbox was no exception. As predicted by journalist Fiona MacCarthy (and Mellor's wife) the new box made 'a lot of enemies: enemies of progress, imbibers of nostalgia; men who shudder at the Council of Industrial Design'.[85] In a rare show of disunity, even the RFAC seemed to dislike it, describing Mellor's F-type as 'rather teutonic', echoing Kenneth Grange's derisory comments about Dieter Rams earlier.[86] By contrast, the CoID perceived it as a vast improvement.[87] While the efficiency of the new design was not disputed – it reduced collection time by half – nevertheless a national campaign developed to preserve the older models. One aggrieved reader wrote to the *Daily Mail* under the strapline 'please let's keep our CURVES' to say that 'the best sort of letterbox is rich, fat, comfortable and round'; *The Scotsman* warned of the effect the new sharp-edged boxes might have on drunks, and a reader of *The Observer* wrote to say, 'how heartily sick we are of straight lines and uniform angles!'[88]

Like other objects of street furniture, particularly the telephone box, an emotional attachment had developed towards the original letterbox. For MacCarthy, they represented 'minor traditions, gently extolled in screeds on the highways and byways of Britain'.[89] Earlier still they had been cited by George Orwell in his 1941 essay 'England your England', allegedly written as German bombers flew overhead. For Orwell, English civilization 'is somehow bound up with solid breakfasts and gloomy Sundays, smoky towns and winding roads, green fields and red pillar-boxes. It has a flavour of its own'; like suet puddings, he added, 'the red pillar-boxes, have entered into your soul'.[90] Orwell's sentiment about the red letterbox survives to this day, and reports appear regularly in the national news concerning their cultural value.[91]

The first of Mellor's letterbox designs went into service in 1968 opposite St Paul's Cathedral in London. However, following eight years of development, only 205 F-type letterboxes were ever produced and even then, they were made of cast iron contrary to Mellor's specifications to use vitreous enamelled steel. Whether this was the result of public opposition or just a nod to tradition is unclear, but Mellor once described the production of street furniture as characterized by a 'design by committee' approach.[92] Mellor became increasingly involved with design for the public sector over the course of the 1960s. The second major project he was involved with concerned the national traffic signal system (see Figure 5.5). Following the Worboys Committee recommendations, Mellor was appointed as design consultant by the MoT in 1963 for its plans to 'reconsider the design of the system as a whole, to reconcile the various traffic light attachments, to examine new materials and techniques and to minimize the costs of production and maintenance'.⁹³ Mellor's approach was to rationalize the existing traffic signal system and make it entirely maintenance free. The traffic lights became more conspicuous, and the designs provided additional assistance for pedestrians. The system has been described as holding 'clarity and simplicity at its core' and it has endured almost unchanged since its introduction in 1968.⁹⁴

Figure 5.5 Traffic light (demonstration prototype) in Cadogan Place, designed by David Mellor for the Ministry of Transport, 1965–70. Courtesy of David Mellor Design.

Like Grange, Mellor considered street furniture design projects like the letterbox and the traffic lights 'as an important opportunity for changing the visual culture of the country as a whole'.[95] But for groups like the CoID, there was also an economic motivation behind such projects. Director Paul Reilly believed that the public sector represented enormous potential for influence, since design standards were perceived to be low, but there were simultaneously considerable sums of money to be spent.[96] What is interesting from a discursive point of view is that, while many of these major street furniture projects were informed by aesthetics, taste and even class, the reoccurring themes within the debate were standardization, modernization and efficiency.[97] Despite the public's resistance, the CoID's street furniture catalogues from the period praised objects that integrated into all environments, especially those which were anonymous and invisible.[98] The *MJ* even went one step further by proposing a flexible form of street furniture design, comprising component parts that could be applied in different ways, unifying the height and depth of objects like guard rails and bus shelters.[99] While the *MJ* acknowledged that such a system would face criticism – and even be perceived as 'bleakly structural and without character' – it stated that 'self-consciously "fine" design' was not appropriate for 'workaday objects' like street furniture, a point it made repeatedly.[100] The language being used to justify these designs is remarkably distinct from the original doctrine of Good Design, employed to improve public taste and society. Did this mean that the design profession had stopped trying to improve the public's taste?

Solving problems with science

Over the course of the 1960s individual taste was increasingly seen by those in the design establishment as troublesome, and perhaps in a drive to excise this controversial element from Good Design, technology and science were gradually understood as capable of solving design problems. One of the ways in which this change was expressed was through the framework of ergonomics. In an introduction to ergonomics in *Design* in 1967, it was described by the general secretary of the DIA Maurice Jay as 'an established design tool', which focused on the relationship of the designer to the user.[101] According to Jay, ergonomics provided a system that could meet the needs of all end users through technology, as long as design became increasingly anonymous and uniform. He called for the situation to be accepted by designers and encouraged 'greater humility on their part and a realisation that, in the twentieth century urban situation, design and architecture (unlike painting) are not valid media for exercises in aesthetics or the expression in visual terms of philosophical comments on society'.[102] Jay's statement appears to overlook the fact that even anonymous and uniformly styled objects express an aesthetic style. Yet in rejecting style, Jay assumes an underlying moral duty on the part of the designer, in which 'the designer must begin to accept a role as a member of a team of social engineers whose aim, in an industrial democracy, can be none other than "the greatest good of the greatest number". Only in the jungle – or the desert – is it possible any longer to justify a more romantic or personal attitude.'[103] What Jay was essentially suggesting was that designers ought to act as social engineers, an expectation that was remarkably similar to that of the 1950s, when design was used as a means of civilizing both people and space. In the context of 1967, however, Jay's comments are remarkable.

Perhaps as a result of these inconsistencies, ergonomics received a mixed welcome. Even *Design* wondered whether ergonomics was a cuckoo in the design nest.[104] It also reported that ergonomics had achieved the status of a science applied as 'a sort of universal panacea' for design problems, or a tool used by the designer to give 'his decisions a scientific backing'.[105] In this respect, ergonomics can be seen as part of the technocratic culture that emerged after the Second World War.[106] And yet, despite observing considerable problems concerning the application of ergonomic theory, *Design* resisted the urge to reject it altogether, reporting instead that the industrial designer 'must regard it as an essential part of the design solution. Otherwise he may find himself doing little more than the job of a stylist.'[107] This point returns to a familiar anxiety, in which design professionals deliberately sought to distance Good Design from questions of appearance, and instead aligned it with a higher social, moral, cultural or even esoteric purpose. Ergonomics represents another way of elevating the design process, and trying to determine behaviour.

In many ways though, the debate about ergonomics relates to broader discussions about technology and function, particularly the aestheticization of function.[108] And it was repeatedly referenced in relation to street furniture. In 1969 a reader of *The Financial Times* described Britain's lamp posts as 'concrete giraffes that hold the light source some 30 feet from the ground; needing at least nine times the power of lights at 10 feet high, to give the same ground intensity'.[109] The point being made was that, not only were these lights ugly, but they were also technically inferior to the lights they had replaced, despite looking functional. Throughout this period doubt about the uses of function sat alongside doubt about the technocratic jargon that accompanied it. In one case in Bath involving lamp posts, highly specialized technical information and statistics was used to justify decisions of taste.[110] Much like the discourse of Good Design, jargon was used as a convenient means of defensive action, while simultaneously disarming the opposition.

A critique of greyness

Overlooking what were now mounting concerns, the functional values of Good Design continued to be promoted by the official organizations involved in street furniture design during the 1970s. In 1971, the CoID staged an exhibition in the Design Centre on the subject of standardized street furniture (see Figure 5.6). Titled 'Streets Ahead', the exhibition included benches, fencing, litter bins and paving that could be used by local authorities as a kit of parts.[111] The underlying message was that such objects would restore dignity to an otherwise cluttered streetscape, ease flow and create order.

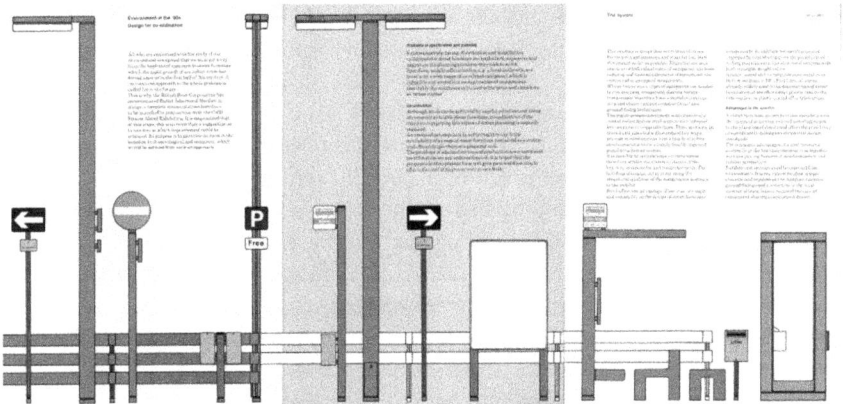

Figure 5.6 'Design for Coordination' sought to eliminate 'the concept of street furniture as single objects'. 'Design for Coordination', brochure, internal view, British Steel Corporation, ND but 1971. Design Council Archive, University of Brighton Design Archives.

Yet response to Streets Ahead was mixed. While the *Journal* from Newcastle upon Tyne, praised systematized street furniture and hoped that the CoID's 'efforts will give pace and direction towards eliminating the concept of street furniture as single objects', others however were less supportive.[112] The *Eastern Daily Press* from Norwich, announced that 'the only trouble is, the grey angular conformity of the designs is as depressing as the present clutter is irritating'.[113] In a similar vein, Neil Steadman writing for *Architectural Design*, characterized the exhibition as a 'dreary display...none of the exhibits obviously improved information flow and while the resulting clutter around Piccadilly may not have the dignity of British Steel's coordinated street furniture, it's good enough for me'.[114] A further complaint was the lack of colour on display, a point that Michael Sharman took up in *Building Design*: 'it's easy to argue that coloured street furniture might intrude... but certain essential public services need to be defined by colour coding... Adding colour would... provide a much-needed identity to the greyness of drab slab streets.'[115] Besides the grey qualities of the exhibits, Sharman also complained about their scale, reporting that 'it's confusing coming eye-to-eye with street lamps – they're just not designed for eye level viewing'.[116] Yet if the colour and scale of the display was considered objectionable, the underlying premise of the exhibition was even more so. The most damning assessment of Streets Ahead was published by *Architect 69*, which declared the exhibition horrifying, not just for the exhibits themselves but also for the CoID's propaganda about clutter, and the author noted,

> I admit that for months I went about looking at the forests of road signs and quite happily selecting the information I needed to know. And I suppose other people have done the same. But we must try to stop thinking like that if we're going to help the cause of good design. We must first pretend that bad design is bad for us. Then we'll be on the way to believing that good design does us good in some way.[117]

While such strong views – and sarcasm – were not necessarily representative, nevertheless, it is striking that by 1971, revulsion about Good Design had reached such levels.

The CoID's street furniture catalogues fared just as badly. Its 1972 edition of the catalogue contained an essay by the architect Neville Conder, in which he disparaged the use of street furniture as 'beauty symbols', particularly planters, and he warned that 'well-designed street furniture cannot be used as a symbolic gesture for salving the conscience of people who have allowed streets and spaces to become rotten'.[118] To remedy such scenarios, Conder encouraged authorities 'to become far more arrogant in their ownership of the road so that they can act as gardeners and insist on a design discipline'.[119] However, given the criticism Conder levelled at those responsible for street furniture, it is perhaps unsurprising that response to the catalogue was mixed. For *Wolverhampton Magazine*, the catalogue demonstrated the CoID's 'very good taste', and it noted that 'this excellent volume should prove both utilitarian and pleasing...all that remains is for those authorities who have to incorporate street amenities in their scheme show good taste. There perhaps is the rub!'[120] *Building Design* observed that 'the more public spirited of the local authorities refuse to accept any item which could be in its pages but isn't'.[121] And in the *Newark Advertiser*, the Secretary of the Nottinghamshire Association of Parish Councils encouraged the people responsible for choosing lighting standards to first refer to the CoID's catalogues.[122]

Unsurprisingly, however, others criticized Conder for exaggerating the problems of the urban realm to further the CoID's agenda. The *Municipal Review* rejected the catalogue's characterization of a cluttered street-scene in that 'design conscious authorities...would never allow their streets to get into such an unsightly mess'.[123] *Surrey Life* took issue with Conder's portrayal of flowers as a 'license for ugliness', and reported that 'in lashing out at local authorities for using flowers in an attempt at brightening things up...he may find few sympathizers in Surrey...Design problems cannot be rectified overnight and if ugliness can be alleviated by the use of well planted floral aids, which many Surrey councils employ, there seems little sense in suffering "squalor" merely to emphasize Mr. Conder's contention.'[124] In a similar vein, Cardiff's *Western Mail* reported that several lamps approved by the CoID had angered villagers of the Lower Wye Valley, which were described as 'suitable for an urban motorway but are completely out of place in the Wye Valley'.[125] For readers of the *Nottingham Evening Post*, modern concrete lighting standards were spoiling some of Nottinghamshire's prettiest villages.[126] And for others in Newark, modern lights were 'totally out of keeping with the rural heritage of our villages...We don't want a return to the ornate wrought ironwork of the Victorian era. We are not against modern design. What we want is good design.'[127] Clearly, anger towards modern street furniture had not abated, but what is particularly revealing is that, by 1972, references to Good Design were increasingly made by the public. Indeed, throughout the 1970s, the public regularly appropriated the discourse of Good Design in their dealings with authority.[128] Yet what did Good Design mean once it was out of the hands of the design profession?

Good Design in the public's hands

Authority within design became much more fragmented during the 1960s and 1970s, and the public more involved in design decisions. This can partly be attributed to the radical democratization and distrust of experts that characterize the period, but also its wider intellectual context. The advance of post-war French linguistic theory, also known as structuralism or semiotics, saw artists, writers and philosophers becoming increasingly aware of ideas like interpretation and subjectivity. And although it is highly unlikely that participants in the post-war street furniture debate were reading semiotic theory, such ideas had significant implications, particularly the notion that an object could be inherently good because of its appearance, function or how it had been produced. Encouraged by figures like Banham – who challenged the notion that Good Design was non-negotiable – such associations meant that the advice given by organizations like the CoID came to be understood as little more than opinion.

Outside this elite intellectual context, some within the design profession were already showing signs of realizing that other opinions existed besides their own. Whether one looks at the non-plan theories of Banham, Peter Hall and Cedric Price, or the iconoclastic work of Archigram, Colin Buchanan's research on pedestrianization, or the increase in community activism, it is clear that the rights of people were being increasingly acknowledged during the 1960s. This change is also reflected in books like *Architecture without Architects* by Rudofsky in 1964, and the 1969 Skeffington Report produced by Arthur Skeffington MP and the Ministry of Housing and Local Government, which encouraged public participation in planning.

Within the context of street furniture design, groups like the RFAC and the *AR* had, even as early as the 1950s, been trying to involve the public in design decisions. Though the efforts by these elite groups had initially privileged their own role as mediators – and therefore limited genuine participation by the public – nevertheless, by the 1960s, their efforts appear more practical. The *AR* for instance, published several articles in 1961 encouraging readers to stand up to their local 'philistine or dictatorial' lighting and borough engineers and even provided a set of arguments to help protect historic gas lamps.[129] The RFAC also sought to offer more practical help, and in its 1961 annual report, the organization suggested ways in which the public could use its services more effectively, and thereby increase their chances of getting their voice heard in street furniture disputes.[130]

Even the CoID eventually began to express its concern for the opinions of others. As early as 1965, *Design* acknowledged that 'somewhere along the line of technological progress *people* have been overlooked'.[131] The following year, the magazine's editors reported that 'if design is to mean anything at all, it must operate at the level of ordinary people'.[132] It is likely that this concern stemmed from the social and political changes taking place in Europe and America, but it could also relate to a growing perception that despite its idealistic beginnings, modern design was failing communities. In light of these changes, *Design*'s editorial noted in 1968 that, 'it would seem the right time for a major rethink along the lines of what people really want'.[133] By 1970 *Design* had declared that the previous decade's design profession had displayed 'quite appalling ignorance and arrogance', and therefore any suggestion that street furniture was more than just a category of inanimate objects in the street, that it could improve the nation's taste, increase export revenue, or even civilize society, no longer seemed credible.[134] In fact *Design* even announced in 1973 that 'the architect cannot and should not be seen as a social policy maker'.[135]

The organizational role of establishment groups like the Civic Trust (CT) can be understood as stepping into the space vacated by the CoID. During this time, the CT had become much more active in advising the public on how to improve their own surroundings. Its founder, Duncan Sandys, considered participation by the public in urban development to be vital, not only because of the extent to which the face of Britain was changing, but also because of his view that 'action in Whitehall and in the town hall was not enough by itself, and that we would never achieve the highest standards unless the public took a much livelier interest in its surroundings'.[136] The CT's objectives were largely accomplished by encouraging the formation of local civic and preservation societies, organizing conferences and events, and by offering grants to restore and improve the environment. Its recognition that the public's views counted, and that architects, designers and planners had a responsibility to respect and listen to those views, was significant. As a result, public participation in the design debate increased dramatically, to the extent that between 1959 and 1972 the number of local amenity societies concerned with the design of the built environment quadrupled.[137] By the end of 1973, the CT estimated that 'some 300,000 people belonged to over 1000 civic and local amenity trusts throughout the UK', of which it had advised over 900.[138] The CT also initiated hundreds of schemes to improve the environments people lived in, and was closely involved with several legislative changes which occurred throughout the 1960s and 1970s.[139] But what underpinned this marked change in policy, and did it signify a break with modernism?

A romantic attachment to the past

According to Kenneth Grange, post-war Britain never quite managed to reconcile 'the theatricality of the old with the novelty of the new'.[140] Grange's statement conforms to a mythologized perception of Britain as a conservative country, resistant to modernity and modernism. However, as Grange himself recognizes, modernism was embraced by the majority of the British public: 'if there was ambivalence', he notes, 'it was probably coming from the entrenched old guard of the conservative middle England'.[141] Certainly what did emerge during the 1960s and 1970s was a confrontation between the traditional and the modern. Yet does this suggest that modernity and traditionalism are oppositional values? Though it might appear to be the case, historian Arthur Marwick argues that the debate between the two is a false antithesis and to dwell too much on it 'is to miss the interactive and iterative nature of all living culture'.[142]

More recently, historian Miles Glendinning has proposed that these ideas about the past are linked to the conservation movement during the 1960s and 1970s. Glendinning credits conservation as 'a part of modernity' rather than a mirror to it, especially during the post-war period.[143] He also suggests that directly after the war the conservation movement adopted a moderate approach largely because of the need to rebuild rather than restore, and as a result, was unable – and to some extent prevented – from occupying a position at the centre of power. Yet as a result of the radical redevelopment of Britain in the years following the war, which was increasingly met with opposition, a voluntary system of national and local pressure groups emerged to fill the vacuum, among them, the CT.[144] According to Glendinning, by this point 'the machinery of modernist renewal became appropriated by the conservationists', which were able to use its structures for alternative ends.[145] Perhaps in recognition of the number of campaigns emerging to save the nation's architectural heritage – for instance, the Euston arch – government also increased its subsidization of conservation activities, and in 1970 – European Conservation Year – the Department of the Environment was established, headed by a Cabinet minister.[146]

There was certainly an increased interest in conserving Britain's historic street furniture. In a report on the subject from 1960, *Country Life* claimed that across Britain 'people with cultural and aesthetic tastes' were protesting against the removal of gas lamps, despite the fact that they were routinely labelled as either 'fusty and muddle-headed' or 'mischief-makers and reactionaries'.[147] It was not a view shared by Reilly, who privately maintained that

> The answer to the lighting problems of today and tomorrow does not exist in the past. Much as we regret the passing of the few fine examples, we should be capable of producing something better than the pathetic reproductions which invariably misuse modern materials and manufacturing techniques. It is our responsibility to make our lampposts as representative of the best of today as those of the past were of their day.[148]

While the position of the CoID and *Country Life* is unsurprising, given their respective audiences, other circles within the design profession did show signs of change. For instance, from the 1960s onwards the *AR* actively campaigned to protect Britain's historic street furniture. Though this might seem surprising for a magazine committed to modernism, the *AR*'s relationship with conservation can be understood in light of Outrage and Counter-Attack. Therefore, the fact that many of the *AR*'s campaigns involving street furniture from 1961 onwards were distinctly pro-tradition and anti-uniformity, is not necessarily the big shift in policy that it might otherwise appear to be. Derek Barton's 1961 article 'Converting Gas Lamps' reflects that modernity and conservation were distinctly not oppositional within the *AR*. Barton claimed that in the right street, Victorian lamp posts 'achieve the requisite blend of solidity, just scale and gently ornate character', and can often be easily changed from gas to electric without excess expense.[149] Though Barton's advice differs somewhat from Townscape, it was as much reflective of the *AR*'s anti-authoritarian position as it was with the democratization of design.

Yet the *AR*'s growing tolerance of historic street furniture brought it into conflict with other organizations, like the RFAC. In 1961, the *AR* criticized the RFAC for approving the removal of the cast-iron lamp posts in Cambridge (see Figure 5.7). According to the *AR*, Cambridge's twenty-six different types of

Figure 5.7 Nicholas Taylor and David Watkin, 'Lamp-posts: Decline and Fall in Cambridge', the *Architectural Review*, June 1961, Vol. 129, No. 772, 425. RIBA Library Books & Periodicals Collection. The *Architectural Review* described the scene in Cambridge in 1961 as 'all very sad and messy'.

street lamp punctuated the intricate systems of courts and passageways of the city, and were an integral way of spatially linking these spaces for the pedestrian. Six years earlier, the city council had implemented an electrification scheme, which not only required the older models to be replaced by newer ones but also that a degree of uniformity be established over the city. For the *AR*, this meant that 'at night one is aware of nothing but a grandiose procession of triumphal columns of light leading nowhere. The Royal Fine Art Commission gave its consent. The lamps have been objects of derision ever since they were put up.'[150] The reason for the derision was said to have little to do with design necessarily, but to do with their siting and variety. It was not due to the fact that 'one is "Georgian" and the other is "modern", but that, unlike the 1823 designs, *they only give lighting*. By day these do nothing but stand in the way'.[151] Clearly, the *AR*'s objection to these lamps was visual, since their anonymous, homogenous qualities made no positive contribution to the landscape of Cambridge. As the *AR* reflected, 'the flexibility of a creative mind and the vision of a dynamic society, variations within a greater unity – these are missing; the standard type is supreme'.[152] But how did these intellectual discussions affect what happened on the ground?

Fighting uniformity on the ground

There are a number of instances during the late 1960s, where public opposition to modern street furniture successfully managed to overturn decisions by local authorities. One of these occurred between 1969 and 1971 when the City of Westminster tried to replace six ornamental gas-lamps with modern electric lamp standards in Manchester Square, Marylebone (see Figure 5.8).[153] Its justification for the scheme was that the old lamps were corroded and it was necessary for safety reasons to replace them.[154] However, following protests from local residents, the re-lighting scheme was suspended in March 1969 until a compromise could be reached.

The row between the residents and the City of Westminster centred upon the style of the lamp posts – characterized by the *Marylebone Mercury* as 'stark, modern design' – and their lack of sympathy with the eighteenth-century environment in which they were installed.[155] According to the *Daily Telegraph*, Westminster Corporation's re-lighting scheme was made in 'the sacred name of uniformity'.[156] And the City of Westminster was also criticized for failing to consult either the Manchester Square Trust or the RFAC, despite its assurances.[157] What is perhaps even more remarkable is that *Design* even criticized the City of Westminster for its plans, and it reported that 'the existing standards are of no great age … but their design (in cast iron and steel tube) is pleasantly elaborate and suggests an earlier period'.[158] By contrast, the new designs were reported as being 'horizontal tubular fluorescent jobs which are now becoming drearily familiar in the West End'.[159] After several alternative options were proposed, the ornamental lamps were eventually replaced and as a result, by 1971 the *Evening Standard* was able to report that the 'council engineers have gone into full retreat. A crane has been moved in to uproot the modern lamps, which have stood unlit for the past two years.'[160]

Figure 5.8 Historic lamp posts in Manchester Square, London, in 'Lowering of Standards', *Design*, No. 245, May 1969, 28. Design Council Archive, University of Brighton Design Archives. Lamp standards in Manchester Square, London 1969. According to *Design*, 'their design (in cast iron and steel tube) is pleasantly elaborate and suggests an earlier period'.

In contrast to the lighting controversies identified earlier, the case in Marylebone illustrates that by the early 1970s, it was clearly much more difficult for local authorities to push decisions past residents without sufficient consultation. And with press support, residents could hope for a more positive outcome than they might have only a few years earlier. But it also reflects a widespread rejection of monotony, uniformity and standardization, resulting in a change in accepted styles of street furniture. Even the CoID was prepared to recognize the value of elaborately designed period street furniture in Marylebone. In fact, the CoID began to recommend the safeguarding of historic street furniture as a means of retaining the character of a town. It even went as far as praising the same Victorian

Embankment lamps that a decade earlier it had criticized as backwards.[161] But what had prompted this stylistic shift?

To some extent, public anger about the monotonous quality of Good Design throughout the post-war period resulted in a drive to preserve existing models of street furniture, but it also resulted in a greater acceptance of different styles. Writing in *The Spectator* in 1967, the American art critic Mario Amaya attributed this shift to a growing consciousness about style, in which 'the preoccupation with the way things look has come to mean that more people are aware than ever before of the visual environment'.[162] This in turn represented 'an upgrading of taste, a keener awareness of the things around us as they infiltrate our lives and our art'.[163] In light of this change, the modern aesthetic adopted by the CoID began to be perceived as 'puritan' and 'damn dreary' in comparison to the other brightly coloured products available.[164] Writing in the *Society of Industrial Arts Journal*, Michael Wolff stated only designers like Ken Adam, Mary Quant and John Stephen had 'given people a bang in the last two years', and that 'it is their zing and their zest and their vigorous understanding of what design is all about which should be one of the main contributions of industrial designers to modern society. It'll be a great day when cutlery and furniture design… swing like the Supremes.'[165] For Fiona MacCarthy, the designs promoted by the CoID most certainly did not swing, but it was slowly coming round to the idea.[166] Writing in *Design* in 1970, the journalist Ken Baynes stated that:

> Today the pedantry and purism of functionalism seems irrelevant, a debased coinage in the riotous but cramped environment of the mid-twentieth century. The direction for design should surely be related to the central theme of the present, to the growing concern with the individual and the expression of his individuality in the context of society. If this means more decoration, more colour, more flamboyance, a closer link between entertainment and everyday life, design has no brief to impose its own more limited morality.[167]

Baynes' statement illustrates the extent of the turnaround of the design elite, which had depended for decades on the idea that design could impose a sense of morality upon society.

By the early 1970s that turnaround was complete. Even *The Times*, normally so conservative, celebrated street lamps that looked like 'giant egg timers with double spheroids balanced on silver clouds'.[168] Just as surprisingly, *Design* promoted the merits of a Mickey Mouse telephone kiosk and a brightly coloured 'cheerful' scheme by José Manser for Shepherds Bush (see Figure 5.9).[169] That a magazine dedicated to promoting Good Design could validate the kitsch and the cheerful, suggests that by the 1970s the street furniture debate had lost its intensity and the opinions of its main contributors had converged. By this point, the volume of coverage specifically about street furniture – articles, essays and letters – rapidly decreased, and the debate lost its heat. Instead, design debates began to reflect the growing economic difficulties of the time, and with it themes like vandalism, neglect, urban decay, social disorder and blight. Evidently, promoting aesthetically pleasing environments and tasteful street furniture would no longer address the complex problems that society faced or design's impact on the world more generally.

Figure 5.9 'Cheerful' street furniture, in José Manser, 'Magic Gardens Round the Bush', *Design*, No. 273, September 1971, 54–5. Design Council Archive, University of Brighton Design Archives.

Notes

1. Paul Reilly, *Lamp Post Feature: Notes Sent to Lord Snowdon (Confidential)*, 19 March 1962, 5, in Council of Industrial Design. 'Street Furniture: Articles and Lectures'. Box 220 (1432.15 Part III).
2. 'Notes for a Lecture Given to Durham County Council Planning Officer', 27 January 1960, in ibid.
3. 'Report on Lighting. (Lighting: Part of the Streetscene)', no date, 2 in ibid.
4. See Arthur Marwick, *The Sixties: Cultural Revolution in Britain, France, Italy, and the United States* (Oxford: Oxford University Press, 1998); Dominic Sandbrook, *Never Had It So Good: A History of Britain from Suez to the Beatles* (London: Little, Brown, 2005); Mark Donnelly, *Sixties Britain: Culture, Society and Politics* (New York: Pearson Longman, 2005).
5. Arthur Marwick, *Culture in Britain since 1945* (Oxford: Basil Blackwell Ltd, 1991), 67–8.
6. John Archer, Letter, *Design*, No. 143, November 1960, 91.
7. Kenneth J. Robinson, 'But Does It Work?', *The Spectator*, 22 January 1960, No. 6865, 122.
8. Katharine Whitehorn, 'Intents and Purposes', *The Spectator*, 20 May 1960, No. 6882, 749.
9. Ibid.
10. Stephen Spender quoted in John and Avril Blake, *The Practical Idealists: Twenty-Five Years of Designing for Industry* (London: Lund Humphries, 1969), 133.
11. Cecilia Scurfield, Cambridge, 'Designs of the Year', Correspondence, *The Spectator*, 27 May 1960, No. 6883, 767.
12. See Nigel Whiteley, *Pop Design: Modernism to Mod* (London: The Design Council, 1987), 38–9.
13. Paul Reilly, 'Designs of the Year', Correspondence, *The Spectator*, 3rd June 1960, No. 6884, 801.
14. *Design*, No. 149, May 1961, 37.
15. 'DCA 1961', *Design*, No. 150, June 1961, 52.
16. 'Comment: The Case for Criticism', *Design*, No. 150, June 1961, 43.
17. Kenneth J. Robinson, 'Antics with Semantics', *The Spectator*, 11 March 1960, No. 6872, 373.
18. Reyner Banham, 'The End of Insolence', *New Statesman*, 29 October 1960, 644.
19. Ibid.
20. Ibid., 644–6.
21. Ibid., 646.
22. Ibid.
23. Stephen Hayward, "Good Design Is Largely a Matter of Common Sense': Questioning the Meaning and Ownership of a Twentieth-Century Orthodoxy. *Journal of Design History*, Vol. 11, No. 3 (1998), 218.
24. Reyner Banham, 'H.M. Fashion House', *New Statesman*, 27 January 1961, 151.
25. Ibid.
26. Ibid.
27. Ibid.
28. Misha Black, 'Taste, Style and the Industrial Designer', *Motif*, No. 4, 1962, in *The Black Papers on Design: Selected Writings of the Late Sir Misha Black*, ed. Avril Blake (Oxford: Pergamon Press, 1983), 39.

29 Ibid.
30 Jennie Lee, *A Policy for the Arts: The First Steps*, White paper, 15 February 1965, 5, in CAB 129/120 0022.
31 Ibid., 6 and 15.
32 Ibid., 16.
33 David Davies, 'Influence of Changing Transport Systems', the *MJ*, 24 November 1967, in Council of Industrial Design. 'Street Furniture: Articles and Lectures'. Box 220 (1432.15 Part III).
34 'Comment: Function and the Aesthetic Free for All', *Design*, No. 213, September 1966, 27.
35 Paul Reilly, 'Comment: The Expanding Frontiers of Industrial Design', *Design*, No. 221, May 1967, 27.
36 'Point of View', *Design*, No. 215, November 1966, 25.
37 Banham, Reyner, 'All That Glitters Is Not Stainless', in *The Aspen Papers: Twenty Years of Design Theory from the International Design Conference in Aspen*, ed. Reyner Banham (London: Pall Mall Press, 1974).
38 Ibid.
39 Ibid.
40 Ibid.
41 Ibid.
42 Fiona MacCarthy, *All Things Bright and Beautiful: Design in Britain 1830–Today* (London: Allen & Unwin, 1972), 83.
43 Ibid.
44 'Comment: Moving Education Upstream', *Design*, No. 200, August 1965, 17.
45 Reyner Banham, 'H.M. Fashion House', *New Statesman*, 27 January 1961, 152.
46 Paul Reilly, 'The Challenge of Pop', the *AR*, October 1967, Vol. 142, No. 848, 255.
47 Ibid.
48 Ibid.
49 Ibid.
50 Ibid., 256.
51 Ibid.
52 Ibid.
53 Ibid.
54 Ibid., 257.
55 Christopher Cornford, 'Cold Rice Pudding and Revisionism', *Design*, No. 231, March 1968, 46.
56 Ibid.
57 Ibid., 47.
58 Ibid., 48.
59 Cartoon about standardization, in *Punch*, 30 January 1946, 108.
60 In a letter to the RFAC in 1950, C. d'O Pilkington Jackson wrote: 'we look with apprehension at too much standardization of Furniture throughout the Country', in a Letter from C. d'O Pilkington Jackson to Haswell Miller [RFAC] 26 April 1950, loose in Royal Fine Art Commission, 'Street Furniture. Design: Correspondence and Minutes'. BP 2/127.
61 'News of the Week: "Standardised Street Lighting Rejected"', the *MJ*, 7 March 1952, Vol. 60, 466.
62 'Why Street Lighting Cannot Conform to One Standard', the *MJ*, 28 March 1952, Vol. 60, 671.

63 Ibid.
64 Rowan Moore, 'Michael Gove's Standardised Schools Not Such a Class Act', *Guardian*, 14 April 2013. Available online: http://www.guardian.co.uk/artanddesign/2013/apr/14/michael-gove-standardised-school-architecture (accessed 30 July 2015).
65 'Why Street Lighting Cannot Conform to One Standard', the *MJ*, 28 March 1952, Vol. 60, 671.
66 *Design*, No. 76, April 1955, 8.
67 John Betjeman, Letter to Miss Mackie, 1 September 1954, Collection of the Lyme Regis Philpot Museum. Available online: http://lymeregismuseum.blogspot.com/2011/10/john-betjeman-and-lyme-regis.html (accessed 30 July2015).
68 Kenneth Browne, 'Streetscape with Furniture', The *AR*, May 1958, Vol. 123, No. 736, 314 and 321.
69 For more information on the impact of cycling on the evolution of road signs, see Nicholas Oddy, 'This Hill Is DANGEROUS', *Technology and Culture*, Vol. 56, No. 2, (2015): 335–69.
70 See Phil Baines and Catherine Dixon, *Signs: Lettering in the Environment* (London: Laurence King, 2008. First published in 2003), 24.
71 One example of a local authority that did modernize its signage includes Westminster City Council, which commissioned the designer Misha Black from the Design Research Unit to design new street nameplates in 1967. For more information, see Westminster Council, 'Highways and Traffic Committee Minutes June 1967–June 1968', 204 and 270-1. See also Cotton, *Design Research Unit 1942-72*, 101.
72 For more information on the Worboys Committee, see Chris's British Road Directory. Available online: http://www.cbrd.co.uk/articles/war-to-worboys/7.shtml (accessed 31 July 2015).
73 Rick Poyner (ed.), *Communicate: Independent British Graphic Design since the Sixties* (London: Laurence King Publishing, 2004), 81.
74 Interview with Margaret Calvert, 4 July 2013.
75 Poyner, *Communicate*, 81.
76 Interview with Margaret Calvert, 4 July 2013. See also 'Battle of the Serif', in *AGI: Graphic Design Since 1950* (London: Thames and Hudson, 2007).
77 Letter from Kindersley to the Minister of Transport and Civil Aviation, Sir Gilmore Jenkins, 18 December 1958, cited in Simon Loxley, *Type: the Secret History of Letters* (London: I.B. Taurus and Co, 204), 192–3.
78 W.P. Jaspert, Letters page, *Design*, No. 168, January 1961, 81.
79 Letter from Kindersley to the Minister of Transport, Ernest Marples, 4 April 1961, cited in Loxley, *Type*, 194 and 197.
80 Ibid., 199. See also Moore and Christie, *Research on Traffic Signs* (1963).
81 See UK Government Digital Service blog. Available online: https://gds.blog.gov.uk/2012/07/05/a-few-notes-on-typography/ (accessed 30 July 2015).
82 Interestingly, Mellor later joined such a committee at the CoID. See *David Mellor: Master Metalworker* (Sheffield: Sheffield Galleries and Museums Trust, 1998), viii.
83 Benn cited in Glendinning, *The Conservation Movement*, 295.
84 'Pillar Box: Proposed New Design', loose in Royal Fine Art Commission, 1946–66. 'General Post Office: Miscellaneous. Pillar Box: Proposed New Design', BP 2/126.
85 Fiona MacCarthy, 'Post Taste', *Guardian*, 5 February 1966, loose in ibid.
86 'Pillar Box: Proposed New Design', loose in ibid.
87 Cover image, *Street Furniture from Design Index 1970/71* (London: CoID, 1970).

88 M. Rollason, *The Observer*, 27 February 1966; Anne Scott James, *Daily Mail*, 1966 cited in *David Mellor: Master Metalworker*, 57. See also Llio Teleri Lloyd-Jones, *David Mellor: Design* (Suffolk: Antique Collectors Club, 2009), 18.
89 Fiona MacCarthy, 'Post Taste', *Guardian*, 5 February 1966, loose in Royal Fine Art Commission, 1946–66. 'General Post Office: Miscellaneous. Pillar Box: Proposed New Design', BP 2/126.
90 George Orwell, 'England your England', in *The Lion and the Unicorn: Socialism and the English Genius* (London: Secker and Warburg, 1941).
91 Alexandra Topping, 'Royal Mail Backs down over Golden Postbox in Ben Ainslie's Home Town', *Guardian*, 16 August 2012. Available online: http://www.theguardian.com/uk/2012/aug/16/royal-mail-golden-postbox-ben-ainslie (accessed 30 July 2015).
92 Lloyd-Jones, *David Mellor*, 26.
93 New Traffic Signal System for Department of the Environment, MoT Design Brief, document part of David Mellor Design Collection.
94 Lloyd-Jones, *David Mellor*, 20.
95 *David Mellor: Master Metalworker*, 30.
96 Ibid., 54.
97 See *Design*, No. 195, March 1965, 40–5; Corin Hughes-Stanton, 'Design Management: Pioneering Policies', *Design*, No. 196, April 1965; Christopher Alexander, *A City Is Not a Tree* [excerpt], *Design*, No. 206, February 1966, 45–55.
98 *Street Furniture: List of Approved Designs 1963* (London: CoID, 1963), 122; *Street Furniture: List of Approved Designs 1965–66* (London: CoID, 1963).
99 'Restoring Order to the Street Scene in Britain', the *MJ*, 15 March 1963, Vol. 71, 737.
100 Ibid; The *MJ*, 17 May 1963, Vol. 71, 1434; The *MJ*, 2 August 1963, Vol. 71, 2241.
101 Maurice Jay, 'Environmental Design: An Introduction', *Design*, No. 218, February 1967, 45.
102 Ibid., 48.
103 Ibid.
104 *Design*, No. 225, September 1967, 19.
105 Ibid.
106 See Theodor Roszak, *The Making of a Counter Culture: Reflections on the Technocratic Society and Its Youthful Opposition* (London: Faber and Faber, 1970)..
107 *Design*, No. 225, September 1967, 19.
108 One reader of *Design* in 1967 defended the functional qualities of a Singer sewing machine against *Design*'s criticism of its apparently superficial qualities, and prejudice towards modernism. See C. Cranford, Letter, *Design*, No. 217, January 1967, 61.
109 James Ker Cowan, Letter to the Editor, 'Standards of Lighting', the *Financial Times*, 21 January 1969.
110 Hugh P. Crallon, Letter to David Davies, 'Street Lighting in Historic Areas', 11 July 1968, in Council of Industrial Design. 'Street Furniture: Articles, Lectures and Correspondence'. Box 220 (1432.15.1 Part I).
111 See 'Restoring Order to the Street Scene in Britain', the *MJ*, 15 March 1963, Vol. 71, 737.
112 Victor Reeve, 'Steeling the Streets to Stop Clutter', the *Journal*, Newcastle upon Tyne, 21 January 1971, in Council of Industrial Design. 'Streets Ahead 76'.
113 'Grey Conformity', *Eastern Daily Press*, Norwich, 7 January 1971, in ibid.
114 Neil Steadman, 'Streets Ahead', *Architectural Design*, March 1971, in ibid.

115 Michael Sharman, 'Streets Ahead: Roads to Freedom', *Building Design*, 15 January 1971, in ibid.
116 Ibid.
117 *Architect 69*, February 1971, in ibid.
118 *Street Furniture from Design Index 1972-73* (London: CoID), 38.
119 Ibid.
120 'Planning the Environment', *Wolverhampton Magazine*, March 1972, 30, in Council of Industrial Design. '(PC15) Street Furniture: Press Cuttings 1972'.
121 'On the Street Where You Live', *Building Design*, 4 February 1972, in ibid.
122 'New Lights Don't Match Villages It Is Claimed', *Newark Advertiser*, 27 May 1972, in ibid.
123 The *Municipal Review*, March 1972, in ibid.
124 *Surrey Life*, April 1972, in ibid.
125 'Too Many New Lamps Anger Villagers', *Western Mail* (Cardiff), 9 June 1972, in ibid.
126 Letters Page, *Nottingham Evening Post*, 6 March 1972, in ibid.
127 'New Lights Don't Match Villages It Is Claimed', *Newark Advertiser*, 27 May 1972, in ibid.
128 For instance, in 1974 H. G. Bellamy, a bus driver, wrote a letter to the MoT on the design of bollards, which Bellamy claimed was merely a 'question of correct design' in 'Letter from HG Bellamy to Minister for the Environment', 7 January 1974, in Ministry of Transport. 'Ministry of Transport and Successors, General Traffic Division: Registered Files. Street Furniture: Traffic Bollard Design and Location; Policy', MT 112/163.
129 Derek Barton, 'Converting Gas Lamps', the *AR*, September 1961, Vol. 130, No. 775, 196.
130 The RFAC, *17th Annual Report - September 1959-August 1960* (London, April 1961), 13, MoDA Ref. 720.6041.
131 *Design*, No. 204, December 1965, 25.
132 'Comment', *Design*, No. 205, January 1966, 17.
133 'Designing for Satisfaction', *Design*, No. 231, March 1968, 19.
134 Peter Hall, 'Who Planned What, and Why?' *Design*, No. 253, 107-9.
135 *Design*, No. 297, September 1973, 64-5.
136 Duncan Sandys, 'Comment: Ten Years of Civic Action', *Design*, No. 224, August 1967, 20.
137 The Civic Trust, *Pride of Place: A Manual for Those Wishing to Improve Their Surroundings* (London: Civic Trust, 1972), 12.
138 Ibid.
139 Including The Civic Amenities Act, 1967; the Town and Country Planning Act, 1971; the Transport Act, 1968; and the Housing Act, 1969; and the Town and Country Planning (Amendment) Act, 1972.
140 Interview with Kenneth Grange, November 2012.
141 Interview with Kenneth Grange, July 2015.
142 Arthur Marwick, *Culture in Britain since 1945* (Oxford: Basil Blackwell Ltd, 1991), 167.
143 Glendinning, *The Conservation Movement*, 4.
144 Ibid., 286.
145 Ibid., 320.
146 Other official agencies were also formed which lobbied for environmental standards, including the Countryside Commissions, the Central Council for Physical Recreation, and the Nature Conservancy.

147 *Country Life*, 29 December 1960, 1592.
148 Paul Reilly, *Lamp Post Feature: Notes Sent to Lord Snowdon (Confidential)*, 19 March 1962, 1, in Council of Industrial Design. 'Street Furniture: Articles and Lectures'. Box 220 (1432.15 Part III).
149 Derek Barton, 'Converting Gas Lamps', the *AR*, September 1961, Vol. 130, No. 775, 194.
150 Nicholas Taylor, David Watkin, 'Lampposts: Decline and Fall in Cambridge', the *AR*, June 1961, Vol. 129, No. 772, 425.
151 Ibid., 426.
152 Ibid.
153 City Engineer's Report to the Highways Committee by F. J. Cave, City Engineer, 23 June 1970, 257, in 'City of Westminster Highways Committee Minutes of Proceedings', February–November 1970.
154 City Engineer's Report to the Highways Committee by F. J. Cave, City Engineer, 16 December 1969, 382, in City of Westminster, 'City of Westminster Highways Committee Minutes of proceedings', July 1969–December 1969; City Engineer's Report to the Highways Committee by F. J. Cave, City Engineer, 29 September 1970.
155 'Keep the Old', the *Marylebone Mercury*, 4 November 1969.
156 'Uniformity before All', the *Daily Telegraph*, 16 March 1969.
157 'Keep the Old', the *Marylebone Mercury*, 4 November 1969.
158 John Allerton, 'Point of View: Lowering of Standards', *Design*, No. 245, May 1969, 28.
159 Ibid.
160 'Manchester Square Lighting', The City of Westminster Highways Committee Minutes of Proceedings, 23rd June 1970, 202; David Wilcox, 'Council Loses Battle of Manchester Square Lamps', the *Evening Standard*, 8 July 1971.
161 *Street Furniture from Design Index 1972-73*, 34.
162 Mario Amaya, 'The Style of the Sixties', *The Spectator*, 1967 quoted in *British Design from 1948: Innovation in the Modern Age* (London: V&A, 2012), 207.
163 Ibid.
164 Leslie Julius, Correspondence, *Design*, No. 293, 81.
165 Michael Wolff, 'The Society of Industrial Arts Journal' quoted in Arthur Marwick, *Society since 1945* (London: Penguin, 1990. First published 1982), 139.
166 Fiona MacCarthy, *A History of British Design: 1830–1970* (London: George Allen and Unwin, 1979). First published in 1972 as *All Things Bright and Beautiful*, 105-6.
167 Ken Baynes, *Design*, No. 253, February 1970, 97.
168 Philip Howard, 'Carnaby Street Restyled in Spectacular Fashion', *The Times*, 4 October 1973, 2.
169 February 1970 issue of *Design*; José Manser, 'Magic Gardens Round the Bush', *Design*, No. 273, September 1971, 54–5.

EPILOGUE

More than half a century later, we've come a long way from discussing the design of lamp posts, but are we any wiser about how the street is put together? Just as in Britain after the Second World War, ideas about 'good' design continue to inform our understanding of street furniture. Today, rather than expecting parking meters, litter bins and lamp posts to raise levels of taste or civilize the landscape, we measure their success through the lens of regeneration, sustainability, local identity, how safe they make us feel, or even how much pleasure they give us. The criteria for good design may have changed but the concept remains intact. It continues to inform decisions about street furniture, which are still made – both directly and indirectly – by legislators, civil servants, planners, anonymous council committees, designers, manufacturers and a host of other bodies on the public's behalf. Some are trained in design and some are not, but strong personalities can still make a difference to what street furniture looks like, who it is meant for and what it means.

Nevertheless many aspects of street furniture have fundamentally changed. For a start, there is no longer any sense of overarching ideology shared by those who collectively 'design' the street. The various agents responsible are increasingly fragmented and have few regulatory standards to work with. State-funded organizations that once educated the British public on matters of design, lobbied for higher standards and sought to use street furniture as an instrument to improve our everyday lives have been substantially weakened. The Design Council, formerly the Council of Industrial Design, has witnessed its state funding dwindle, and now occupies a peripheral role where design policy is concerned. Formerly powerful pressure groups like the Royal Fine Art Commission, the Georgian Group and the Civic Trust have either been massively reduced in scale, merged with other bodies or dismantled altogether. Magazines like the *Architectural Review* are no longer considered the go-to authority on design; they exist as a single voice amidst a sea of journals, blogs and podcasts.

Replacing this diverse range of bodies now sits the private sector. Late capitalism's insatiable need for growth eventually redefined whole sectors of everyday life that were not previously considered to be for sale. Consequently, cities today find themselves in competition with each other, as the rise in place promotion and city branding testifies. In turn, furnishing the street has become a lucrative business opportunity. The urban landscape is ever more reliant on the 'market', which is perceived as able to provide services better and more efficiently and cheaply than public authorities. Multinational firms are becoming increasingly responsible for designing street furniture, a process sanctioned by local councils keen to reduce costs. These profit-making private firms offer a 'free' service in return for advertising space, but in doing so they have fractured the state's role in street furniture design, making the post-war period even more remarkable. As a result, international differences between such objects are considerably less marked than they used to be. This extraordinary aesthetic convergence might be linked to economies of scale – after all, just how many different kinds of bus shelter can the world afford to have? – but it also reflects some of the challenges posed by globalization, the death of the nation-state and the privatization of public space.

These changes didn't happen overnight. In the years following the end of the street furniture debate, there was a huge power shift in Britain. In 1979 Margaret Thatcher's Conservative government began dismantling the post-war vision of a powerful welfare state with its belief in state-ownership and centralized committees, replacing it with a different set of values based on the primacy of the individual, free enterprise and financial deregulation. These ideological changes had a specific effect upon the design of the public realm. The state-supported committees that had significantly influenced street furniture design up until that point were perceived as strangling creativity and smothering innovation. The planning system was deliberately weakened so as to reduce the scope of planning regulations, and planners were encouraged to support market-led development. In turn, the public realm was stripped of its assets. The commercial sale of the British telephone network, for instance, meant that Gilbert Scott's classic red telephone kiosk became subject to market forces and was replaced with an alternative British Telecom model bearing advertising on its metal back. The ensuing public protests saved some of the kiosks – many of which are assigned different uses today – but the act was considered an attack on the very fabric of British identity, as well as what architectural historian Gavin Stamp describes as 'a complete rejection of the civilized attitude towards public amenities which prevailed earlier this century'.[1]

Such an apparently uncivilized approach to street furniture also had an effect upon the built environment's relationship with history. Unlike earlier efforts to preserve period street furniture, the political climate of the 1980s was more than willing to commodify the past. Municipal authorities consequently reintroduced cobblestones, Victorian-style street lamps (complete with make-believe gas flicker) and cast iron bollards (usually made from fibre glass) as a means of reinstating the past – as well as Victorian values – within the public realm. The Marxist historian Raphael Samuel described these objects as 'a kind of talisman of historicity', but that underneath this 'period dress' was actually modernization in disguise.[2] New 'old' street furniture signalled a change in ideological occupancy, just as municipal authorities tried to signal a change in occupancy with concrete lamp posts and ornament-free railings during the early 1950s.

These ideas about occupancy are fundamentally about control, and during post-war Britain the struggle to control the design of street furniture was intense. The reason why so many people from all walks of life were enraged by modern street furniture wasn't only because of how it looked or its effect on local identity and the British landscape – though these were major factors – it was also due to a perceived imbalance of power. Ultimately what the debate exposes is a power struggle, in which powerful, interlocking professional bodies were forced to work together on an issue in which no one had complete autonomy, but which the untrained public and professionals felt very strongly about. There was a widespread feeling that the public's liberty was being threatened by the tyranny of those in charge. Even those who genuinely tried to improve the design of Britain's streets were perceived as tyrants. The post-war period was relatively unique in this respect, largely because of the power that local government possessed to almost single-handedly effect change over the designed environment, but it is important to remember that central government was ultimately responsible for empowering them. Government clearly took a view on standards of design and taste, despite its claims to the contrary, and by doing so, was able to radically alter Britain's urban landscape, as well as inadvertently create the perfect conditions for a passionate debate that polarized the country.

The picture today is no less complex and questions about power, influence and class in the shaping of public life continue to be relevant. In some ways these questions are especially timely, particularly if we consider the influence of the private sector on street furniture, a sector which is not democratically elected, transparent in its decision-making or accountable to the public. What is good for the private sector does not necessarily benefit the public. Those who are democratically elected issue guidance on the subject every few years, but generally appear to have more pressing urban issues to contend with, not least rising inequality, house prices, gentrification, transport infrastructure and air pollution.[3] Few politicians today express a personal interest in street furniture; and those that do, such as the current Labour leader Jeremy Corbyn – an admirer of drain and manhole covers – tend to be mocked for their niche interests. Local councils continue to engage directly with street furniture, and Westminster Council even makes money from licensing the reproduction rights to its iconic street signs designed by Misha Black in 1967. What was once considered good design is now a design classic. For its part, central government tends to be more interested in 'design thinking' than improving the design of objects within the civic realm. To some extent this is because the very nature of the 'public' has changed. New technologies have accelerated a retreat from public life and undermined the need for some forms of street furniture – for instance, personal mobile phones reduce the need for public telephone boxes and email communication has replaced our reliance on the postal system and therefore letterboxes – but this retreat is also linked to the privatization of public space. At the same time, other objects have taken their place or swollen in number. Public charging stations for electric cars now exist in many major cities, CCTV cameras increasingly monitor our movements, anti-homeless spikes and other forms of defensive architecture are becoming more common, and the number of bollards and barrier-style benches and planters that protect our public spaces from terrorism have multiplied. Just as street furniture from the past reflected anxieties and discontents, so too do our objects today.

The topic of street furniture design also continues to prompt debate. Though the institutional framework may have changed, efforts to improve the design of the street have persisted. Campaigns like 'Save Our Streets' by English Heritage or 'Street Pride' by Civic Voice demonstrate a continued interest in how our streets are put together. They support local communities and promote civic pride, the value of heritage, and the removal of urban clutter; but their existence also reflects dissatisfaction with the current state of the public realm. Increasingly members of the public are finding ways to re-appropriate responsibility for designing the street. Around the world flowers are being planted in pavement cracks, bollards are being covered with knitting and bus shelters are being filled with the comforts of home. During the 2012 London Olympics members of the British public subverted Royal Mail's scheme to paint athletes' hometown postboxes gold in recognition of their gold medals, by covertly painting postboxes gold themselves. Others have been addressing the problems of inadequate road signage by installing their own, and therefore performing a public service.[4] Critics argue that these 'guerrilla' acts are not just examples of subversion, but 'a sign that the local community is not functioning properly; that citizens are not talking to elected local councillors; that people feel isolated; that the urban environment is poor'.[5] Others suggest that they closely resemble current Conservative Party ideology of the 'Big Society' where local groups take on the duties of the state.[6] What is unmistakable however is that such acts can quietly transform the street – and the objects within it – for aesthetic, personal or local reasons. And they are driven by the same motivation that underpinned protests about street furniture in post-war Britain – the belief that what our streets look like, and who gets to decide, matters.

Today's community engagement with street furniture is certainly small in scale, but it reminds us that the street is a civic space and we have the right to be consulted on how it is shaped, especially since most of us would rather have a beautiful street than an ugly one. The book has tried to show that a complex network of relations among individuals, companies and organizations is responsible for furnishing the street. Unpicking the process by which these decisions are made and the agenda and objectives of those who made them, exposes the reasons why our streets look the way they do. There are no clear solutions, but what is certain is that, for as long as street furniture is designed for the public, and not in consultation with the public, the design of such objects will remain subject to the tastes, beliefs and prejudices of those making the decisions.

Notes

1. Stamp, *Telephone Boxes*, 25–6.
2. Raphael Samuel, *Theatres of Memory* (London: Verso, 1994), 73–5.
3. Department for Communities and Local Government and the Rt Hon Sir Eric Pickles MP, 'Councils Urged to Cut Street Clutter', 26 August 2010. Available online: https://www.gov.uk/government/news/councils-urged-to-cut-street-clutter-2 (accessed 4 December 2015).

4   Michael Buser, Carlo Bonura, Maria Fannin and Kate Boyer, 'Cultural Activism and the Politics of Place-Making', *City: Analysis of Urban Trends, Culture, Theory, Policy, Action*, Vol. 17, No. 5 (2013), 614–16. See also 99 per cent Invisible, 'Guerrilla Public Service', 10 February 2015. Available online: http://99percentinvisible.org/episode/guerrilla-public-service/ (accessed 9 July 1980).
5   Martin Allen, 'Guerrilla Gardening in the UK Is a Sign of Failure', Gardening Blog, *The Guardian*, 22 October 2014. Also available online: http://www.theguardian.com/lifeandstyle/gardening-blog/2014/oct/22/guerrilla-gardening-uk-failure (accessed 11 August 2015).
6   The Conservative Party, 'Building a Big Society'. Available online: https://www.conservatives.com/~/media/Files/Downloadable%20Files/Building-a-Big-Society.ashx (accessed 11 August 2015).

SELECT BIBLIOGRAPHY

Aitchison, Matthew, ed. *Visual Planning and the Picturesque: Nikolaus Pevsner*. Los Angeles: Getty Research Institute, 2010.
'APLE Conference'. *The Municipal Journal*, 6 October 1961, Vol. 69, 3208.
Archer, L. Bruce. 'What Is Good Design?' *Design*, No. 137, May 1960, 28–33.
'Association of Public Lighting Engineers Conference'. *The Municipal Journal*, 17 September 1954, Vol. 62, 2213–15.
Attfield, Judy. *Wild Things*. Oxford: Berg, 2000.
Aynsley, Jeremy. *Designing Modern Germany*. London: Reaktion Books, 2009.
Baines, Phil and Catherine Dixon. *Signs: Lettering in the Environment*, 2003. Repr. London: Laurence King, 2008.
Banham, Reyner. *Theory and Design in the First Machine Age*. London: The Architectural Press, 1960.
Banham, Reyner. 'The End of Insolence'. *The New Statesman*, 29 October 1960, 644.
Banham, Reyner. 'A Gong for the Welfare State'. *The New Statesman*, 6 January 1961, 26.
Banham, Reyner. 'H.M. Fashion House'. *The New Statesman*, 27 January 1961, 151–2.
Banham, Reyner. 'Handsome Doesn't'. *The New Statesman*, 19 May 1961, 806.
Banham, Reyner. 'All That Glitters Is Not Stainless' in *The Aspen Papers: Twenty Years of Design Theory from the International Design Conference in Aspen*, edited by Reyner Banham, London: Pall Mall Press, 1974, 155–60.
Banham, Reyner. *Age of the Masters: A Personal View of Modern Architecture*, 1960. Repr. London: The Architectural Press Ltd, 1975.
Banham, Mary, Paul Barker, Lyall Sutherland and Cedric Price, eds., *A Critic Writes: Collected Essays by Reyner Banham*. Berkeley/London: University of California Press, 1996.
Barman, Christian. *The Man Who Built London Transport: A Biography of Frank Pick*. London: David & Charles, 1979.
Barton, Derek. 'Lamp-posts: At Home and Abroad'. *The Architectural Review*, August 1961, Vol. 130, No. 774, 134.
Barton, Derek. 'Converting Gas Lamps'. *The Architectural Review*, September 1961, Vol. 130, No. 775, 194–6.
Bertram, Anthony. *Design*. Harmondsworth, Middlesex: Pelican Special, Penguin Books Ltd, 1938.
Betjeman, John. 'Ugly Lamp Posts'. *The Times*, 16 August 1950.
Betjeman, John. *Ghastly Good Taste: Or the Depressing Story of the Rise and Fall of English Architecture*, 1933. Repr. London: Anthony Blond Ltd, 1970.
Blake, Avril, ed. *The Black Papers on Design: Selected Writings of the Late Sir Misha Black*. Oxford: Royal Designers for Industry by Pergamon Press, 1983.
Blake, John and Avril Blake. *The Practical Idealists: Twenty-five Years of Designing for Industry*. London: Lund Humphries, 1969.

Board of Trade. *Art and Industry Report. Of the Committee Appointed by the Board of Trade under the Chairmanship of Lord Gorell on the Production and Exhibition of Articles of Good Design and Every-day Use.* London: Board of Trade, 1932.
Brett, Lionel. 'Detail on the South Bank'. *Design*, No. 32, August 1951, 3–6.
Breward, Christopher and Ghislaine Wood, eds. *British Design from 1948: Innovation in the Modern Age*. London: V&A, 2012.
Brief City: The Story of London's Festival Building, Dir. Maurice Harvey/Jacques Brunius. Richard Massingham Productions in association with *The Observer*, 1951.
Briggs, Asa. *Victorian Things*. London: Batsford, 1988.
Brock, Arthur Clutton. *A Modern Creed of Work: The 4th Pamphlet of the Design and Industries Association*. London: Design and Industries Association, 1917.
Cabinet. 'Cabinet Conclusions of a Meeting held at 10 Downing Street on 2nd December 1954'. [Manuscript] CAB 128/27 0081. National Archives of the United Kingdom, 1954a.
Cabinet. 'Draft Cabinet Statement: Parking Meters'. [Manuscript] CAB 129/72 0051. National Archives of the United Kingdom, 1954b.
Cabinet. 'Memorandum by the Minister of Transport and Civil Aviation, 26th November 1954, Road Traffic Bill: Parking Meters'. [Manuscript] CAB 129/72 0011. National Archives of the United Kingdom, 1954c.
Cabinet. 'Cabinet Conclusions of a Meeting held at 10 Downing Street on the 25th June 1964'. [Manuscript] CAB 128/38 0047. National Archives of the United Kingdom, 1964.
Cabinet. 'A Policy for the Arts: The First Steps'. [Manuscript] CAB 129/120 0022. London: National Archives of the United Kingdom, 1965.
Calder, Angus and Dorothy Sheridan. *Speak for Yourself: A Mass Observation Anthology*. Oxford: Oxford University Press, 1985.
Calvert, Margaret. [Interview] 2013–15.
Campbell, Donald. 'Townscape: Municipal Rustic'. The *Architectural Review*, October 1952, Vol. 111, No. 670, 285–90.
Campbell, Joan. *The German Werkbund: The Politics of Reform in the Applied Arts*. Princeton: Princeton University Press, 1978.
'Can We Measure Appearance?' *Design*, No. 217, January 1967, 11.
Carrington, Noel. *The Shape of Things: An Introduction to Design in Everyday Life*, 1939. Repr. London: Nicholson and Watson, 1945.
Carrington, Noel. *Industrial Design in Britain*. London: George Allen & Unwin Ltd, 1976.
Casson, Hugh. 'Quality in Danger/Defence against Subtopia'. *The Municipal Journal*, 4 May 1956, Vol. 64, 969–95.
Chase, John, Margaret Crawford and John Kaliski, eds. *Everyday Urbanism*. New York: The Monacelli Press Inc., 1999.
City of Westminster. 'Highways and Traffic Committee'. [Minutes of Proceedings]. London: Westminster City Archives, 1968–69.
City of Westminster. 'Highways Committee'. [Minutes of Proceedings]. London: Westminster City Archives, 1969.
City of Westminster. 'Highways Committee'. [Minutes of Proceedings]. London: Westminster City Archives, 1970.
City of Westminster. 'Press Cuttings'. Box T138 Ma. London: Westminster City Archives, 1969–71.
Civic Trust. *Pride of Place: A Manual for Those Wishing to Improve Their Surroundings*. London: Civic Trust, 1972.

'CoID Progress Report'. The *Architectural Review*, December 1951, Vol. 110, No. 660, 349–52.

Collins, Michael. *Towards Postmodernism: Design since 1851*, 1987. Repr. London: British Museum Press, 1994.

Cook, E.T. and Alexander Wedderburn, eds. *The Works of John Ruskin*. London: George Allen, 1903–4.

Cool Hand Luke. Film. Dir. Stuart Rosenberg, USA: Jalem Productions, 1967.

Cornford, Christopher. 'Cold Rice Pudding and Revisionism'. *Design*, No. 231, March 1968, 46–8.

Cotton, Michelle. *Design Research Unit 1942–72*. Köln: Walther Koenig Books Ltd, 2011.

Council for Art and Industry. *Report by the Council for Art and Industry: Design and the Designer in Industry*. London: His Majesty's Stationary Office, 1937.

Council of Industrial Design. 'Street Furniture: South Bank Exhibition'. Box 220 (1432.21.1). Brighton: Design Council Archive, University of Brighton Design Archives.

Council of Industrial Design. 'Street Furniture: Articles, Lectures and Correspondence'. Box 220 (1432.15.1 Part I). Brighton: Design Council Archive, University of Brighton Design Archives.

Council of Industrial Design. 'Street Furniture: Articles and Lectures'. Box 220 (1432.15 Part III). Brighton: Design Council Archive, University of Brighton Design Archives.

Council of Industrial Design. 'Royal Chelsea Flower Show: Display of Outdoor Seats'. Box 220 (1401.1). Brighton: Design Council Archive, University of Brighton Design Archives.

Council of Industrial Design. '1972 Seminar on Street Furniture/Street Furniture'. Box 220 (1432.33.1 Part I). Brighton: Design Council Archive, University of Brighton Design Archives.

Council of Industrial Design. 'Annual Reports 1945–79'. Brighton: Design Council Archive, University of Brighton Design Archives.

Council of Industrial Design. 'Book L: Street Furniture: A Design Folio Prepared by the CoID'. Brighton: Design Council Archive, University of Brighton Design Archives.

Council of Industrial Design. 'Streets Ahead 76'. Brighton: Design Council Archive, University of Brighton Design Archives.

Council of Industrial Design. 'Street Furniture (General) 1/2'. Brighton: Design Council Archive, University of Brighton Design Archives.

Council of Industrial Design. 'Street Furniture for Design Index'. Brighton: Design Council Archive, University of Brighton Design Archives.

Council of Industrial Design. '(PC15) Street Furniture: Press Cuttings 1972'. Brighton: Design Council Archive, University of Brighton Design Archives.

'Counter-Attack: The Next Stage in the Fight against Subtopia'. The *Architectural Review*, June 1957, Vol. 121, No. 725, 405–7.

'Counter Attack'. The *Architectural Review*, February 1958, Vol. 123, No. 733, 141.

Cullen, Gordon. 'Focus on Floor'. The *Architectural Review*, January 1952, Vol. 111, No. 661, 33.

Cullen, Gordon. 'Townscape: Common Ground'. The *Architectural Review*, March 1952, Vol. 111, No. 663, 183–4.

Cullen, Gordon. *Townscape*. London: The Architectural Press Ltd, 1961.

Dahl, Robert A. *Who Governs?* Yale: Yale University, 1961.

Darling, Elizabeth. *Re-forming Britain: Narratives of Modernity before Reconstruction*. Abingdon: Routledge, 2007.

Davison, Ian Hay. [Interview and Personal Papers] 2015.
de Maré, Eric. 'Buttoning up'. *The Architectural Review*, April 1952, Vol. 111, No. 664, 233–5.
de Maré, Eric. [Correspondence] *The Architectural Review*, April 1953, Vol. 112, No. 675, 273–4.
'Design Must Not Be Forgotten in Creating Parking System'. *The Municipal Journal*, 22 February 1957, Vol. 65, 390.
Design & Industries Association. *Design and Industry: A Proposal for the Foundation of a Design and Industries Association*. London: Design and Industries Association, 1916.
Design & Industries Association. *Design in Modern Industry: The Yearbook of the Design & Industries Association*. London: Design and Industries Association, 1922.
Design Council. *Streetscene*. London: Design Council, 1976.
Design Council. *Streets Ahead*. London: Design Council, 1979.
Design Museum. *Kenneth Grange: Making Britain Modern*. London: Design Museum and Black Dog Publishing, 2011.
'Design of Street Furniture'. The *Municipal Journal*, 9 November 1956, Vol. 64, 2673.
Ekirch, A. Roger. *At Day's Close: Night in Times Past*. New York: W.W. Norton and Co. Inc., 2005.
Emmett, John T. 'The Profession of an "Architect"'. *British Quarterly Review*, April 1880, 335–68.
Emmett, John T. 'The Bane of English Architecture'. *British Quarterly Review*, April 1881.
'Eton Street Lighting Is Not Just a Local Authority Matter'. *The Municipal Journal*, 14 September 1956, Vol. 64, 2115–2117.
Farr, Michael. *Design in British Industry: A Mid-Century Survey*. Cambridge: Cambridge University Press, 1955.
Forshoe, C., 'Street Furniture: History of the Bollard'. The *Architectural Review*, September 1953, Vol. 112, No. 681, 191.
Forty, Adrian. *Concrete and Culture: A Material History*. London: Reaktion, 2012.
Gage, Michael and Maritz Vandenberg. *Hard Landscape in Concrete*. London: The Architectural Press Ltd, 1975.
Games, Stephen. *Pevsner: The Early Life*. London: Continuum, 2010.
Glendinning, Miles. *The Conservation Movement: A History of Architectural Preservation*. London: Routledge, 2013.
Glendinning, Miles and Stefan Muthesius. *Tower Block: Modern Public Housing in England, Scotland, Wales, and Northern Ireland*. New Haven/London: The Paul Mellon Centre for Studies in British Art by Yale University Press, 1993.
Gloag, John, ed. *Design in Modern life*. London: George Allen and Unwin Ltd, 1934a.
Gloag, John. *Industrial Art Explained*. London: George Allen and Unwin Ltd, 1934b.
Goldhagen, Sarah and Réjean Legault, eds. *Anxious Modernisms: Experimentation in Postwar Architectural Culture*. Montréal: Canadian Centre for Architecture and Massachusetts Institute of Technology, 2000.
Gorman, Carma. *The Industrial Design Reader*. New York: Allworth Press, 2003.
Grange, Kenneth. Interview. 2012–15.
Greenhalgh, Paul, ed. *Modernism in Design*. London: Reaktion Books, 1990.
Greenhalgh, Paul. *Quotations and Sources on Design and the Decorative Arts*. Manchester: Manchester University Press, 1993.
Hamilton, Nicola, ed. *From the Spitfire to the Microchip: Studies in the History of Design from 1945*. London: The Design Council, London, 1985.
Harries, Susie. *Nikolaus Pevsner: The Life*. London: Chatto & Windus, 2011.

Harris, Alexandra. *Romantic Moderns: English Writers, Artists and the Imagination from Virginia Woolf to John Piper*. London: Thames and Hudson, 2010.
Hayward, Stephen. '"Good Design Is Largely a Matter of Common Sense": Questioning the Meaning and Ownership of a Twentieth-Century Orthodoxy'. *Journal of Design History*, Vol. 11, No. 3, 1998, 217–33.
Highmore, Ben. *Cityscapes: Cultural Readings in the Material and Symbolic City*. London: Palgrave MacMillan, 2005.
Highmore, Ben. *The Design Cultures Reader*. Oxon: Routledge, 2009.
Hussey, Christopher. *The Picturesque: Studies in a Point of View*. London: G.P. Putnam & Sons, 1927.
'Individualism in Street Furniture'. [Correspondence] *The Municipal Journal*, 4 January 1957, Vol. 65, 10.
'Industrial Design: Special Number'. *The Architectural Review*, October 1946.
Jack Howe: A Designed Life. Film. Dir. Martin Mortimore. Prod. Susan Wright, 2015.
Jones, Michelle. 'Design and the Domestic Persuader: Television and the British Broadcasting Corporation's Promotion of Post-war Good Design'. *Journal of Design History*, Vol. 16, No. 4, 2003: 307–18.
Leith, Ian. 'British Litter Bins 1950–66'. *Photoworks*, No. 15, Winter 2010.
LeMahieu, D.L. *A Culture for Democracy: Mass Communication and the Cultivated Mind between the Wars*. Oxford: Clarendon Press, 1988.
'Lighting: Annual Report of the Georgian Group'. *The Municipal Journal*, 9 July 1954, Vol. 62, 1569.
Lloyd-Jones, Llio Teleri. *David Mellor: Design*. Suffolk: Antique Collectors Club, 2009.
London County Council. 'Lansbury Housing sites 1–5'. [Documents and Correspondence] CL HSG 2 31. London Metropolitan Archives, c. 1950.
London County Council. 'Litter bins'. [Letter] MCC-PL-GEN-3-138. London Metropolitan Archives, 1954.
London County Council. 'General Purposes Committee Minutes'. [Minutes and Records] London Metropolitan Archives, 1962.
Loxley, Simon. *Type: The Secret History of Letters*. London: I.B. Taurus and Co, 2004.
Lubbock, Jules. *The Tyranny of Taste: The Politics of Architecture and Design in Britain 1550–1960*. New Haven and London: Paul Mellon Centre for British Art, Yale University Press, 1995.
Lucie-Smith, Edward. *A History of Industrial Design*. Oxford: Phaidon, 1983.
MacCarthy, Fiona. 'Post Taste'. *Guardian*, 5 February 1966.
MacCarthy, Fiona. *A History of British Design: 1830–1970*, 1972. Repr. London: George Allen and Unwin 1979.
Maguire, Paddy. 'Designs on Reconstruction: British Business, Market Structures and the Role of Design in Post-War Recovery'. *Journal of Design History*, 1991, Vol. 4, No. 1, 15–30.
Malt, Harold Lewis. *Furnishing the City*. New York: McGraw-Hill Book Company, 1970.
Marples, Eric and Peter Whitworth. 'Street Furniture: A Report on Current Progress in the Industry', *Design*, No. 134, February 1960, 33–9.
Marwick, Arthur. *British Society since 1945*, 1982. Repr. London: Penguin, 1990.
Marwick, Arthur. *Culture in Britain since 1945*. Oxford: Basil Blackwell Ltd, 1991.
'Matters of Taste'. [Correspondence] *The Times*, 10 October 1957, 11.
McNay, Michael. 'An End to Dull Theory', *Design*, No. 253, January 1970, 104–6.
Ministry of Housing and Local Government. 'Street Lighting: General Questions and Correspondence on Design Amenity and Aesthetics'. [Correspondence and Papers] HLG 51/847. London: National Archives of the United Kingdom, 1951–54.

Ministry of Housing and Local Government. 'Records Created or Inherited by the Ministry of Housing and Local Government, and of Successor and Related Bodies. Street Furniture for Town Centre'. [Correspondence and Papers] HLG 91/744. London: National Archives of the United Kingdom, 1959–60.

Ministry of Transport. 'Highways Engineering: Registered Files. Street Lighting. Design of Lamp Standards: Including Painting and Guidance by Royal Fine Art Commission'. [Correspondence and Papers] MT 95/210. London: National Archives of the United Kingdom, 1949–67.

Ministry of Transport. 'Ministry of Transport and Successors, Highways Management and Services Division: Registered Files. Street Lighting. Council of Industrial Design: Design of Street Lighting Equipment'. [Correspondence and Papers] MT 109/132. London: National Archives of the United Kingdom, 1958–64.

Ministry of Transport. 'Ministry of Transport and Successors, General Traffic Division: Registered Files. Street Furniture: Traffic Bollard Design and Location; Policy'. [Correspondence and Papers] MT 112/163. London: National Archives of the United Kingdom, 1969–74.

Moriarty, Catherine. 'A Backroom Service? The Photographic Library of the Council of Industrial Design 1945–1965'. *Journal of Design History*, 2000, Vol. 13, No. 1, 39–57.

Motoring News – London. [Film] London: British Pathé, 1956.

Nairn, Ian. *Outrage*. London: The Architectural Press, 1955.

Nairn, Ian. 'Counter-Attack'. The *Architectural Review*, December 1956, Vol. 120, No. 179.

Nairn, Ian. *Nairn's Towns*, 1967. Repr. London: Notting Hill Editions, 2013.

Nairn, Ian. 'Outrage 20 Years After'. The *Architectural Review*, 1975, Vol. 158, No. 946, 327–37.

Nye, Joseph S. 'Soft Power'. *Foreign Policy*, No. 80, Autumn 1990, 153–71.

O'Dea, William T. *The Social History of Lighting*. London: Routledge and Kegan Paul Ltd, 1958.

Office of Works. 'Ancient Monuments and Historic Buildings: Registered Files. General. Proposed Scheduling of Old Lampposts and Other 'Street Furniture'. [Correspondence and Papers] WORK 14/2302. London: National Archives of the United Kingdom, 1960.

Olins, W. 'Good Design'. *The Municipal Journal*, 31 July 1964, Vol. 72, 2449–71.

Otter, Chris. *The Victorian Eye: A Political History of Light and Vision in Britain, 1800–1910*. Chicago and London: The University of Chicago Press, 2008.

Pahl, R.E. *Whose City? And Further Essays on Urban Society*. Middlesex, UK: Penguin, 1970.

Parking Meters. [Film] London: British Pathé, 1965.

Pevsner, Nikolaus. *Pioneers of Modern Design: From William Morris to Walter Gropius*, 1936. Repr. Middlesex: Penguin Books, 1960.

Pevsner, Nikolaus. *An Enquiry into Industrial Art in England*. Cambridge: Cambridge University Press, 1937.

Pevsner, Nikolaus. *The Englishness of English Art: An Expanded and Annotated Version of the Reith Lectures Broadcast in October and November 1955*. London: The Architectural Press, 1956.

Pick, Frank. 'To the Master and Brethren of the Art Worker's Guild. 15th February 1916'. The Frank Pick Collection, PB1. London: London Transport Museum.

Pick, Frank. 'Art in commerce and in life'. [Transcript of a talk to an audience in Leicester] 8 March 1916. The Frank Pick Collection, PB2a. London: London Transport Museum.

Pick, Frank. 'Art in Household Things'. [A paper for the Art Workers Guild] 23 February 1917. The Frank Pick Collection, PB6. London: London Transport Museum.

Pick, Frank. 'An Edinburgh Address on Design and Industry'. [Transcript of a talk delivered to the Design & Industries Association in Edinburgh in October 1916]. The Frank Pick Collection, 1998/105574 B6 BOX 4. London: London Transport Museum.

Pick, Frank. 'Standards of Art and Standards of Trade'. The Art Teachers' Guild Record, No. 34, September 1917, pp. 10–13. The Frank Pick Collection, PB7. London: London Transport Museum.

Pick, Frank. 'The Art of the Street'. 9 March 1923. The Frank Pick Collection, PB13. London: London Transport Museum

Pick, Frank. 'Holiday After-thoughts'. DIA Quarterly Journal, 1929, New Series, No. 9, October 1929. The Frank Pick Collection, PB20. London: London Transport Museum.

Pick, Frank. 'Design in Modern Life. The Design of the Street. Discussion between Mr Frank Pick and Mr John Gloag'. 6 June 1933. The Frank Pick Collection, PB23. London: London Transport Museum.

Pick, Frank. 'The Meaning and Purpose of Design'. 19 June 1933. Frank Pick Collection, PB49. London: London Transport Museum.

Pick, Frank. 'Draft for discussion. Proposed new DIA "Aims leaflet"'. 1935. The Frank Pick Collection, PB44. London: London Transport Museum.

Plummer, Raymond. *Nothing Need Be Ugly*. London: Design and Industries Association, 1985.

Poggioli, Renato. *Theory of the Avant-Garde*. Cambridge, MA: Belknap Press, 1968.

Poynor, Rick, ed. *Communicate: Independent British Graphic Design since the Sixties*. London: Laurence King Publishing, 2004.

'Public Lighting'. *The Municipal Journal*, 8 March 1957, Vol. 65, 503.

Pugin, Augustus Welby. *The True Principles of Pointed or Christian Architecture*, 1841. Repr. Edinburgh: John Grant, 1895.

Pugin, Augustus Welby. *An Apology for the Revival of Christian Architecture in England*, 1843. Repr. Edinburgh: John Grant, 1895.

Read, Herbert. *Art and Industry*, 1934. Repr. London: Faber and Faber Ltd, 1952.

Reilly, Paul. 'A Hallmark for Good Design'. *Design*, No. 20, August 1950, 2.

Reilly, Paul. 'The Shape of Things: Who Cares for Street Furniture?' *Art News and Review*, Vol. 11, No. 22, 2 December 1950, 6.

Reilly, Paul. 'The Challenge of Pop'. The *Architectural Review*, October 1967, Vol. 142, No. 848, 255–7.

'Restoring Order to the Street Scene in Britain'. *The Municipal Journal*, 15 March 1963, Vol. 71, 737–9.

Richards, J.M. 'Townscape: Lampposts'. The *Architectural Review*, December 1954, Vol. 116, No. 696, 399–400.

Richards, J.M. *Memoirs of an Unjust Fella: An Autobiography*. London: Weidenfeld and Nicholson, 1980.

Richards, J.M., Nikolaus Pevsner, Osbert Lancaster and H. de C. Hastings (eds). 'The Second Half Century'. The *Architectural Review*, January 1947, Vol. 103, 21–26.

Royal Fine Art Commission. 'General Post Office: Miscellaneous. Pillar Box: Proposed New Design'. [Correspondence and Papers] BP 2/126. London: National Archives of the United Kingdom, 1946–66.

Royal Fine Art Commission. 'Street Furniture. Design: Correspondence and Minutes'. [Correspondence and Papers] BP 2/127. London: National Archives of the United Kingdom, 1948–52.

Royal Fine Art Commission. 'Annual Reports'. 720.6041. London: The Museum of Domestic Design & Architecture Collections Centre, 1948-68.
Royal Fine Art Commission. 'Discussions on Design of Street Furniture'. [Correspondence and Papers] BP 2/279. London: National Archives of the United Kingdom, 1952-71.
Royal Fine Art Commission. 'Crooms Hill: Opposition to Design of Lamp Standards'. [Correspondence and Papers]. BP 2/103. London: National Archives of the United Kingdom, 1956-60.
Ruskin, John. *The Seven Lamps of Architecture*, 1849. Repr. London: George Allen and Sons, 1907.
Russell, Gordon. 'What Is Good Design?' *Design*, No. 1, January 1949, 2-5.
Russell, Gordon. *A Designer's Trade*. London: Allen and Unwin, 1968.
Samuel, Raphael. *Theatres of Memory*. London: Verso, 1994.
Sandys, Duncan. 'Ten Years of Civic Action', *Design*, No. 224, August 1967, 20.
Schivelbusch, Wolfgang. *Disenchanted Night: The Industrialization of Light in the Nineteenth Century*. Berkeley, CA and London: The University of California Press, 1988.
Schwartz, Frederic, J. *The Werkbund: Design Theory and Mass Culture before the First World War*. New Haven and London: Yale University Press, 1996.
'Self-appointed Expert Is the Curse of Local Government'. The *Municipal Journal*, 26 April 1957, Vol. 65, 887.
'Shedding More Light on a Lipstick Problem'. *The Municipal Journal*, 10 April 1959, Vol. 67, 965.
Sheffield Galleries and Museums Trust. *David Mellor: Master Metalworker*. Sheffield: Sheffield Galleries and Museums Trust, 1998.
Shepheard, Peter. 'Landscape in the Town'. *The Municipal Journal*, 22 July 1955, Vol. 63, 1981.
Solkin, David. *Painting for Money*. New Haven and London: Paul Mellon Centre for British Art, Yale University Press, 1993.
Sparke, Penny, ed. *Did Britain Make It? British Design in Context 1946-1986*. London: Design Council, 1986.
Sparke, Penny. *An Introduction to Design and Culture: 1900 to the Present*, 1986. Repr. London: Routledge, 2004.
Stamp, L. Dudley. 'Municipal Engineer a "Despoiler of Britain"', *The Municipal Journal*, 30 November 1956, Vol. 64, 2823.
Stamp, Gavin. *Telephone Boxes*. London: Chatto and Windus, 1989.
Stevenson, Robert Louis. 'A Plea for Gas Lamps' in *The Travels and Essays of Robert Louis Stevenson*. New York: Charles Scribner's Sons, 1895, Vol. 13, 165-9.
'Street Furniture'. The *Architectural Review*, August 1951, Vol. 110, No. 656, 119-20.
'Street Furniture Need Not Mar the Scene'. The *Municipal Journal*, 16 October 1959, Vol. 67, 2877.
'Subtopia, "Engineer Is Not the Culprit"'. [Correspondence] *The Municipal Journal*, 7 December 1956, Vol. 64, 2869.
Taylor, Nicholas and David Watkins. 'Lamp-posts: Decline and Fall in Cambridge'. The *Architectural Review*, June 1961, Vol. 129, No. 772, 424-6.
The Great Hold Up. Film. London: British Pathé, 1953.
'The Royal Fine Art Commission'. *The Architectural Review*, April 1951, Vol. 109, No. 652, 205-7.
The Story of Magdalen Street. [Film] Dir. Pamela Wilcox Bower. UK: The Civic Trust, 1960.
'The Submerged Third'. The *Architectural Review*, August 1948, Vol. 104, No. 620, 50.

Timpson, John. *Requiem for a Red Box*. London: Pyramid Books, 1989.
'Value of Experience in Street Light Planning'. *The Municipal Journal*, 25 September 1959, Vol. 67, 2647.
Varney, Peter. 'Miscellany – Survey of Street Lighting'. *The Architectural Review*, July 1951, Vol. 110, No. 655, 51–4.
Vidler, Anthony. 'Scenes of the Street: Transformations in Idea and Reality, 1750–1871', in *On Streets*, edited by Stanford Anderson, Cambridge, MA/London: MIT Press, 1986.
Wardens Are So Courteous. [Film] London: British Pathé, 1960, 28–111.
Warren, Geoffrey. *Vanishing Street Furniture*. Newton Abbott, Devon: David and Charles Ltd, 1978.
Waugh, Evelyn. 'Victorian Taste'. *The Times*, 3 March 1942.
Whiteley, Nigel. *Pop Design: Modernism to Mod*. London: The Design Council, 1987.
Whitworth, Lesley. *Inscribing Design on the Nation: The Creators of the British Council of Industrial Design. Business and Economic History Online* (3), 2005. Available online: www.thebhc.org/sites/default/files/whitworth.pdf (accessed 31 July 2015).
Whitworth, Peter. 'Techniques: Street lighting'. *The Architectural Review*, March 1958, Vol. 123, No. 734, 216–20.
Whitworth, Peter. 'Street Lighting: New Designs Reviewed', *Design*, No. 114, June 1958, 45–6.
Williams, George. 'Street Furniture', *Design*, No. 69, September 1954, 15–33.
Williams, George. 'Street Furniture: A Review of the Use and Abuse of Lampposts and Parking Meters'. *Design*, No. 88, April 1956, 27–35.
Williams, George. 'Street Furniture', *Design*, No. 99, March 1957, 46–7.
Williams, Richard J. *The Anxious City*. London: Routledge, 2004.
Winter, James. *London's Teeming Streets 1830–1914*. Abingdon: Routledge, 1993.
Woodham, Jonathan. *The Industrial Designer and the Public*. London: Pembridge Press, 1983.
Woodham, Jonathan. 'Managing British Design Reform I: Fresh Perspectives on the Early Years of the Council of Industrial Design'. *Journal of Design History*, 1996, Vol. 9, No. 1, 55–65.
Woodham, Jonathan. *Twentieth Century Design*. Oxford: Oxford University Press, 1997.
Wright, Patrick. *On Living in an Old Country*. London: Verso, 1985.
York, Peter. *Style Wars*. London: Sidgwick and Jackson Limited, 1980.

INDEX

Abingdon 51, 151
advertising 82, 146, 198
Amaya, Mario 189
America 49, 61–2, 65, 173
Ampthill 98
Anderson Committee 172
Architects Journal 75
Architectural Review (*AR*) 5, 14, 33, 41, 68, 75–109, 136–7, 147–52, 168, 171, 173, 183, 185–7, 197
Architecture without Architects 183
Art News and Review 40
Arts and Crafts 9–10, 12
Association of Municipal Corporations 116
Association of Public Lighting Engineers 53
avant-garde 18

bandstand 7–8, 10
Banham, Reyner 5, 52, 76, 79, 164–8, 183
Banstead 150
Barton, Derek 137
Bath 180
Beatles, The 66
Belfast 140
bench 1–3, 10, 12, 47, 49, 51, 57–8, 76, 87, 101, 105, 108, 147, 180, 190, 199
Benn, Anthony (Tony) Wedgwood 175
Bertram, Anthony 21, 31
Betjeman, John 21, 50–1, 57, 76, 93, 97, 108, 117, 123, 132, 171
Bevan, Aneurin 40
bicycle rack 1
'Big Society' 200
Black, Misha 47, 99, 165, 199
Blackheath Society 130, 138
Board of Trade 29, 89, 118
bollard 1–2, 10, 76, 79, 84, 119, 198–200
Bradford 138
Brett, Lionel 47, 120
Brief City 49

Brighton 140
Britain Can Make It (exhibition) 56
British Broadcasting Corporation 21–2, 40, 87
Brunel, Isambard Kingdom 12
Buchanan, Colin 183
bus shelter 1, 20, 22, 42, 48, 51–2, 58, 119, 147–8, 175, 179, 198, 200
bus stop 2, 41, 54, 56

Cadbury Brown, H. T. 47
Calvert, Margaret 6, 172–5
Cambridge 186–7
Cardiff 182
Carlisle 104
Carrickfergus 141
Carrington, Noel 10, 29, 173–4
Casson, Hugh 49, 105, 173
Chesterton, G.K. 13
Chippenham 51
Chipping Camden 139
Churchill, Winston 2, 61
Civic Trust 5, 75, 91, 98–101, 109, 123, 184, 197
Civic Voice 200
Clark, Kenneth 39, 93
class 3, 10, 17, 21, 39–40, 115, 123, 150, 164, 173
cleanliness 15, 21
clutter 2, 85, 169, 170, 175, 180–1, 200
concrete 20, 79, 130–1, 146
Concrete Utilities Ltd. 80–1, 123, 125–6
Conder, Neville 182
conservation 185
Cool Hand Luke (film) 68
Cornford, Christopher 169
Council for Art and Industry 23, 29
Council of Industrial Design (CoID) 4–5, 14, 23–4, 29–69, 89–90, 97, 99, 115–20, 123, 128, 133–4, 137, 143, 161–9, 173, 177, 179, 180–2, 197
Counter-Attack 147–52, 185

Counter-Attack Bureau 150
Country Life 66–7
Cubitt, James 47
Cullen, Gordon 5, 82–7, 89, 103–4

Dalton, Hugh 29, 118, 123
Day, Robin 47
Defensive street furniture 199
Design (magazine) 45–53, 63, 90, 162
Design Awards 162
Design Centre 30
design folio 53–6
Design Index 36, 60
Design and Industries Association 14–16, 23, 29, 173, 179
Design Research Unit 21, 99
Deutsche Werkbund 14
Devizes 51
Dover 141
drain cover 78–9, 199
Durham 141, 143

Eden, Anthony 61
Edinburgh 142
electricity 13, 22, 32, 98, 138–9, 185, 187
Ely 142
Emmett, John T. 13
English Heritage 200
ergonomics 169, 179–80
Eton College 135
Exeter 51

Festival of Britain 46–9, 56, 85, 89, 115–17, 122, 140
fire hydrant 79
First World War 14
fountain 7, 10–11, 140
Freud, Sigmund 79
Fry, Maxwell 93
Fry, Roger 15, 23

gas lighting 2, 10, 22, 32, 34, 138, 140, 183, 185, 187, 198
General Post Office 175
Georgian Group 91, 93, 109, 118, 123, 197
Gibberd, Frederick 120
Glasgow 10
Gloag, John 18, 22, 143

Good Design
  discourse 14–18, 21, 97, 137, 148, 167, 180, 182, 197
  and government 3, 15, 23–4, 38, 41, 90, 127, 161, 169, 175, 199
  and morality 7, 46, 166–7, 189
  and taste 7, 16, 21, 39–40, 65, 68, 76, 127, 161–6, 173, 182
Grange, Kenneth 5, 34, 60–9, 76, 177, 179
Gray, Milner 47
Great Exhibition 9
Gropius, Walter 61, 75

Hastings, Hubert de Cronin 75–6, 84
His Royal Highness the Duke of Edinburgh 58–9
horse trough 1
Howe, Jack 35, 47, 51–2, 61, 173

imperialism 10
individualism 22, 54

Jacobs, Jane 89
Jay, Maurice 179

Kendal 105
Kindersley, David 174–5
Kinneir, Richard (Jock) 6, 172–5

Labour Party 38, 46–7, 49, 199
Lakeland 105
lamp post 1, 6, 10, 12, 22, 31, 33, 35, 44, 50–1, 54, 57–9, 79–81, 84, 98, 105, 115, 124, 125, 128–40, 147, 164, 180, 189, 197–8
Lancashire 105
Le Corbusier 15, 52, 75
Leamington 105
Lee, Jennie 165
Leslie, S. C. 39
Lethaby, William Richard 14
letterbox 1, 13, 136, 169, 175–7, 199–200
lettering 83–4, 99, 169
Lincoln 51
light (quality) 13, 125, 144
litterbin 1–2, 36, 47–9, 58, 60, 84, 87, 105, 119, 141, 162–3, 180, 197
local government 5, 22, 42–3, 53, 61, 98, 101, 103, 105–8, 116–17, 125–28, 147

London 4, 12–14, 22, 41, 47, 53, 57–9, 61, 63, 90, 125–38, 140, 150–2, 166, 169–70, 177, 181, 187, 189
London Transport 14, 20, 22, 48, 52, 55
Loos, Adolf 15, 52
Lord Snowdon 43, 161
Lower Wye Valley 182
Lyme Regis 171
Lynch, Kevin 89

MacCarthy, Fiona 177, 189
Machin, Arnold 138
MacMillan, Harold 61, 123
Manchester 116, 143
manhole cover 77–9, 199
manufacturing 9, 16–17, 29, 32–4, 36–7, 39–40, 43, 45, 49, 53, 55, 58–63, 68, 90, 106, 116–17, 122, 132, 144–5, 162
Maré, Eric de 91
Mass Observation 77–8
Mellor, David 6, 131, 175–9
Merthyr Tydfil 140
Messel, Oliver 135–7
milestone 1
Ministry of Housing and Local Government 120–2, 124, 125, 127–8, 130–2, 135–7, 183
Ministry of Transport 34, 36–7, 41–2, 61, 63, 93, 96, 98, 107, 115, 117, 120–5, 131–2, 170, 172–5, 177
modernism 2, 6, 19–1, 23, 34, 49–50, 65–6, 75, 78, 85, 94, 135, 137, 161–2, 166, 184–5
monotony 5, 8, 143, 169–71, 175, 188
Moore, Henry 93, 120
Morecambe 124
Morris, William 9, 13–14, 52, 167
Morrison, Herbert 47
municipal authorities. *See* local government
Municipal Journal, The 41, 44–5, 62, 93
municipal rustic 101–2, 105

Nairn, Ian 79, 89, 99, 103–6, 142, 147–8
Nash, Paul 21, 76
National Brassfoundry Association 51, 90
nationalism 7, 34, 49, 63, 84
New Statesman 164
New Town 2, 32–3, 50–1, 82

Newcastle upon Tyne 181
Northampton 32
Norwich 99, 144, 181
Nottingham 51, 181–2

Observer 49, 54
Office of Works 135–6
Old Bosham 139
Omega Workshop 15
Orwell, George 150, 177
Outrage 79, 101–8, 142, 144–5, 147, 152, 185
Oxford 105, 173

parking meter 1, 3–4, 46, 49, 60–9, 164, 197
Pevsner, Nikolaus 21–2, 76, 84–5, 87, 93
photography 4, 45, 60, 77, 85
Pick, Frank 14–16, 22, 76
picturesque 84–5, 87
pillarbox. *See* letterbox
Pioneers of Modern Design 21
Piper, John 21, 77–8, 93
planning 1, 37, 38, 84–5, 88, 97–9, 108, 136–7, 150, 152, 174, 183, 198
planning legislation (Town and Country Planning Act 1947) 37–8, 117, 136
planning officers 37, 43, 79, 101, 123, 142, 147
planning permission 38, 123, 141
planter 1, 47, 182, 199
Plummer, Raymond 17
Poggioli, Renato 18
police boxe 138
postbox. *See* letterbox
Preston 172–4
privacy 13, 31
privatization 197–8
Prudhoe 141
public
  exclusion of 38, 53, 116–17, 125, 137
  opinion 18, 94, 101, 107, 116, 122, 150, 183
  resistance 5, 21, 125–40, 174, 177, 187–9
  space 1–3, 87–8, 101, 108, 198–200
  taste 2, 9, 13, 15–7, 23, 39, 76, 82–3, 122, 134, 164–5, 179

Pugin, Augustus Welby 7–9, 168
Punch 23, 30, 66, 94–5, 148–9, 170

Race, Ernest 47
railing 1, 10, 31–2, 54–5, 147, 198
Rams, Dieter 66, 177
Raymond, Ernest 13
Read, Herbert 16–17, 21
regeneration 1, 197
Reilly, Paul 40, 43, 161–2, 168–9, 179, 185
Richards, J. M. 76–8, 89, 92–4, 97–8, 119–20, 173
Richardson, Sir Albert E. 98, 142
Road Traffic Bill 61
Roehampton 150
Royal Commission on Historical Monuments 130
Royal Fine Art Commission 5, 32, 34, 36, 40, 50, 63, 75, 91–101, 109, 115–23, 128–33, 135, 137, 143–4, 150, 170, 173, 177, 183, 186–7, 197
Royal Institute of British Architects 40
Rural District Councils Association 116
Ruskin, John 9, 52, 138, 167
Russell, Gordon 30, 31, 34, 39, 41–2, 45–6, 54, 90, 97, 117–19, 123

Salisbury 51
Sandys, Duncan 98, 184
Scarborough 141
Scott, Giles Gilbert 19, 198
Seating. *See* bench
Second World War 2, 4, 7, 23, 31–3, 105, 180
semiotic theory 183
Shepheard, Peter 142
Shrewsbury 138
signage 1, 49, 169, 171–5, 200
signal box 1
Skeffington Report 183
Snobbery. *See* class
soft power 75, 92–3, 97
Solkin, David 108
Southampton 104
Spectator 162
Spence, Sir Basil 99
Spender, Stephen 162
Stafford 105
Stamp, Lawrence Dudley 142

standardization 22, 51, 162, 169–75
steel 20, 47, 115, 130–2, 173
Stevenson, Robert Louis 13
Stoke-on-Trent 138
Street Furniture Advisory Committee 36, 37, 39, 43, 51
street furniture booklet 118–25
street lamp. *See* lamp post
style 7, 53, 96
subtopia 105, 107, 128, 136, 138, 143, 147
Summerson, John 93, 119
surrealism 76, 79
Surrey 20, 182
Swanage 76
systems design 169, 181

taste. *See* good design; public
telephone box 19, 177, 189, 198–9
Temperance Movement 7
Thatcher, Margaret 198
townscape 82, 84–9, 185
traffic lights 1, 169, 177–9
Trollope, Anthony 13

uniformity 19, 54, 99, 105, 170–1, 177, 179, 185, 187–8
unobtrusiveness 42, 57, 87, 130–1, 141
Urban District Councils Association 116
urinal 1
Utility Scheme 23, 37, 39

Venner Ltd. 61–4
Voysey, Charles Frances 12
Vuillamy, George John 12, 140

Walter Macfarlane & Co. 10
Wantage 51
Wardens are so Courteous (film) 66
Warwick 105
Waugh, Evelyn 31, 105
Webb, Geoffrey 120
Wheeler, Charles 120
Whickham 141
Whittlesey 98
Windsor 141
Wokingham 51
Worboys Committee 173, 177

www.ingramcontent.com/pod-product-compliance
Ingram Content Group UK Ltd.
Pitfield, Milton Keynes, MK11 3LW, UK
UKHW021151230426
470268UK00015B/267